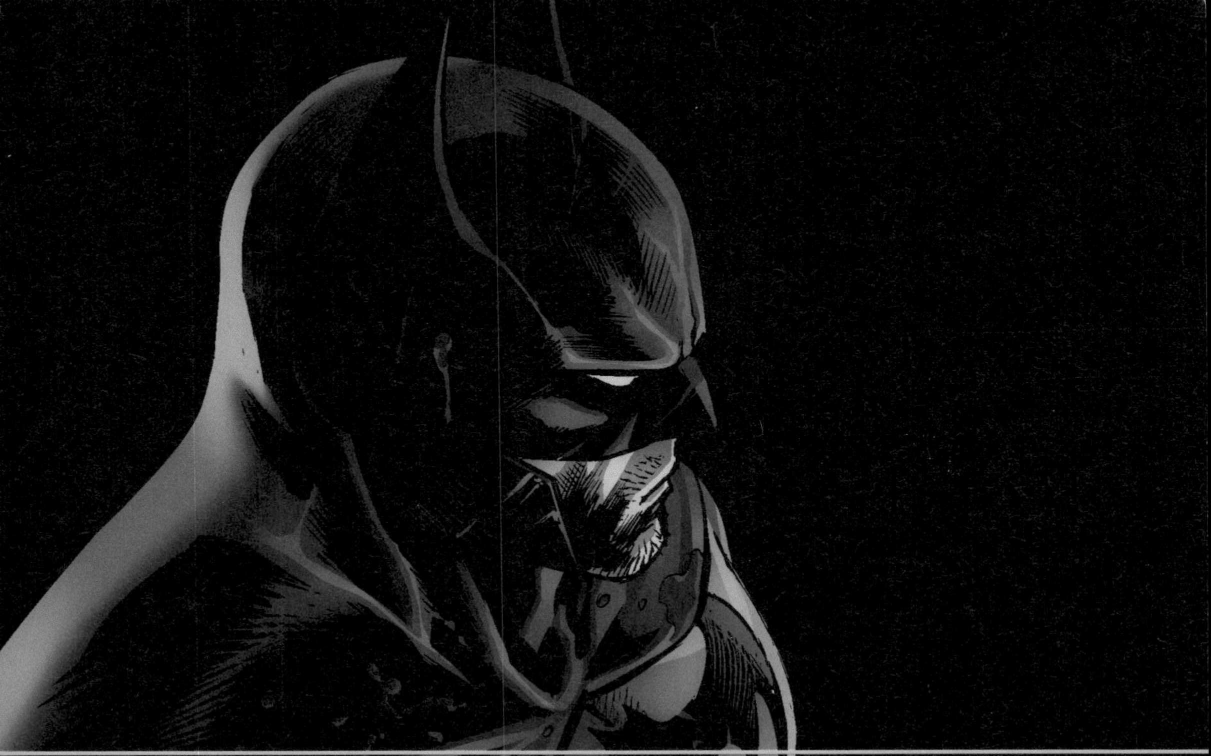

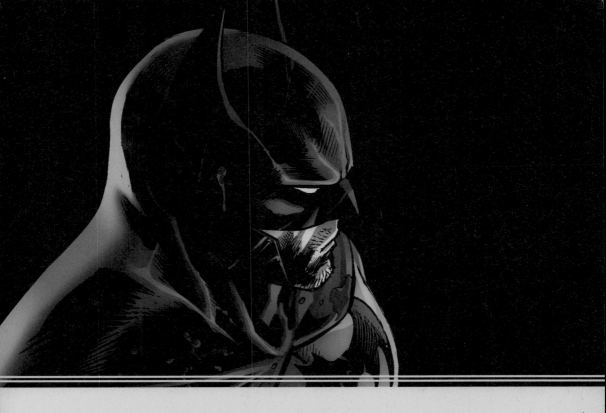

BATMAN
DETECTIVE COMICS

VOL. 3:
GREETINGS FROM GOTHAM

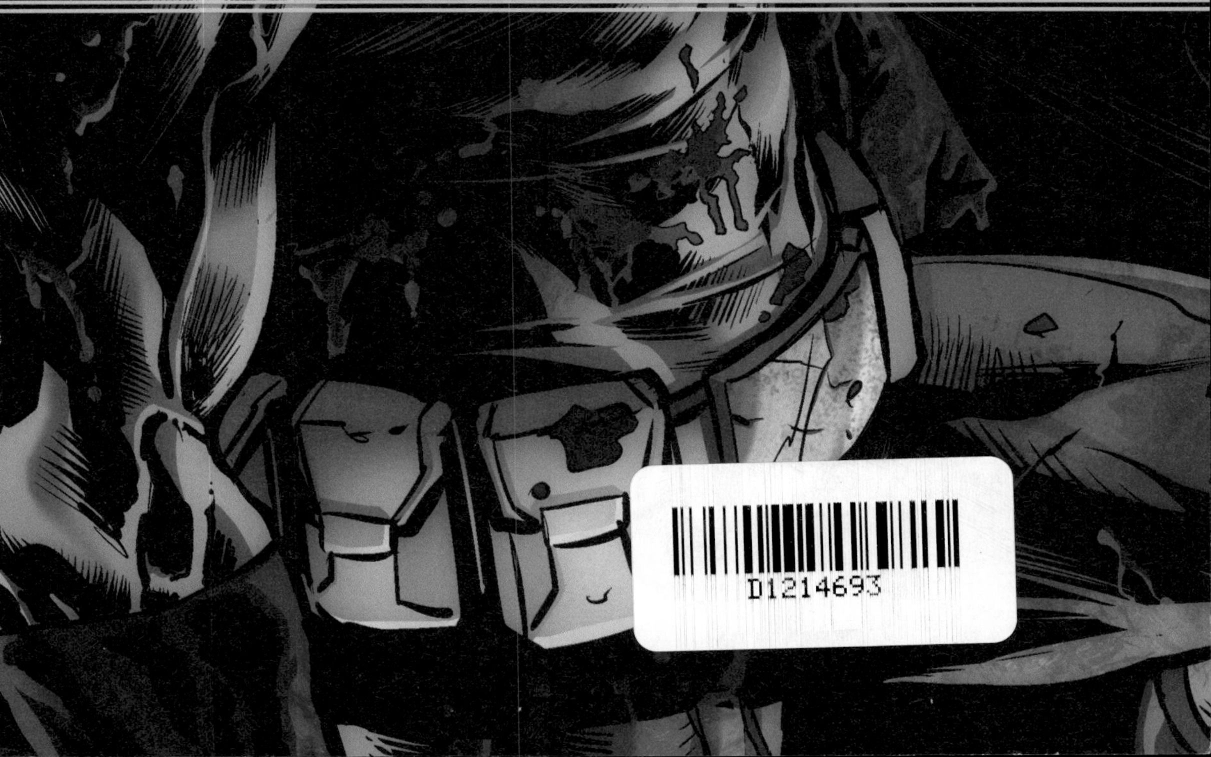

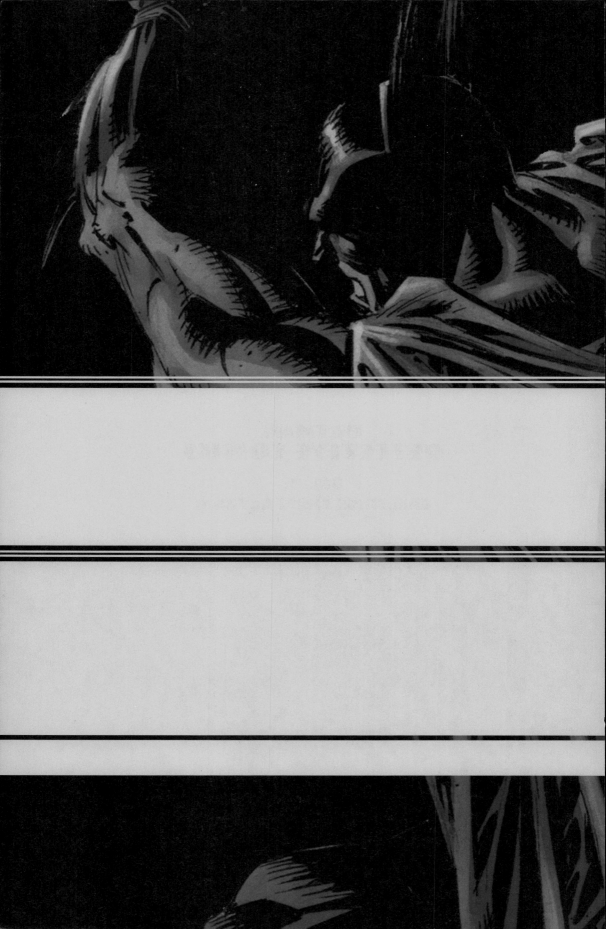

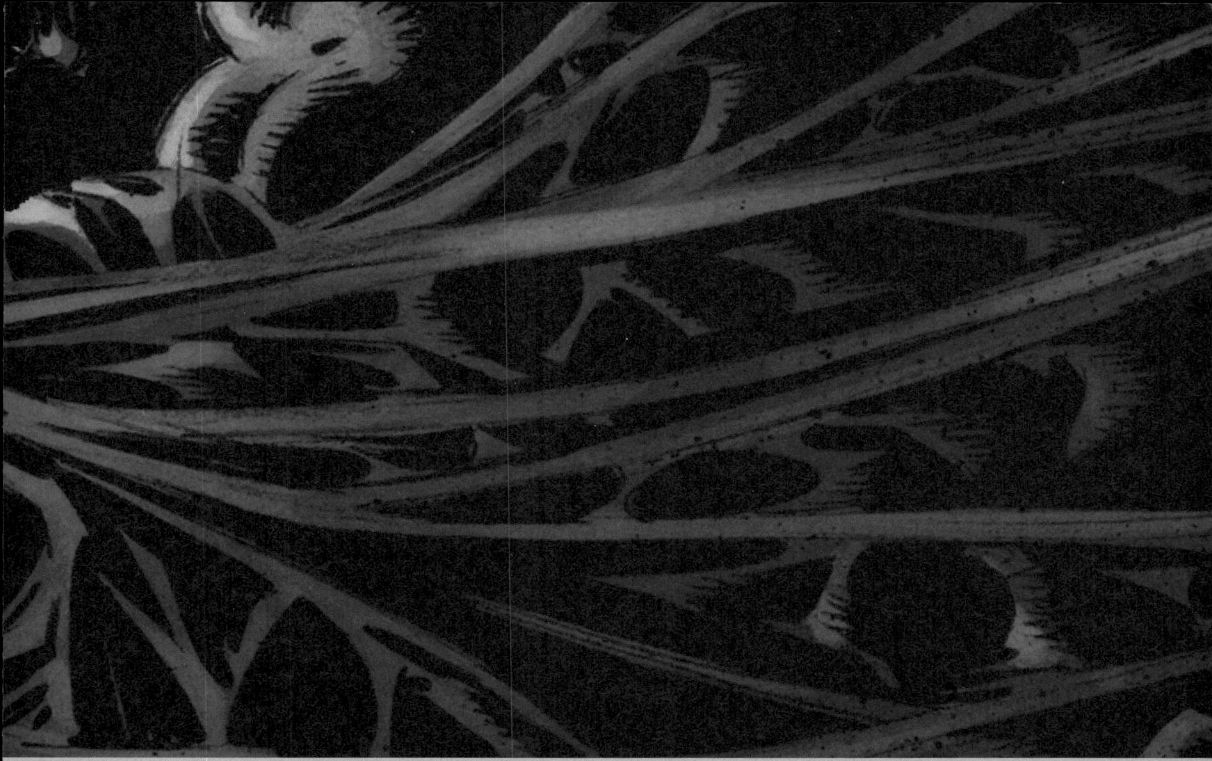

BATMAN
DETECTIVE COMICS

VOL. 3:
GREETINGS FROM GOTHAM

PETER J. TOMASI
WRITER

CHRISTIAN DUCE
KYLE HOTZ
DOUG MAHNKE
JAIME MENDOZA
ARTISTS

DAVID BARON
LUIS GUERRERO
COLORISTS

ROB LEIGH
LETTERER

DOUG MAHNKE, JAIME MENDOZA, and DAVID BARON
COLLECTION COVER ARTISTS

BATMAN CREATED BY **BOB KANE** WITH **BILL FINGER**

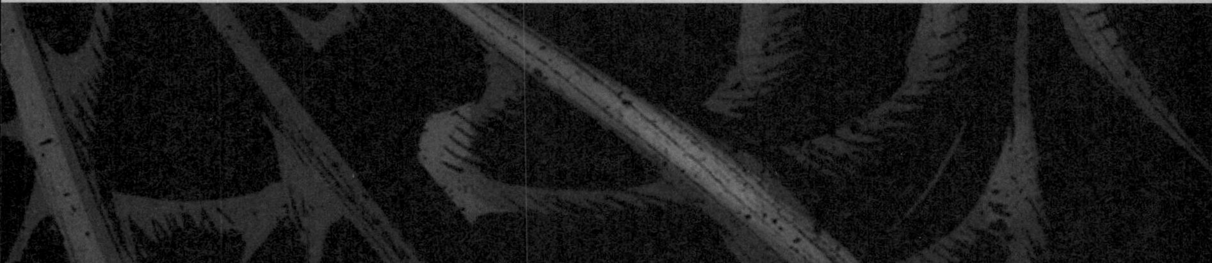

JAMIE S. RICH Group Editor – Original Series
MOLLY MAHAN Editor – Original Series
DAVE WIELGOSZ Assistant Editor – Original Series
JEB WOODARD Group Editor – Collected Editions
ERIKA ROTHBERG Editor – Collected Edition
STEVE COOK Design Director – Books
LOUIS PRANDI Publication Design
SUZANNAH ROWNTREE Publication Production

BOB HARRAS Senior VP – Editor-in-Chief, DC Comics

JIM LEE Publisher & Chief Creative Officer
BOBBIE CHASE VP – Global Publishing Initiatives & Digital Strategy
DON FALLETTI VP – Manufacturing Operations & Workflow Management
LAWRENCE GANEM VP – Talent Services
ALISON GILL Senior VP – Manufacturing & Operations
HANK KANALZ Senior VP – Publishing Strategy & Support Services
DAN MIRON VP – Publishing Operations
NICK J. NAPOLITANO VP – Manufacturing Administration & Design
NANCY SPEARS VP – Sales
JONAH WEILAND VP – Marketing & Creative Services
MICHELE R. WELLS VP & Executive Editor, Young Reader

BATMAN: DETECTIVE COMICS VOL. 3: GREETINGS FROM GOTHAM

DC Comics, 2900 West Alameda Ave., Burbank, CA 91505
Printed by LSC Communications, Owensville, MO, USA. 8/21/20. First Printing.
ISBN: 978-1-77950-554-5

Library of Congress Cataloging-in-Publication Data is available.

PEFC Certified

This product is from sustainably managed forests and controlled sources

PEFC

PEFC/29-31-337   www.pefc.org

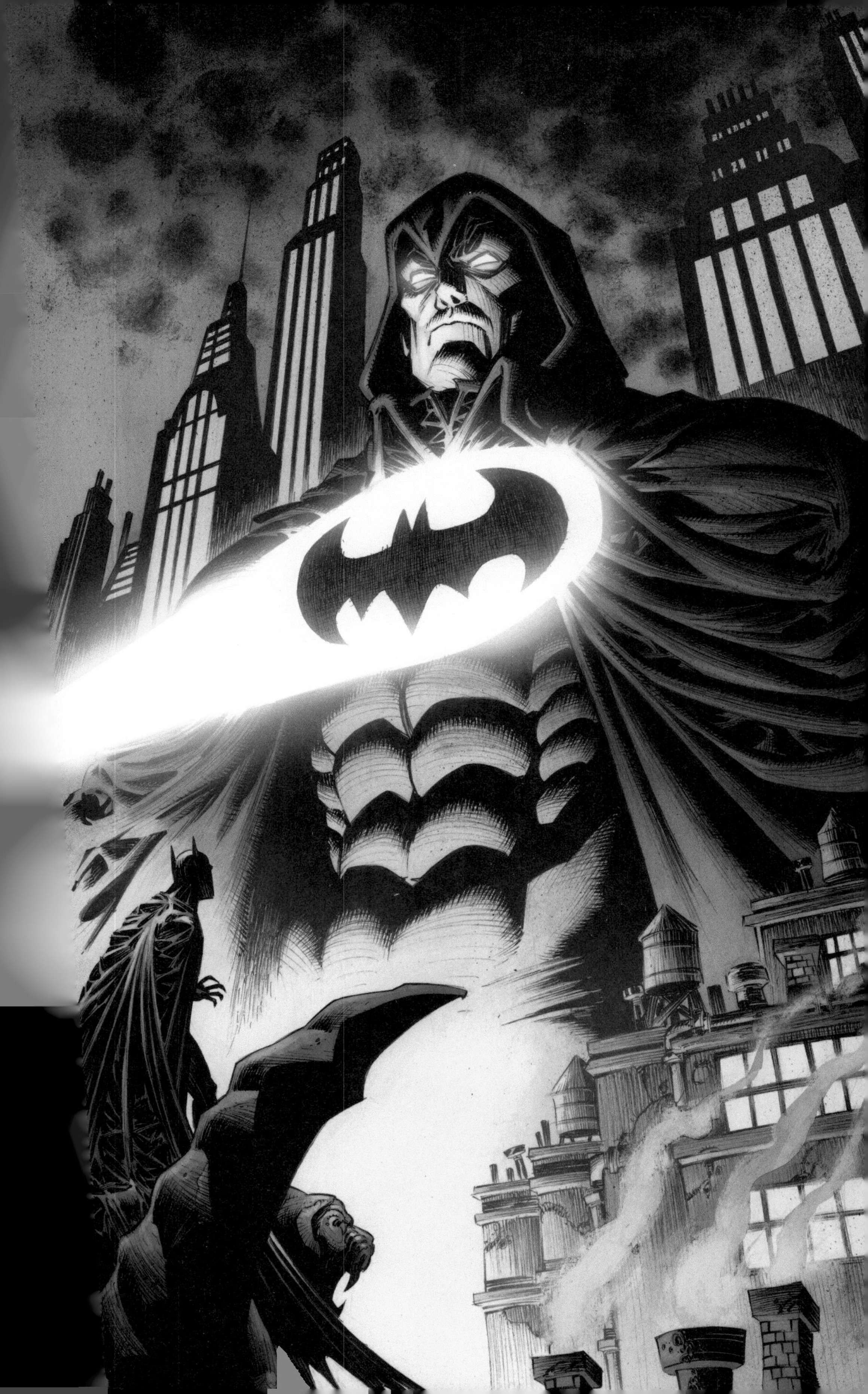

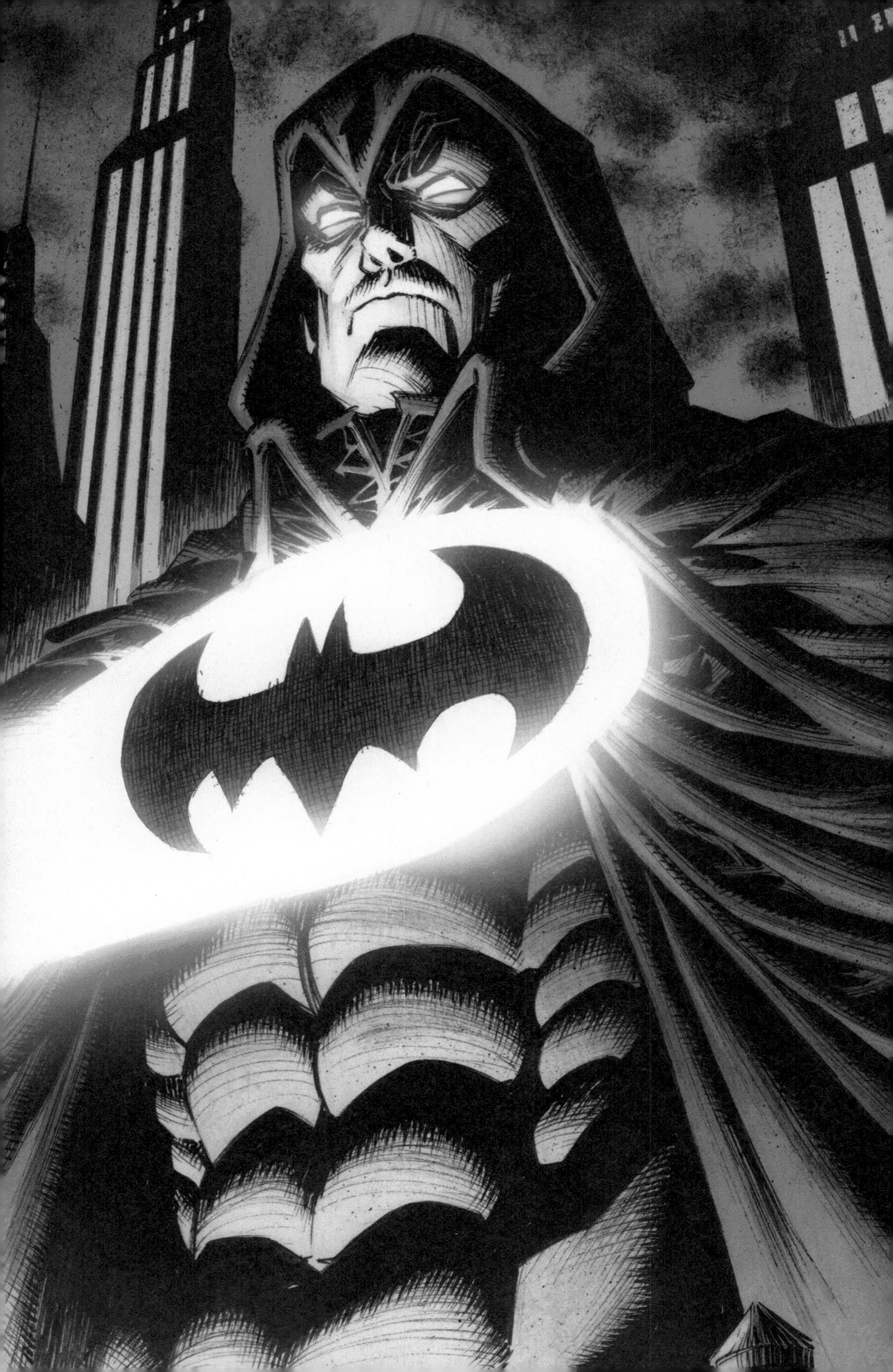

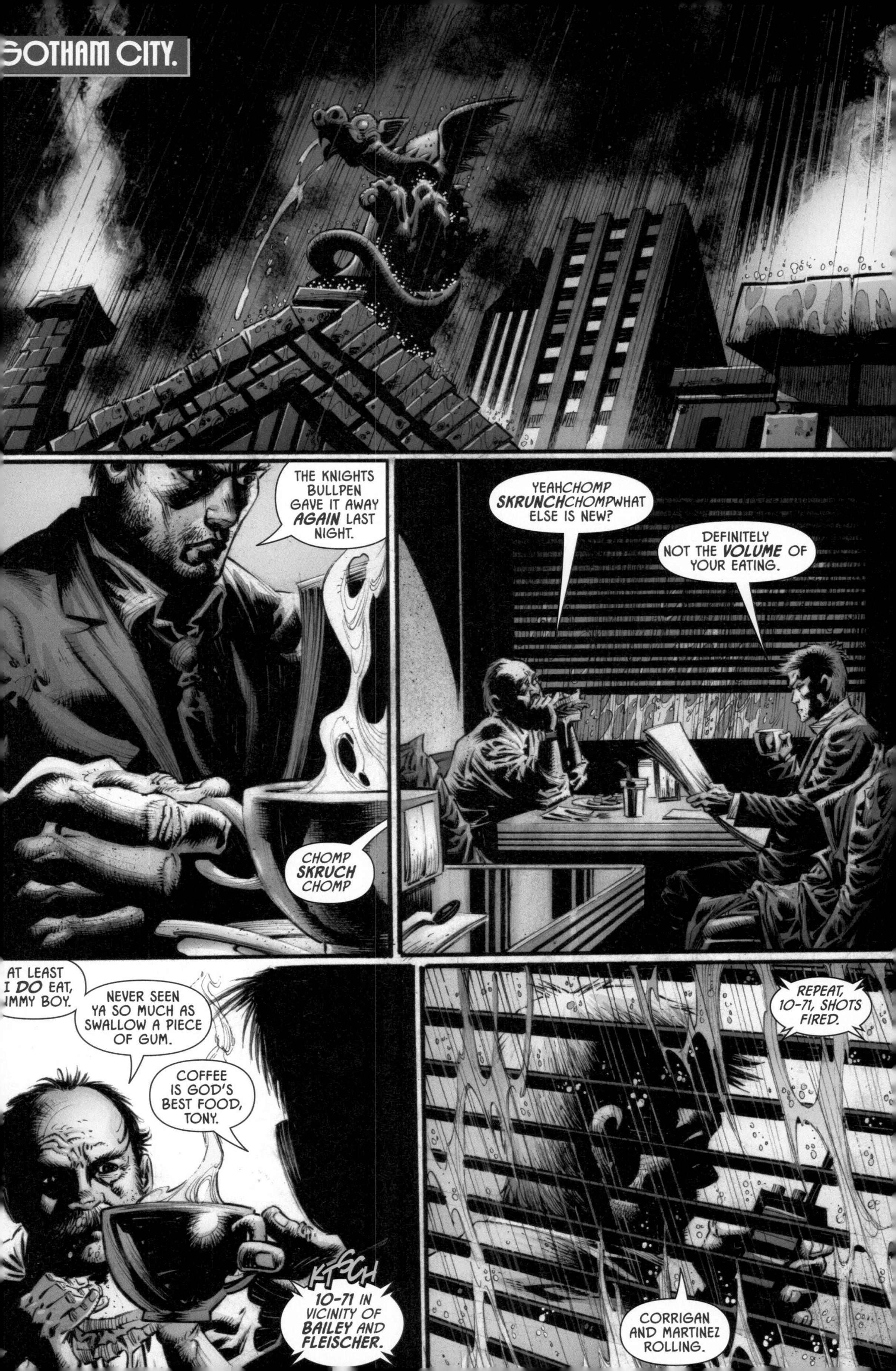
GOTHAM CITY.
THE KNIGHTS BULLPEN GAVE IT AWAY AGAIN LAST NIGHT.
CHOMP SKRUCH CHOMP
YEAHCHOMP SKRUNCHCHOMPWHAT ELSE IS NEW?
DEFINITELY NOT THE VOLUME OF YOUR EATING.
AT LEAST I DO EAT, IMMY BOY.
NEVER SEEN YA SO MUCH AS SWALLOW A PIECE OF GUM.
COFFEE IS GOD'S BEST FOOD, TONY.
KTSCH
10-71 IN VICINITY OF BAILEY AND FLEISCHER.
REPEAT, 10-71, SHOTS FIRED.
CORRIGAN AND MARTINEZ ROLLING.

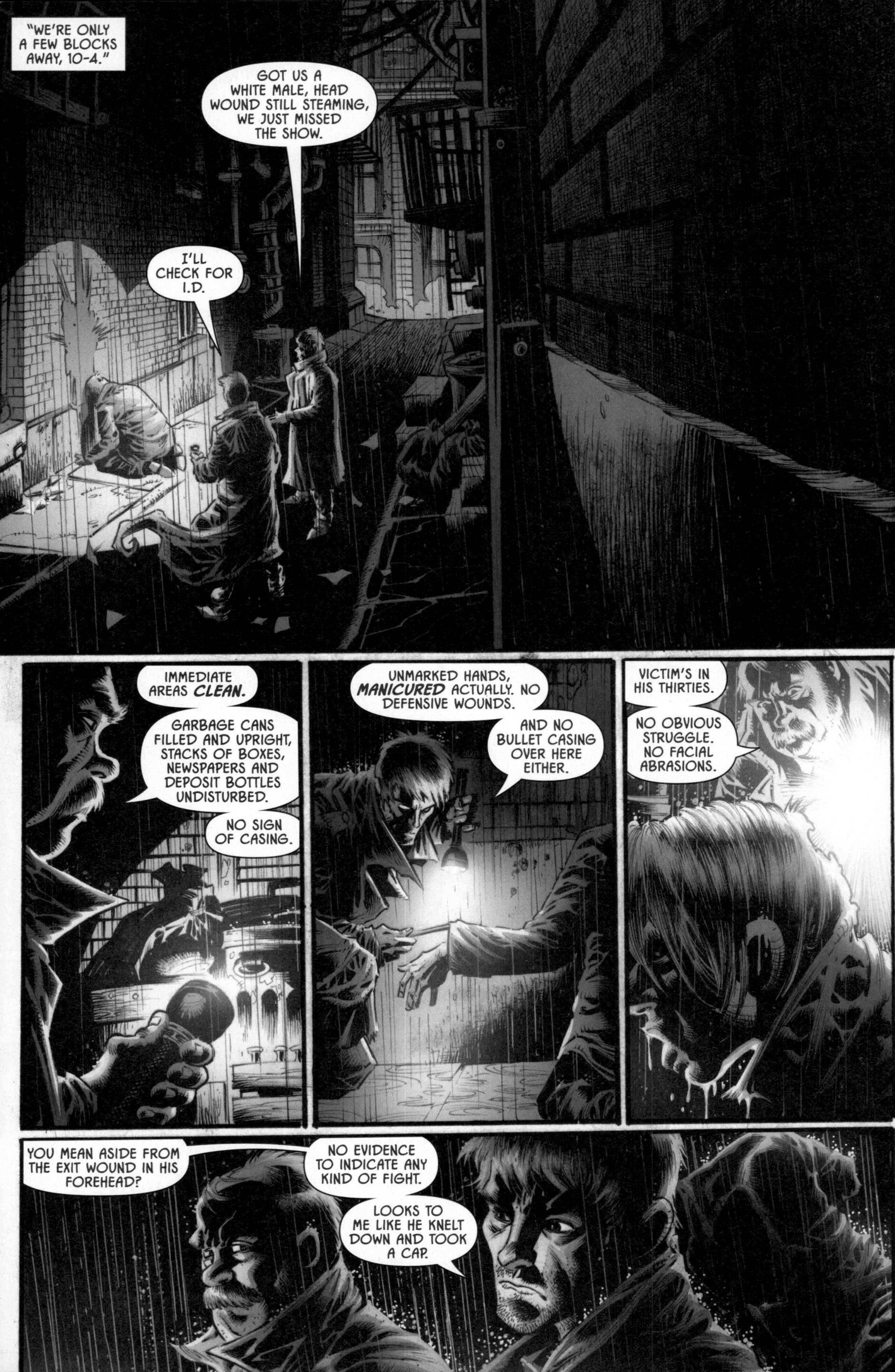
"WE'RE ONLY A FEW BLOCKS AWAY, 10-4."
GOT US A WHITE MALE, HEAD WOUND STILL STEAMING, WE JUST MISSED THE SHOW.
I'LL CHECK FOR I.D.
IMMEDIATE AREAS CLEAN.
GARBAGE CANS FILLED AND UPRIGHT, STACKS OF BOXES, NEWSPAPERS AND DEPOSIT BOTTLES UNDISTURBED.
NO SIGN OF CASING.
UNMARKED HANDS, MANICURED ACTUALLY. NO DEFENSIVE WOUNDS.
AND NO BULLET CASING OVER HERE EITHER.
VICTIM'S IN HIS THIRTIES.
NO OBVIOUS STRUGGLE. NO FACIAL ABRASIONS.
NO EVIDENCE TO INDICATE ANY KIND OF FIGHT.
YOU MEAN ASIDE FROM THE EXIT WOUND IN HIS FOREHEAD?
LOOKS TO ME LIKE HE KNELT DOWN AND TOOK A CAP.

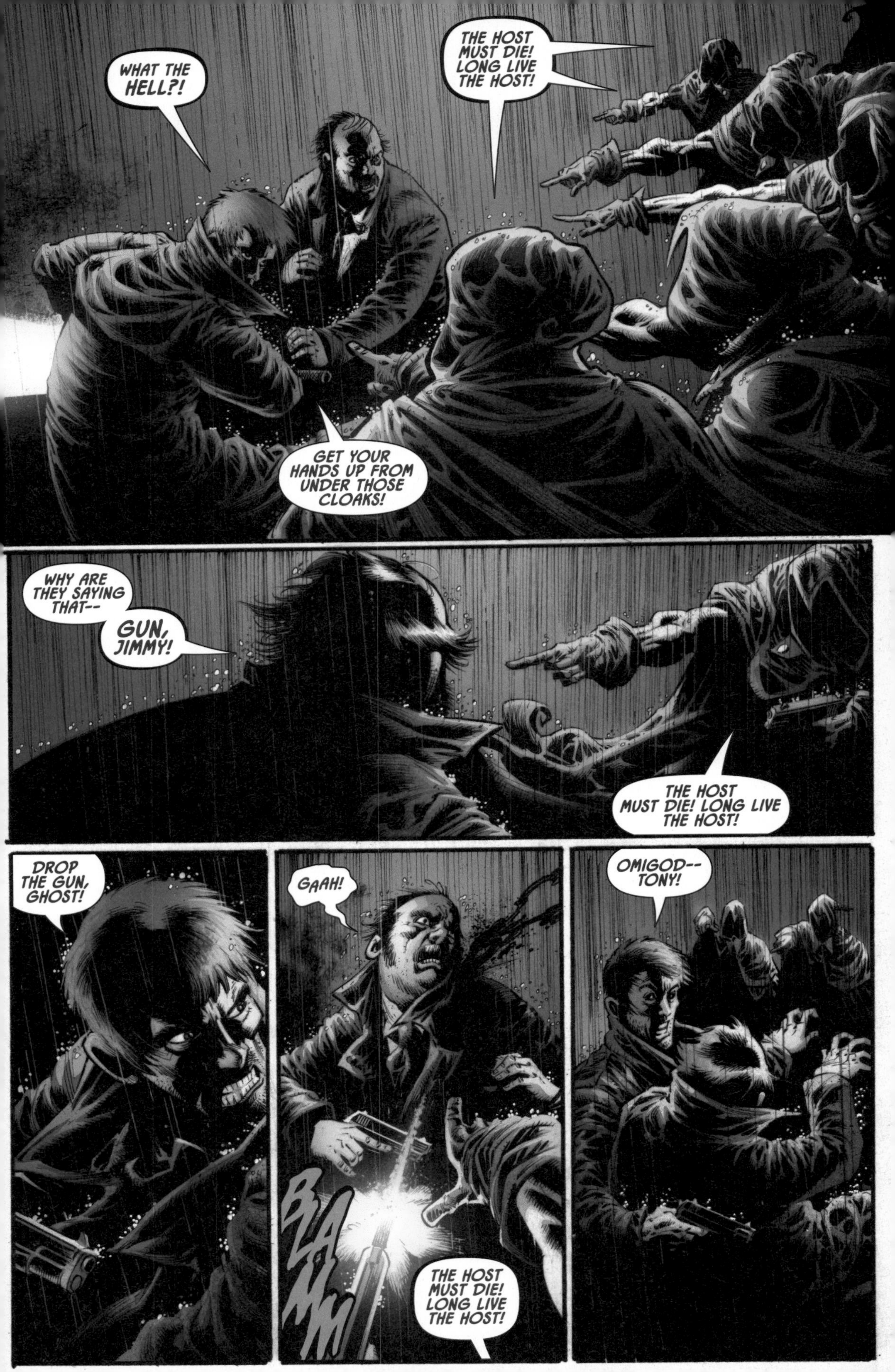
WHAT THE HELL?!
THE HOST MUST DIE! LONG LIVE THE HOST!
GET YOUR HANDS UP FROM UNDER THOSE CLOAKS!
WHY ARE THEY SAYING THAT--
GUN, JIMMY!
THE HOST MUST DIE! LONG LIVE THE HOST!
DROP THE GUN, GHOST!
GAAH!
BLAMM
THE HOST MUST DIE! LONG LIVE THE HOST!
OMIGOD-- TONY!

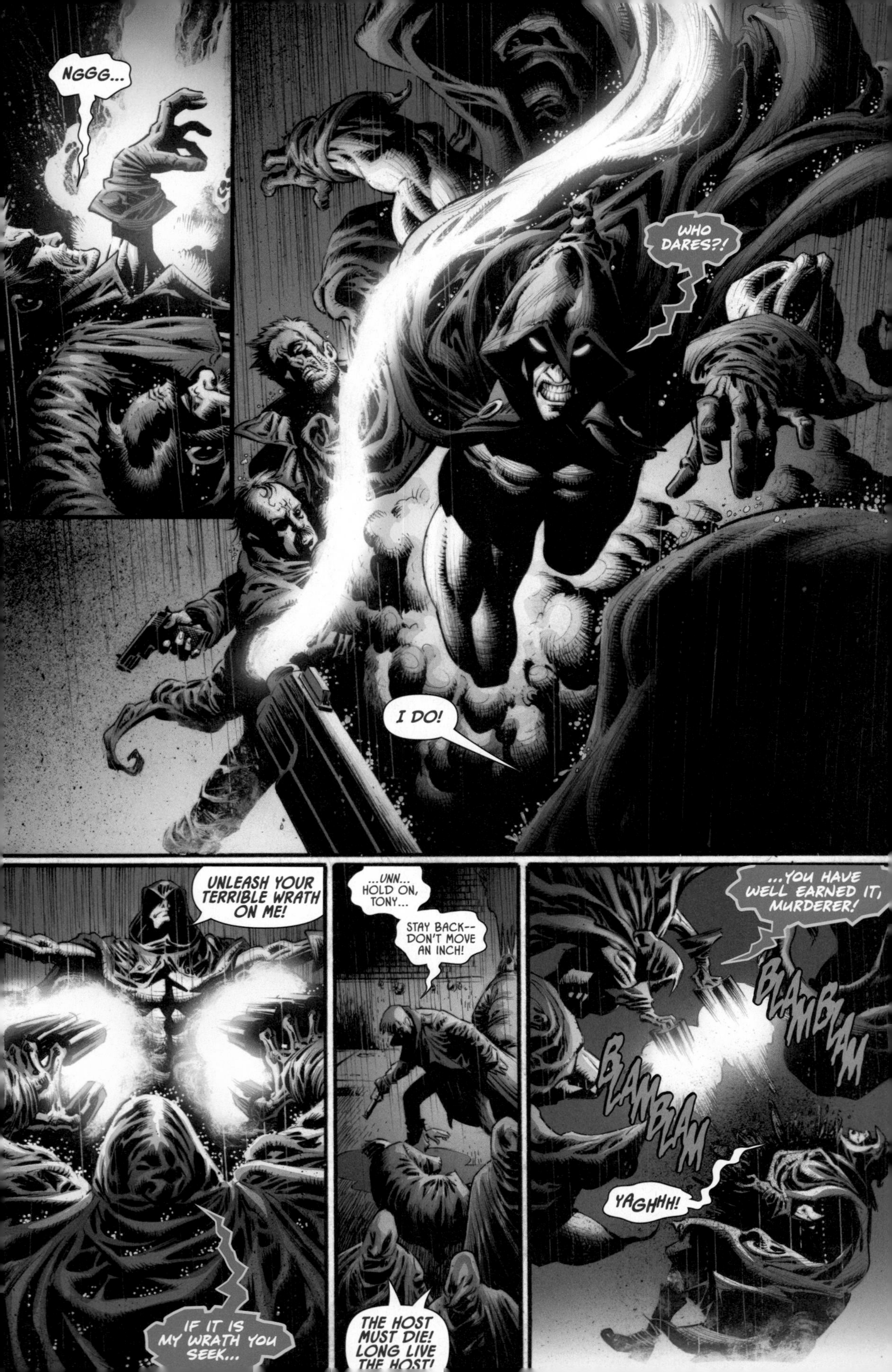
NGGG...
WHO DARES?!
I DO!
UNLEASH YOUR TERRIBLE WRATH ON ME!
IF IT IS MY WRATH YOU SEEK...
...UNN... HOLD ON, TONY...
STAY BACK-- DON'T MOVE AN INCH!
THE HOST MUST DIE! LONG LIVE THE HOST!
...YOU HAVE WELL EARNED IT, MURDERER!
BLAMBLAM
BLAMBLAM
YAGHHH!

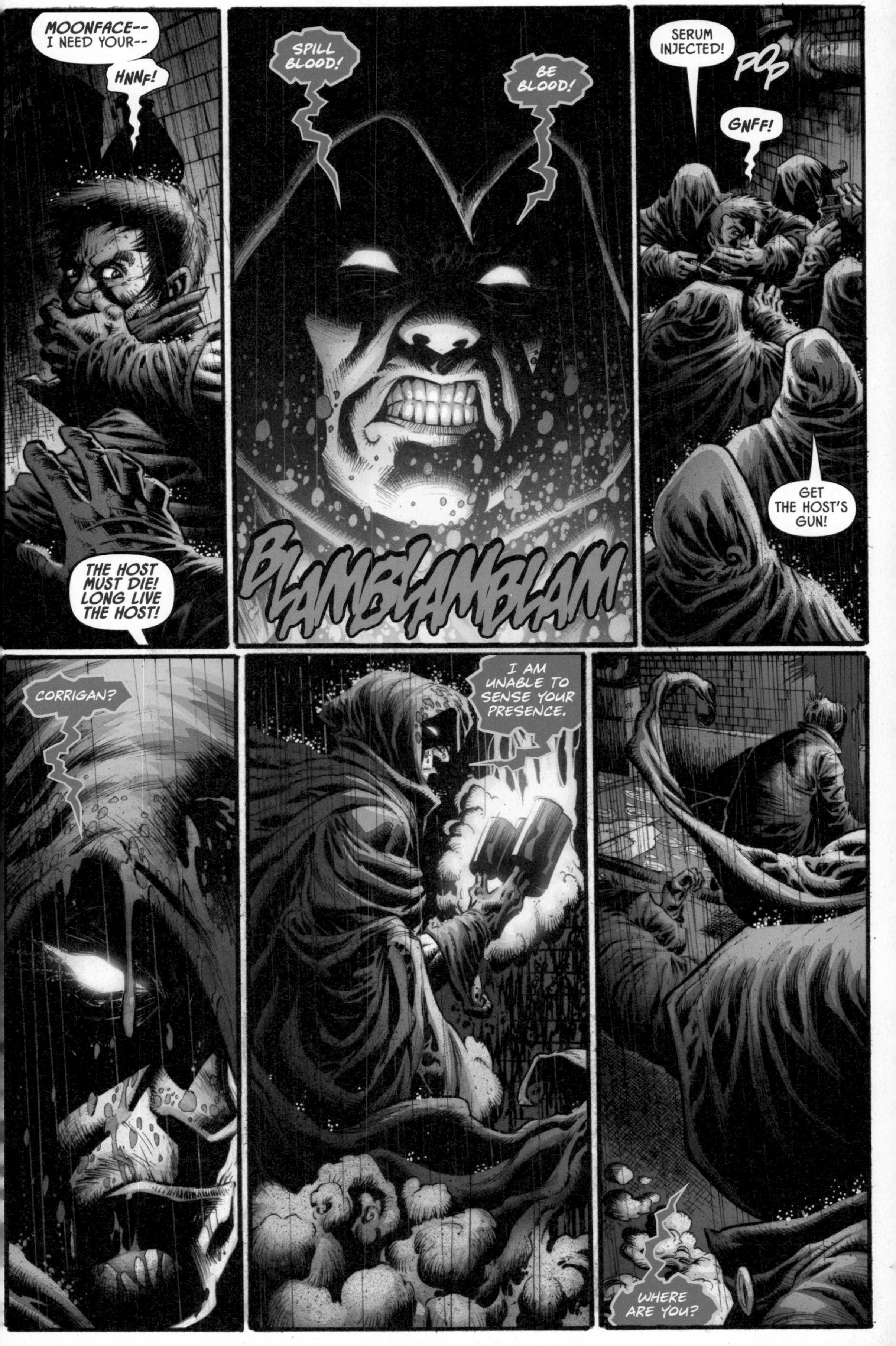
MOONFACE-- I NEED YOUR--
HNNF!
THE HOST MUST DIE! LONG LIVE THE HOST!
SPILL BLOOD!
BE BLOOD!
BLAMBLAMBLAM
SERUM INJECTED!
POP
GNFF!
GET THE HOST'S GUN!
CORRIGAN?
I AM UNABLE TO SENSE YOUR PRESENCE.
WHERE ARE YOU?

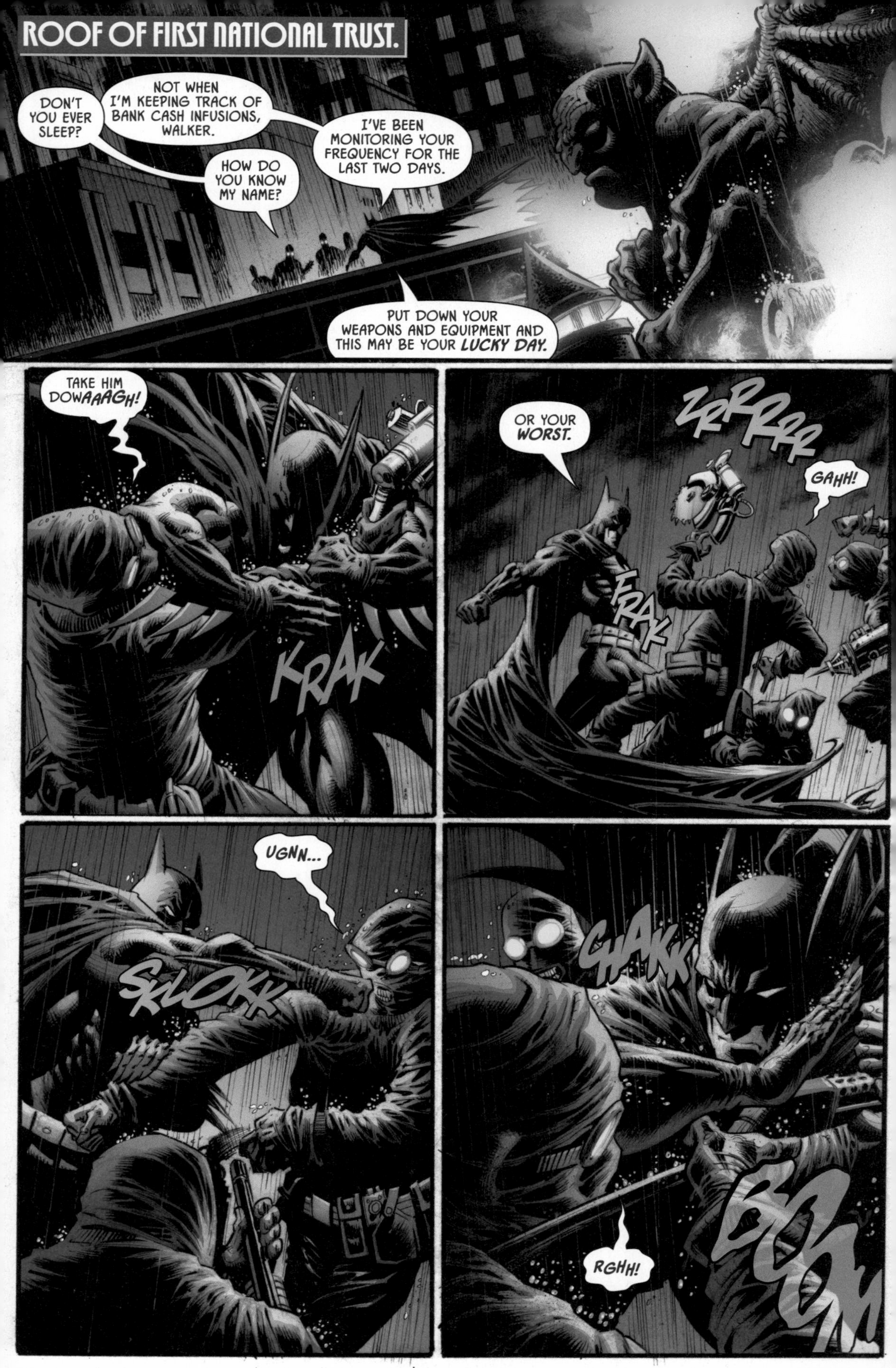
ROOF OF FIRST NATIONAL TRUST.
DON'T YOU EVER SLEEP?
NOT WHEN I'M KEEPING TRACK OF BANK CASH INFUSIONS, WALKER.
HOW DO YOU KNOW MY NAME?
I'VE BEEN MONITORING YOUR FREQUENCY FOR THE LAST TWO DAYS.
PUT DOWN YOUR WEAPONS AND EQUIPMENT AND THIS MAY BE YOUR LUCKY DAY.
TAKE HIM DOWAAAGH!
KRAK
OR YOUR WORST.
ZRRRRRR
GAHH!
FRAK
UGNN...
SKLOKK
CHAKK
RGHH!
BOOM

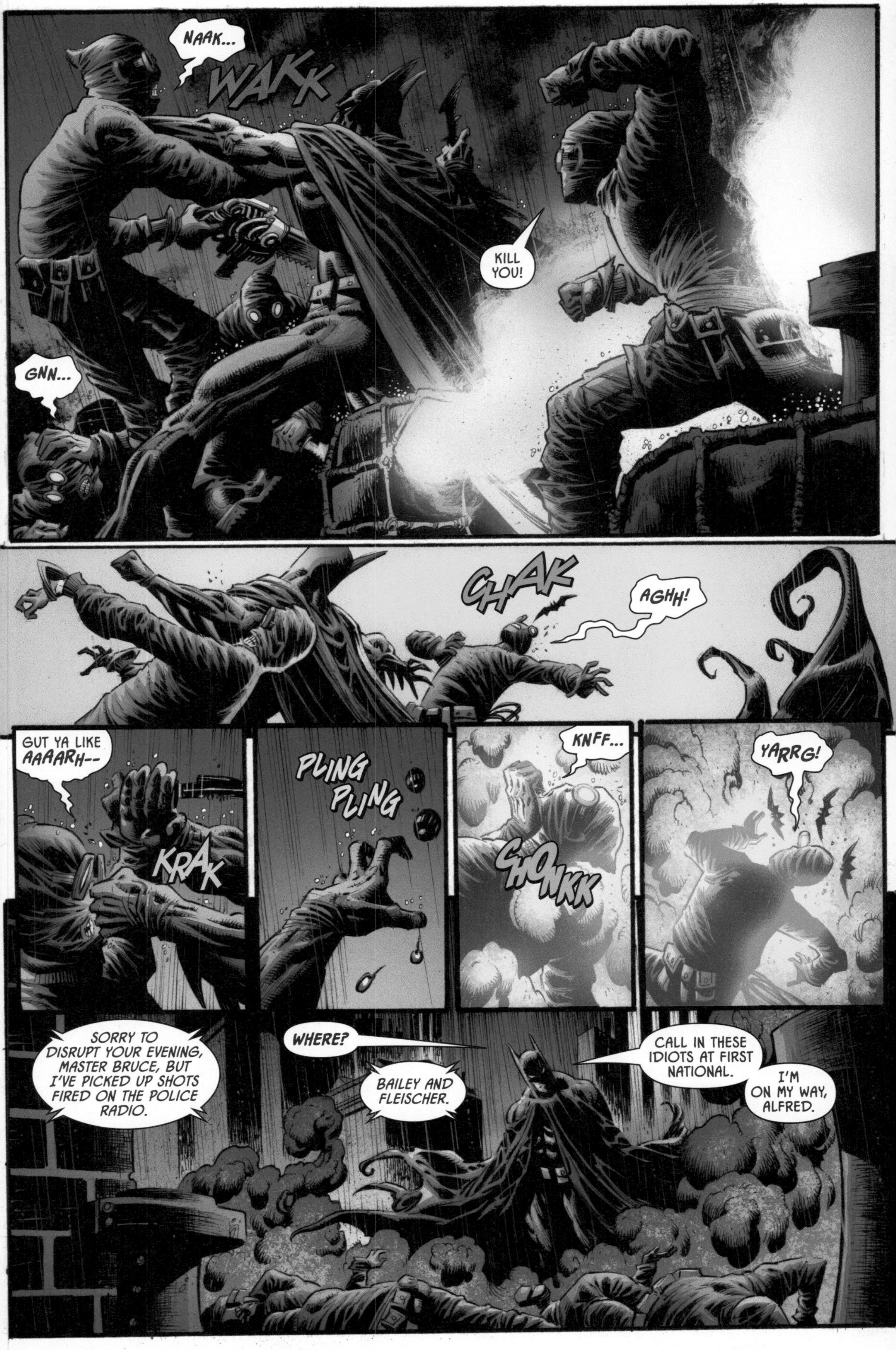
NAAK...
WAKK
KILL YOU!
GNN...
CHAK
AGHH!
GUT YA LIKE AAAARH--
KRAK
PLING PLING
KNFF...
CHONKK
YARRG!
SORRY TO DISRUPT YOUR EVENING, MASTER BRUCE, BUT I'VE PICKED UP SHOTS FIRED ON THE POLICE RADIO.
WHERE?
BAILEY AND FLEISCHER.
CALL IN THESE IDIOTS AT FIRST NATIONAL.
I'M ON MY WAY, ALFRED.

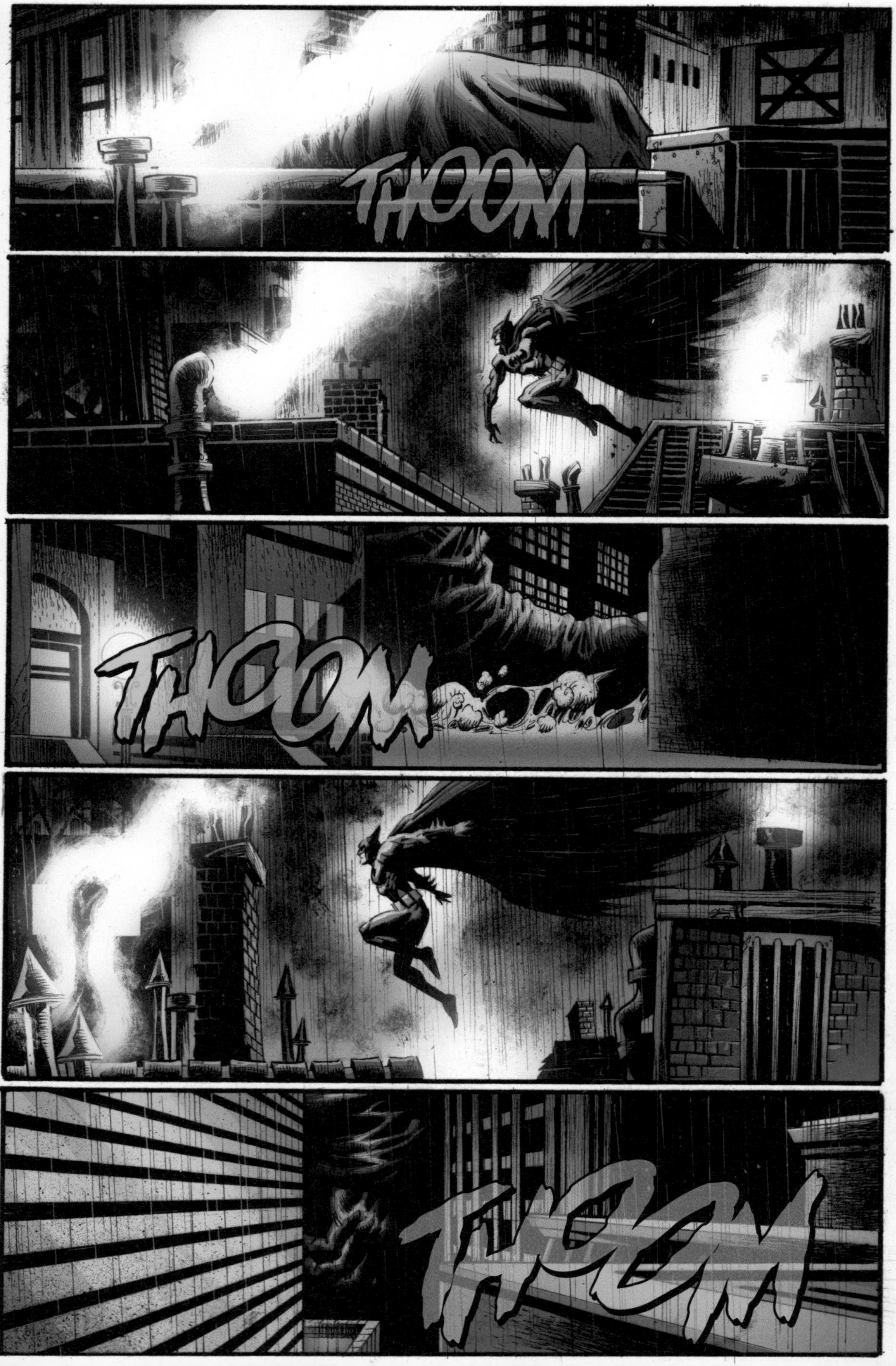
THOOM
THOOM
THOOM

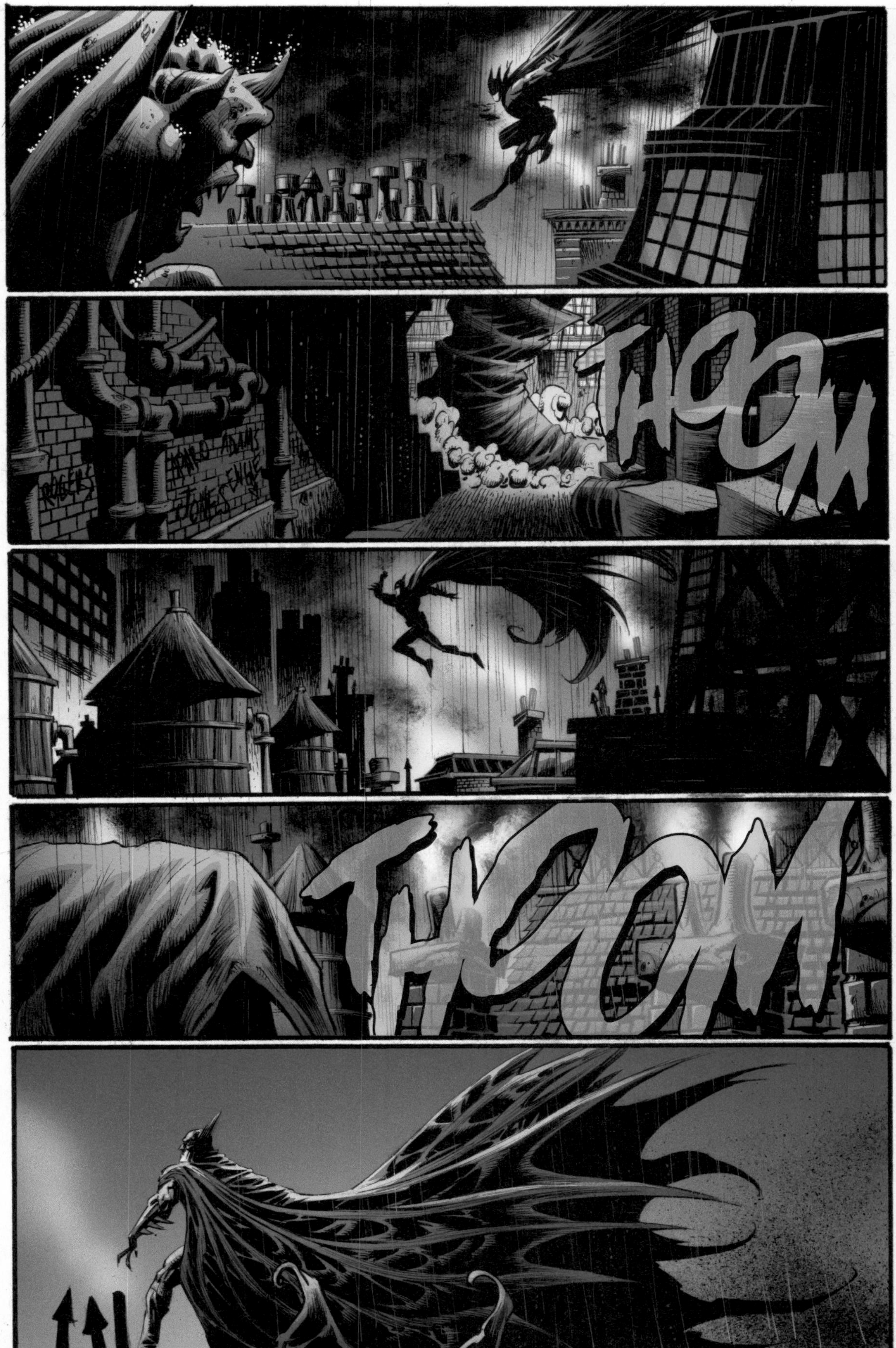
THOOM
THOOM

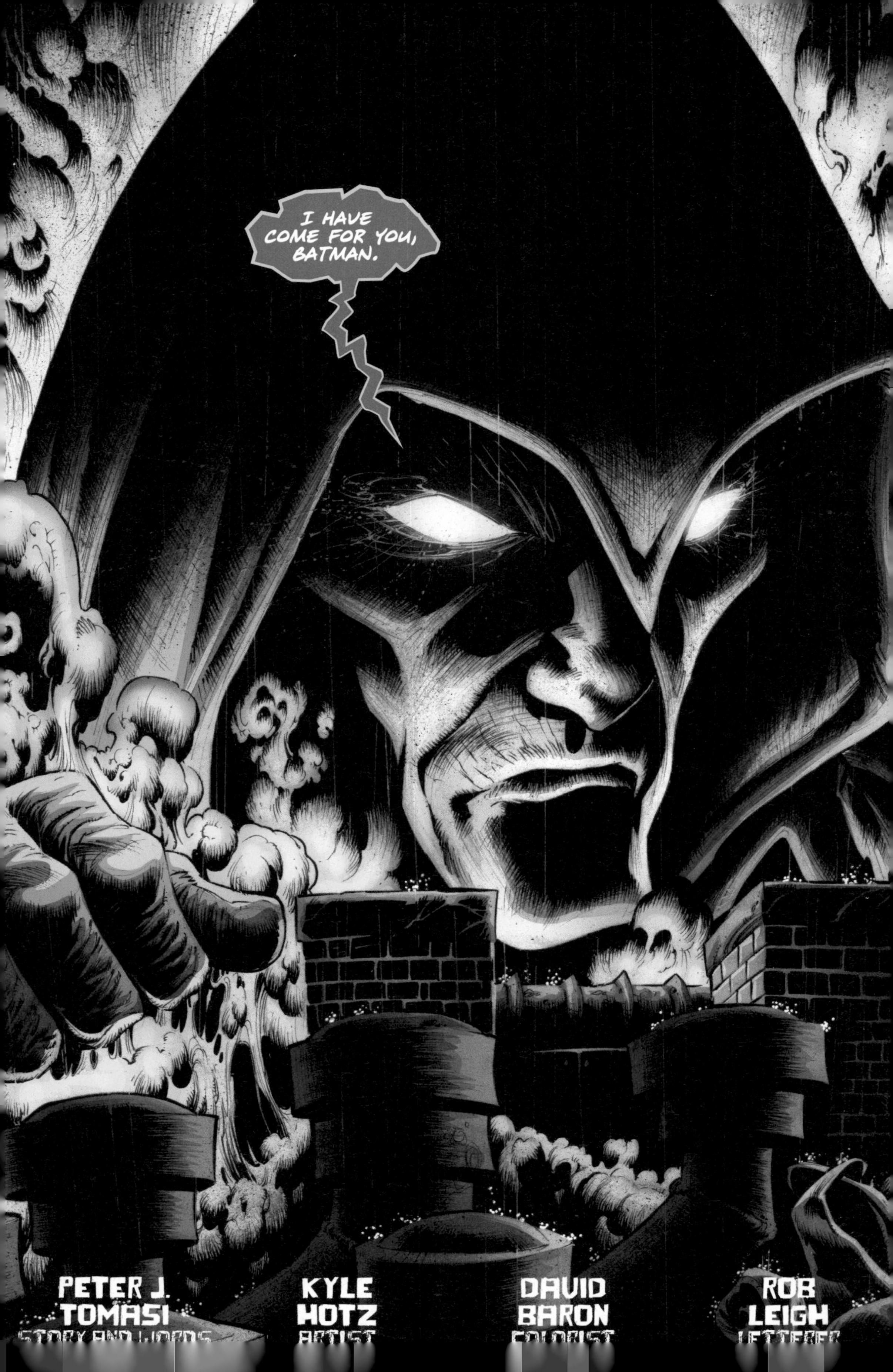
I HAVE COME FOR YOU, BATMAN.
PETER J. TOMASI
KYLE HOTZ
DAVID BARON
ROB LEIGH

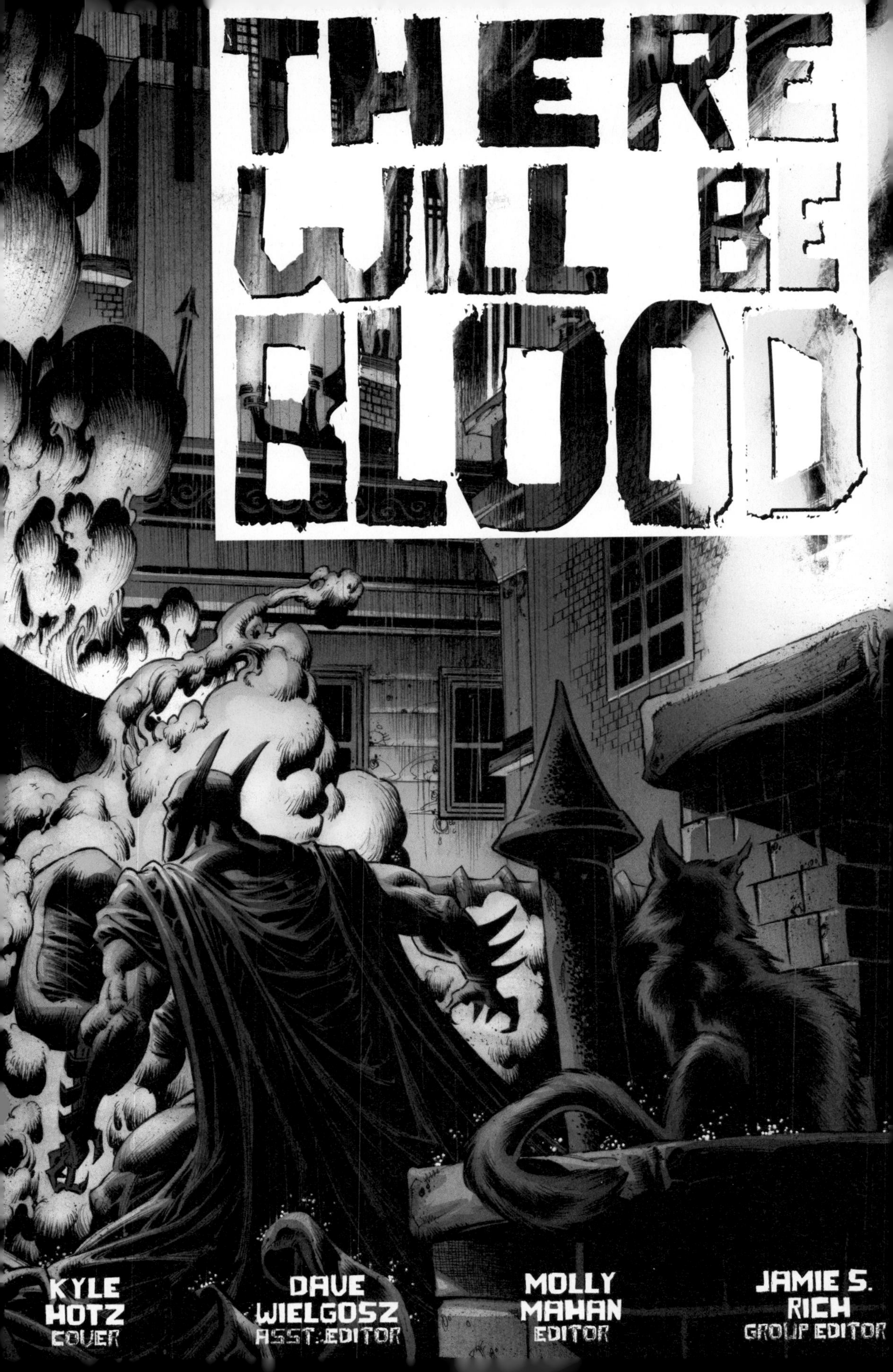

THERE WILL BE BLOOD
KYLE HOTZ COVER
DAVE WIELGOSZ ASST. EDITOR
MOLLY MAHAN EDITOR
JAMIE S. RICH GROUP EDITOR

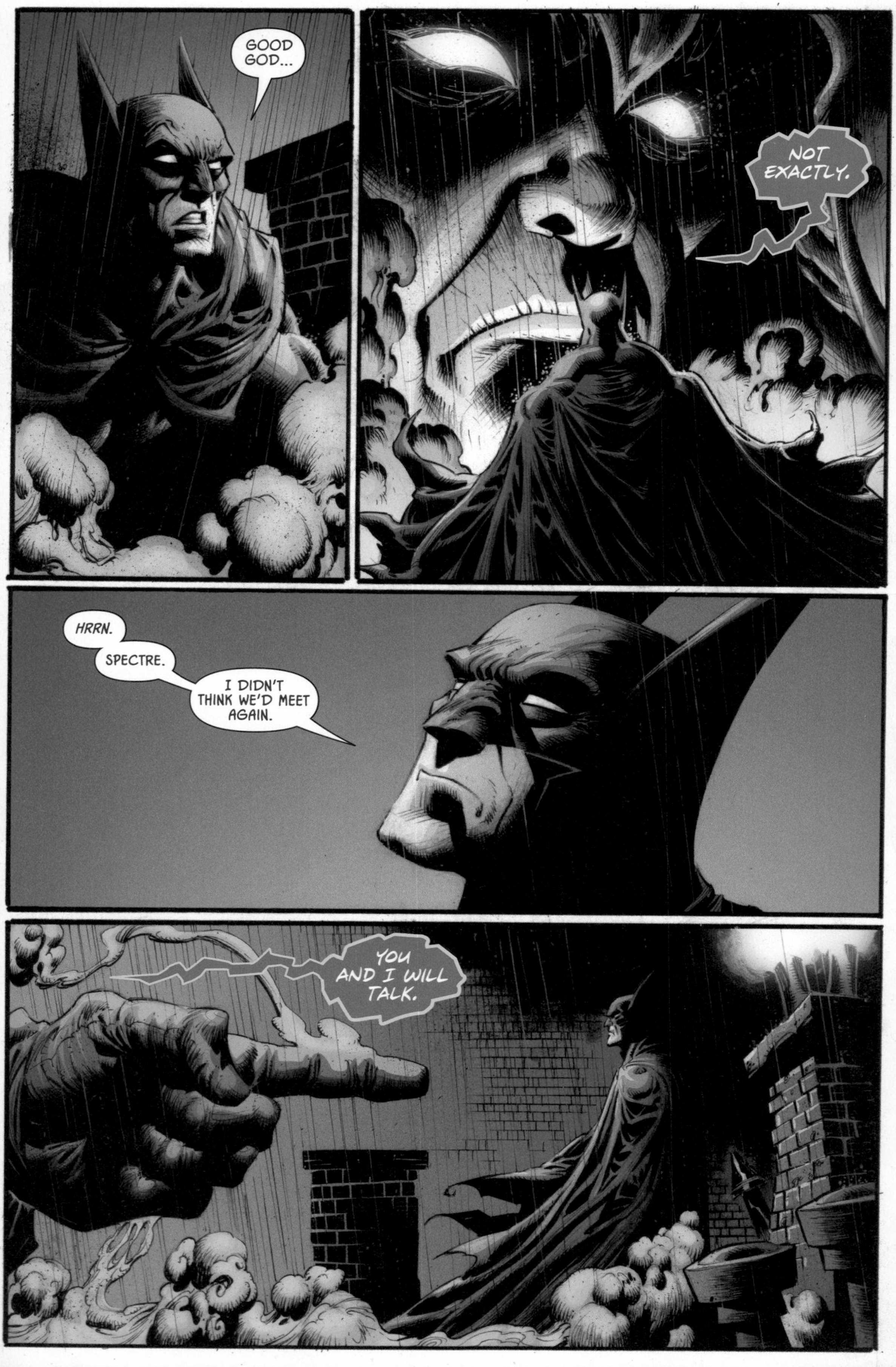
GOOD GOD...
NOT EXACTLY.
HRRN.
SPECTRE.
I DIDN'T THINK WE'D MEET AGAIN.
YOU AND I WILL TALK.

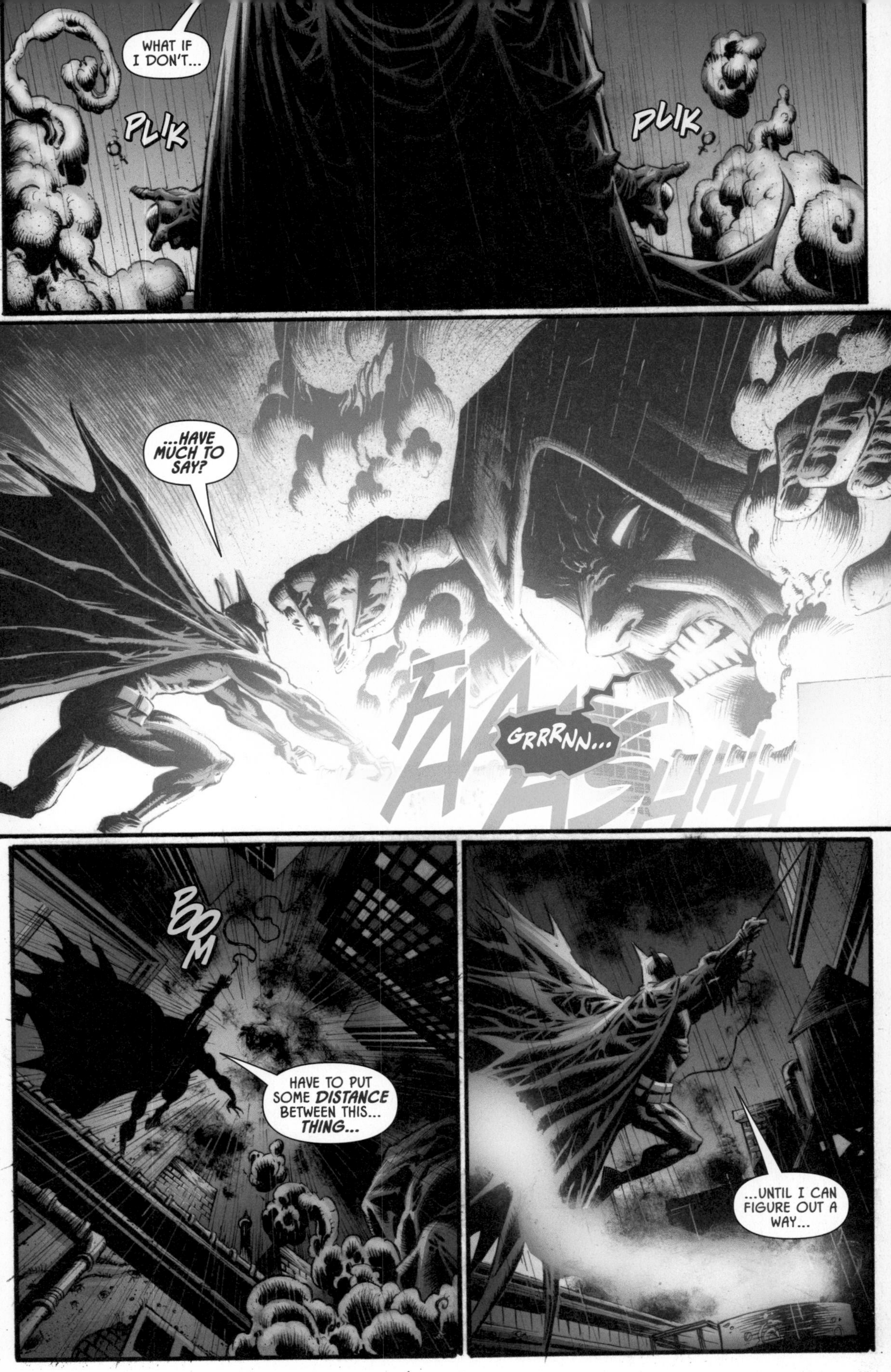

WHAT IF I DON'T...
PLIK
PLIK
...HAVE MUCH TO SAY?
GRRRNN...
BOOM
HAVE TO PUT SOME DISTANCE BETWEEN THIS... THING...
...UNTIL I CAN FIGURE OUT A WAY...

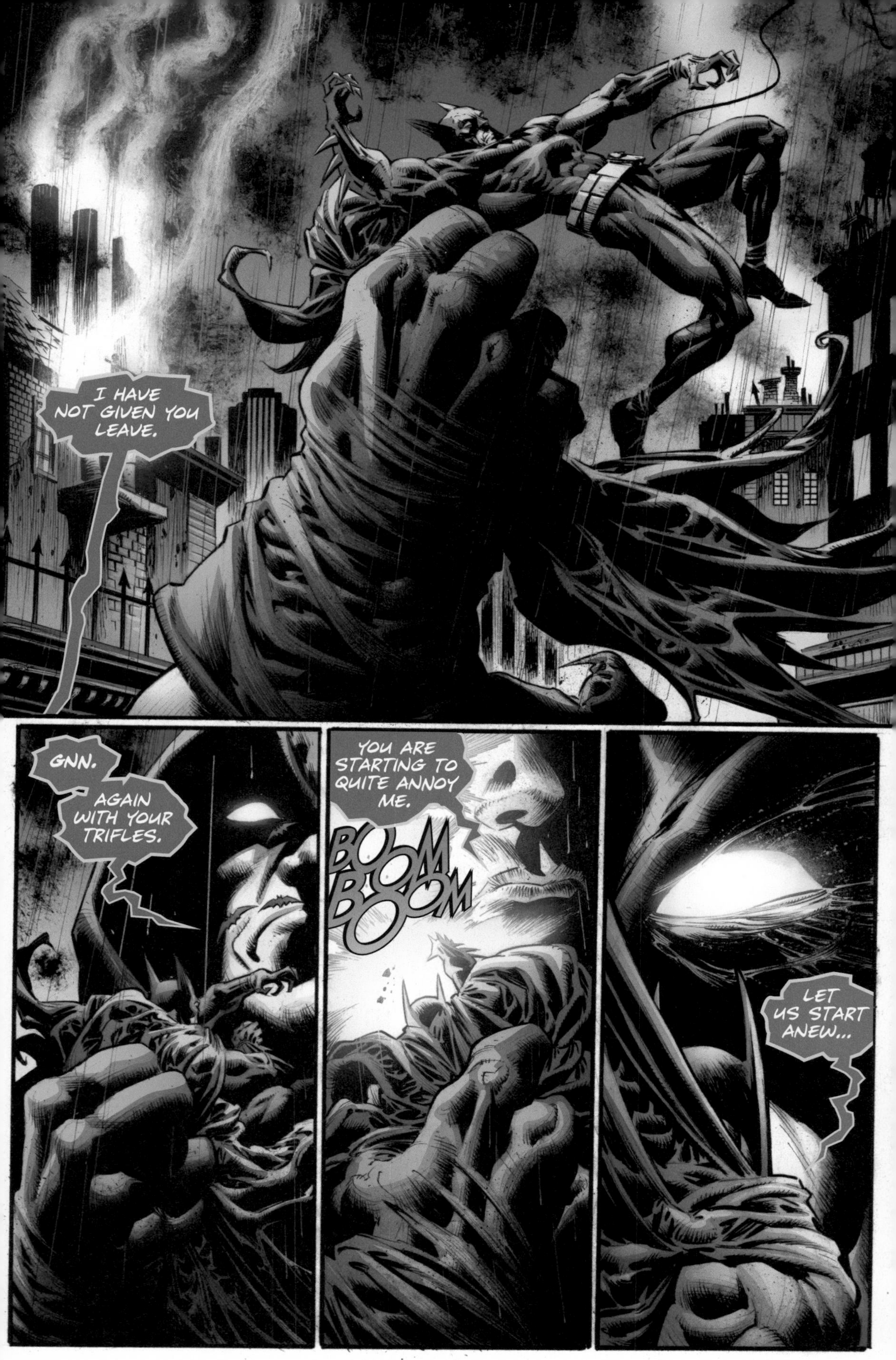
I HAVE NOT GIVEN YOU LEAVE.
GNN.
AGAIN WITH YOUR TRIFLES.
YOU ARE STARTING TO QUITE ANNOY ME.
BOOM BOOM BOOM
LET US START ANEW...

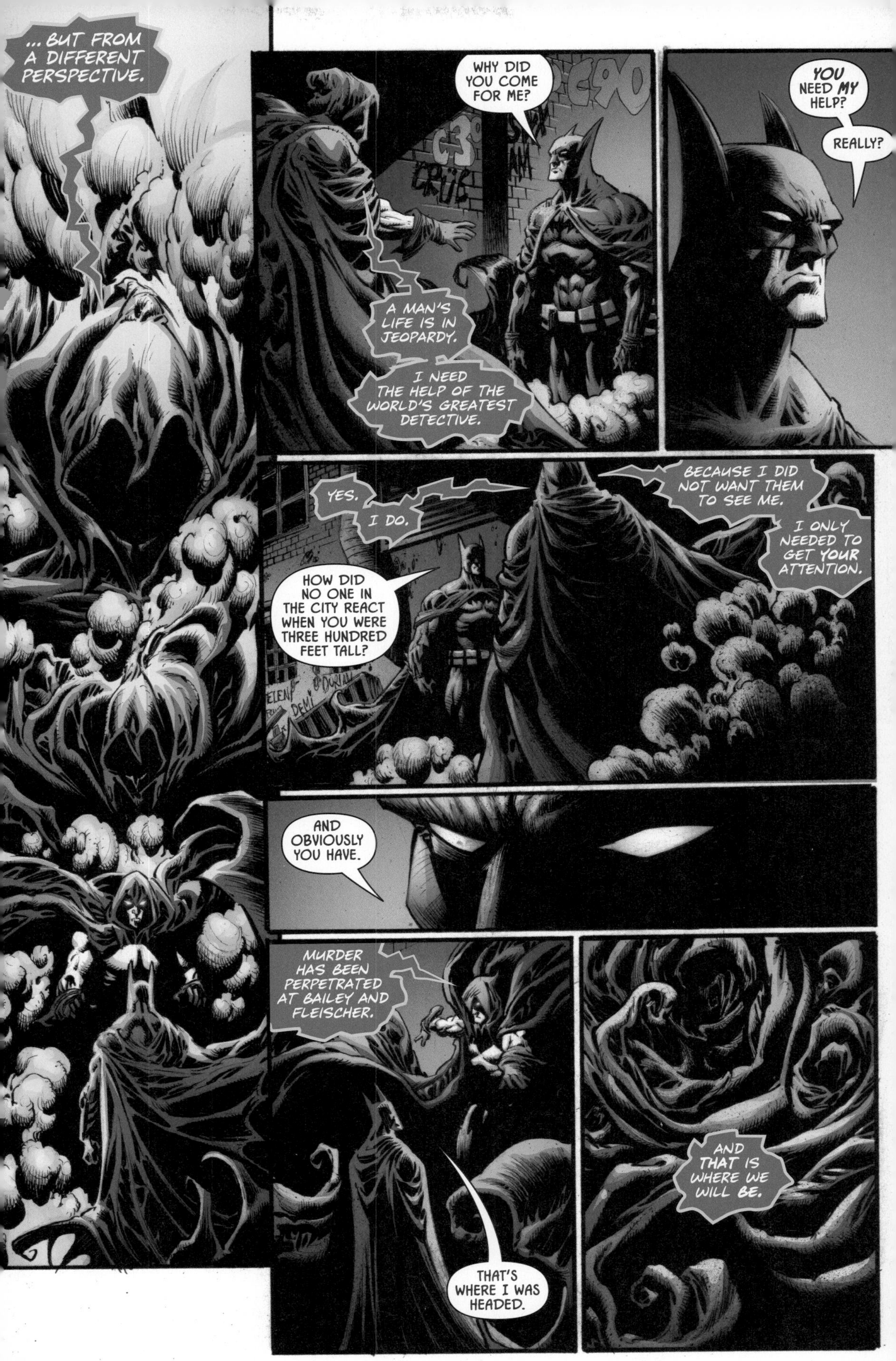
...BUT FROM A DIFFERENT PERSPECTIVE.
WHY DID YOU COME FOR ME?
A MAN'S LIFE IS IN JEOPARDY.
I NEED THE HELP OF THE WORLD'S GREATEST DETECTIVE.
YOU NEED MY HELP?
REALLY?
YES.
I DO.
HOW DID NO ONE IN THE CITY REACT WHEN YOU WERE THREE HUNDRED FEET TALL?
BECAUSE I DID NOT WANT THEM TO SEE ME.
I ONLY NEEDED TO GET YOUR ATTENTION.
AND OBVIOUSLY YOU HAVE.
MURDER HAS BEEN PERPETRATED AT BAILEY AND FLEISCHER.
THAT'S WHERE I WAS HEADED.
AND THAT IS WHERE WE WILL BE.

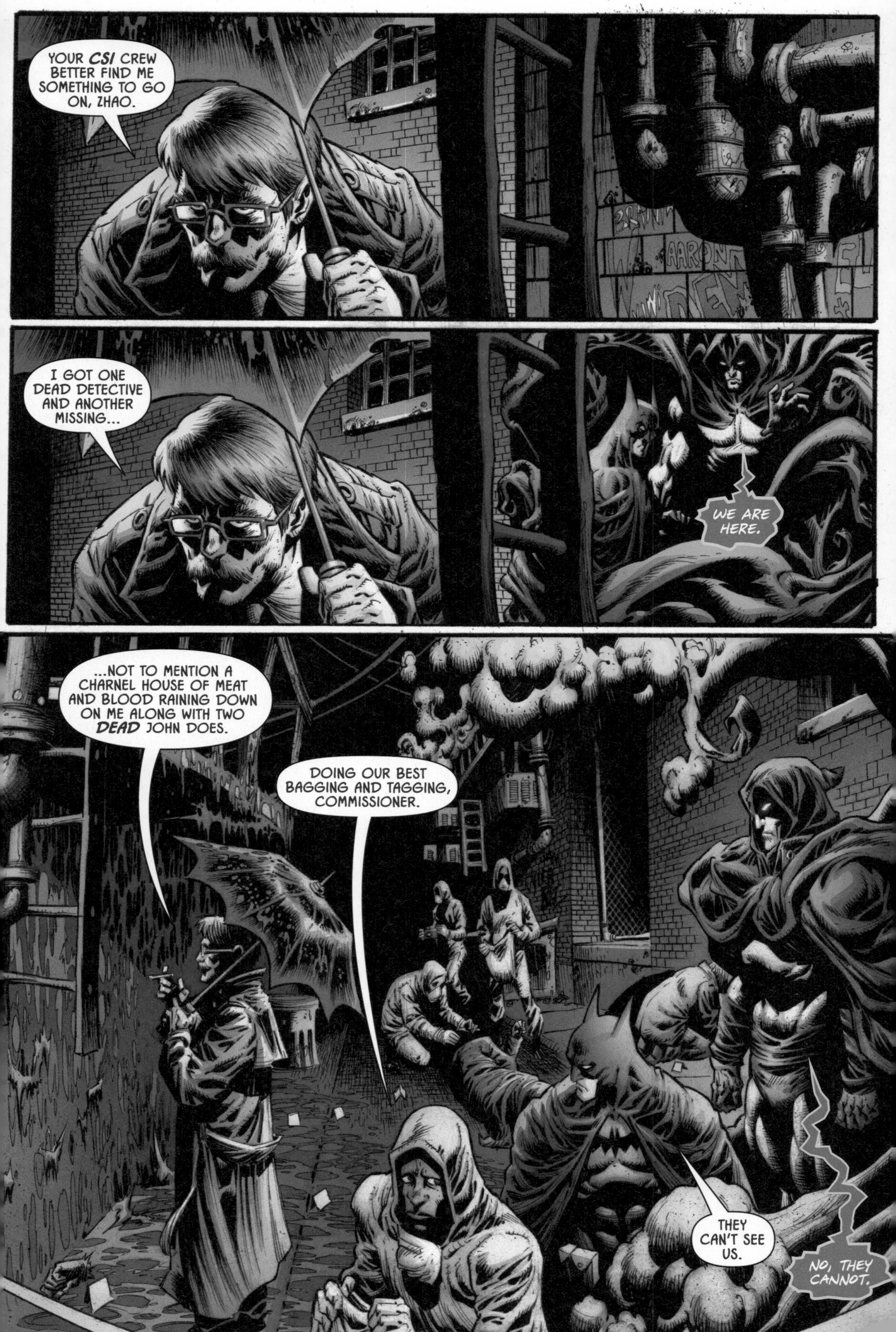
YOUR CSI CREW BETTER FIND ME SOMETHING TO GO ON, ZHAO.
I GOT ONE DEAD DETECTIVE AND ANOTHER MISSING...
WE ARE HERE.
...NOT TO MENTION A CHARNEL HOUSE OF MEAT AND BLOOD RAINING DOWN ON ME ALONG WITH TWO DEAD JOHN DOES.
DOING OUR BEST BAGGING AND TAGGING, COMMISSIONER.
THEY CAN'T SEE US.
NO, THEY CANNOT.

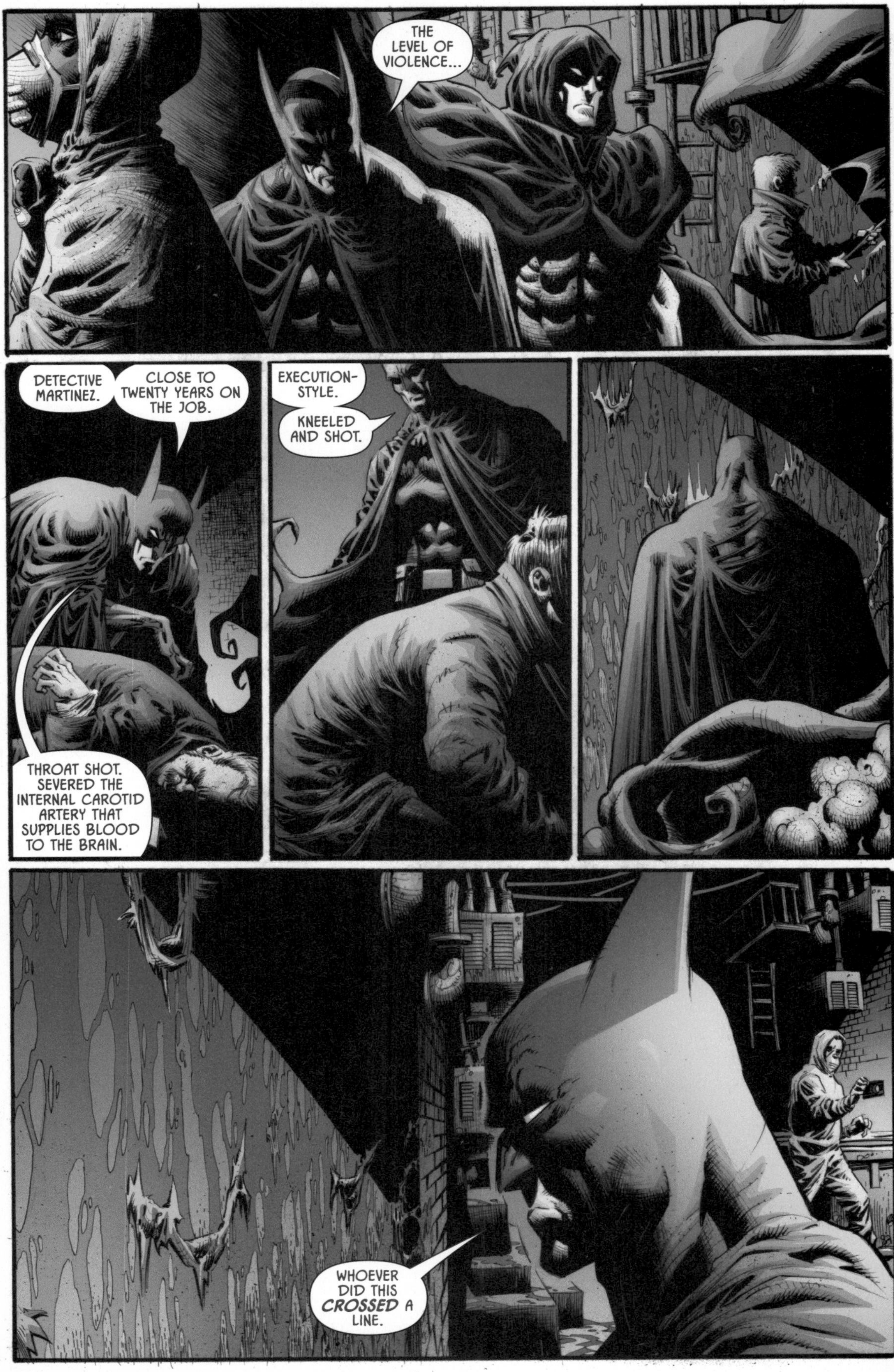
THE LEVEL OF VIOLENCE...
DETECTIVE MARTINEZ.
CLOSE TO TWENTY YEARS ON THE JOB.
THROAT SHOT. SEVERED THE INTERNAL CAROTID ARTERY THAT SUPPLIES BLOOD TO THE BRAIN.
EXECUTION-STYLE.
KNEELED AND SHOT.
WHOEVER DID THIS CROSSED A LINE.

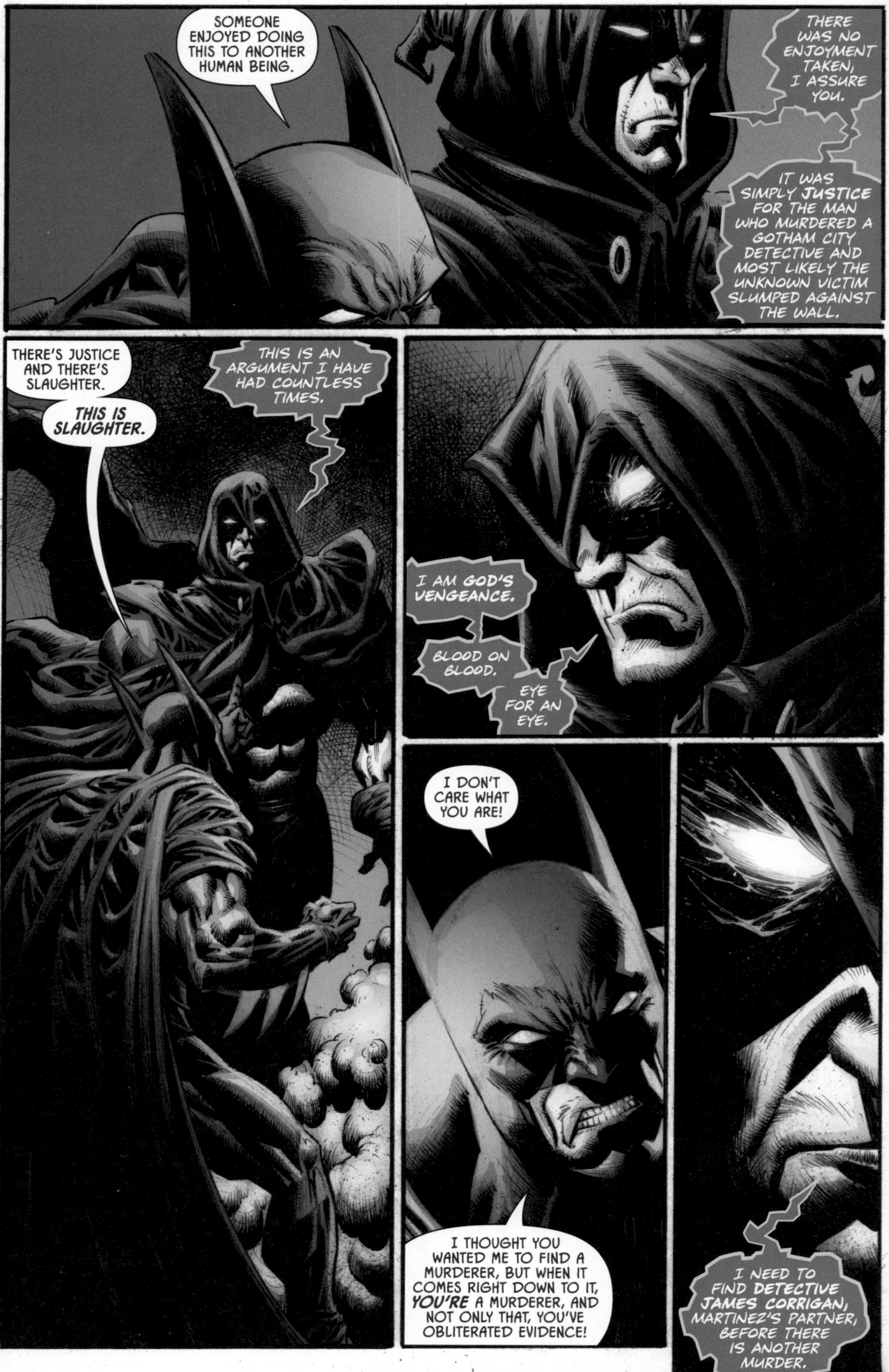
SOMEONE ENJOYED DOING THIS TO ANOTHER HUMAN BEING.
THERE WAS NO ENJOYMENT TAKEN, I ASSURE YOU.
IT WAS SIMPLY JUSTICE FOR THE MAN WHO MURDERED A GOTHAM CITY DETECTIVE AND MOST LIKELY THE UNKNOWN VICTIM SLUMPED AGAINST THE WALL.
THERE'S JUSTICE AND THERE'S SLAUGHTER.
THIS IS SLAUGHTER.
THIS IS AN ARGUMENT I HAVE HAD COUNTLESS TIMES.
I AM GOD'S VENGEANCE.
BLOOD ON BLOOD.
EYE FOR AN EYE.
I DON'T CARE WHAT YOU ARE!
I THOUGHT YOU WANTED ME TO FIND A MURDERER, BUT WHEN IT COMES RIGHT DOWN TO IT, YOU'RE A MURDERER, AND NOT ONLY THAT, YOU'VE OBLITERATED EVIDENCE!
I NEED TO FIND DETECTIVE JAMES CORRIGAN, MARTINEZ'S PARTNER, BEFORE THERE IS ANOTHER MURDER.

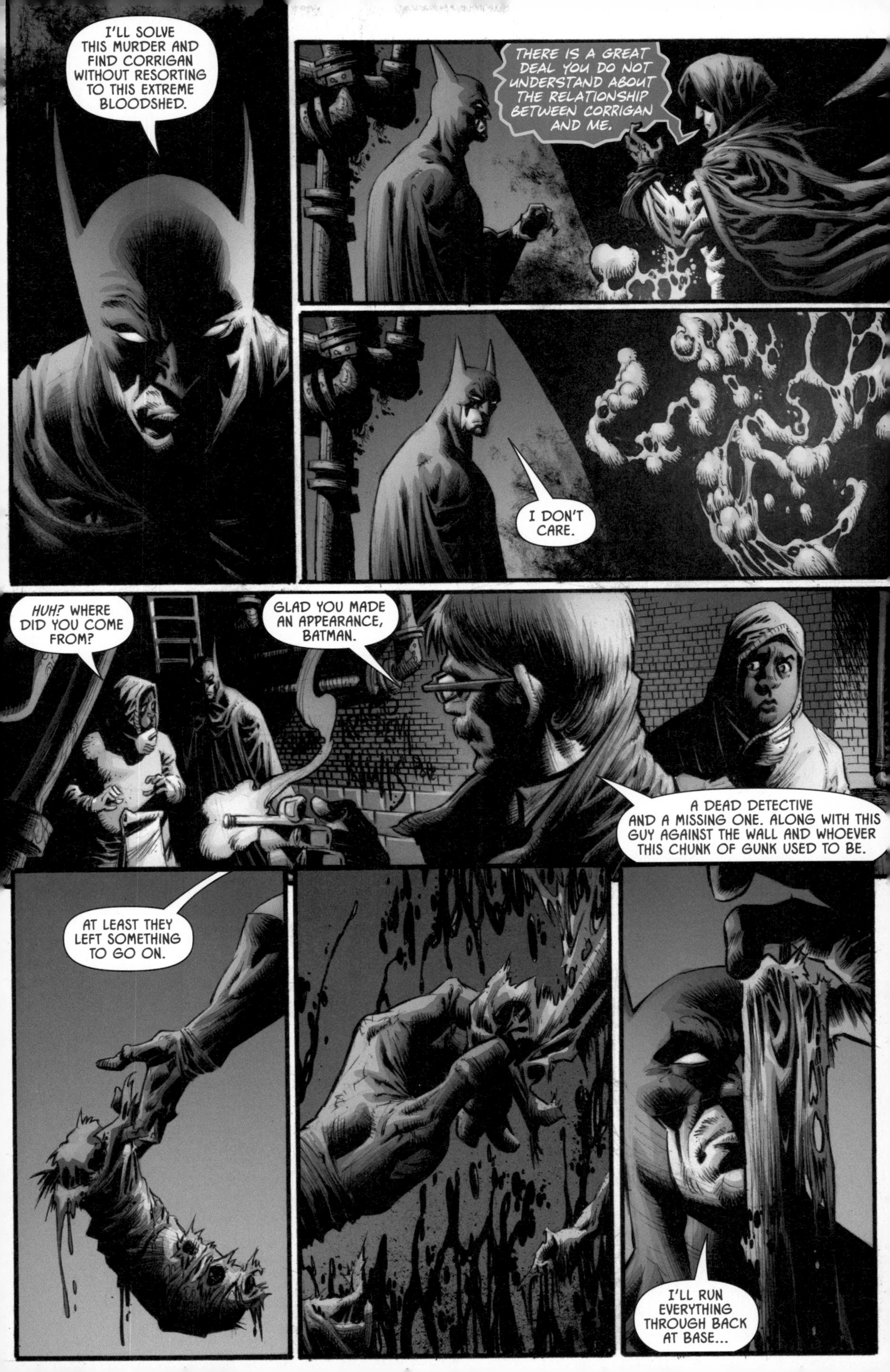
I'LL SOLVE THIS MURDER AND FIND CORRIGAN WITHOUT RESORTING TO THIS EXTREME BLOODSHED.
THERE IS A GREAT DEAL YOU DO NOT UNDERSTAND ABOUT THE RELATIONSHIP BETWEEN CORRIGAN AND ME.
I DON'T CARE.
HUH? WHERE DID YOU COME FROM?
GLAD YOU MADE AN APPEARANCE, BATMAN.
A DEAD DETECTIVE AND A MISSING ONE. ALONG WITH THIS GUY AGAINST THE WALL AND WHOEVER THIS CHUNK OF GUNK USED TO BE.
AT LEAST THEY LEFT SOMETHING TO GO ON.
I'LL RUN EVERYTHING THROUGH BACK AT BASE...

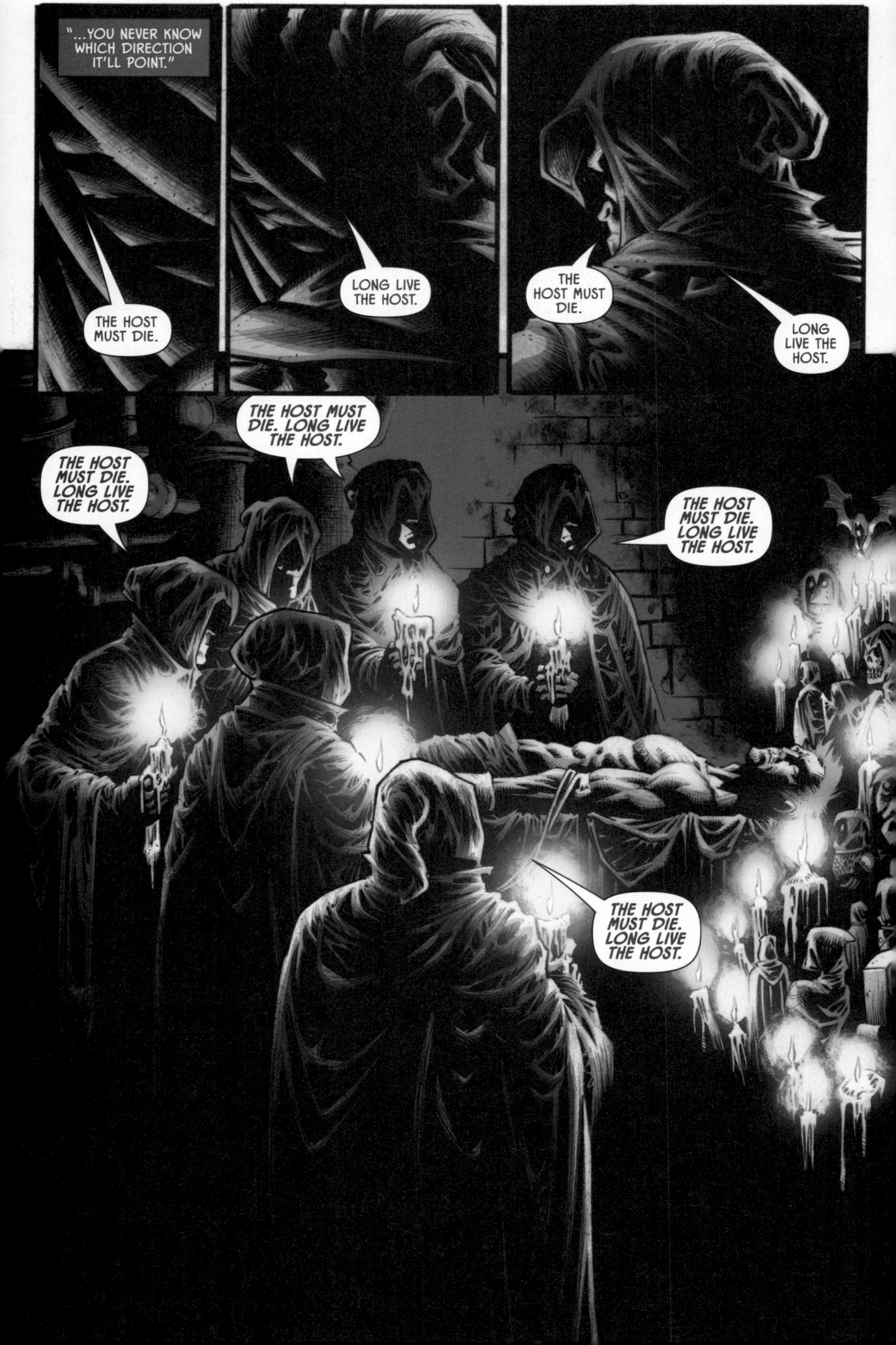
"...YOU NEVER KNOW WHICH DIRECTION IT'LL POINT."
THE HOST MUST DIE.
LONG LIVE THE HOST.
THE HOST MUST DIE.
LONG LIVE THE HOST.
THE HOST MUST DIE. LONG LIVE THE HOST.
THE HOST MUST DIE. LONG LIVE THE HOST.
THE HOST MUST DIE. LONG LIVE THE HOST.
THE HOST MUST DIE. LONG LIVE THE HOST.

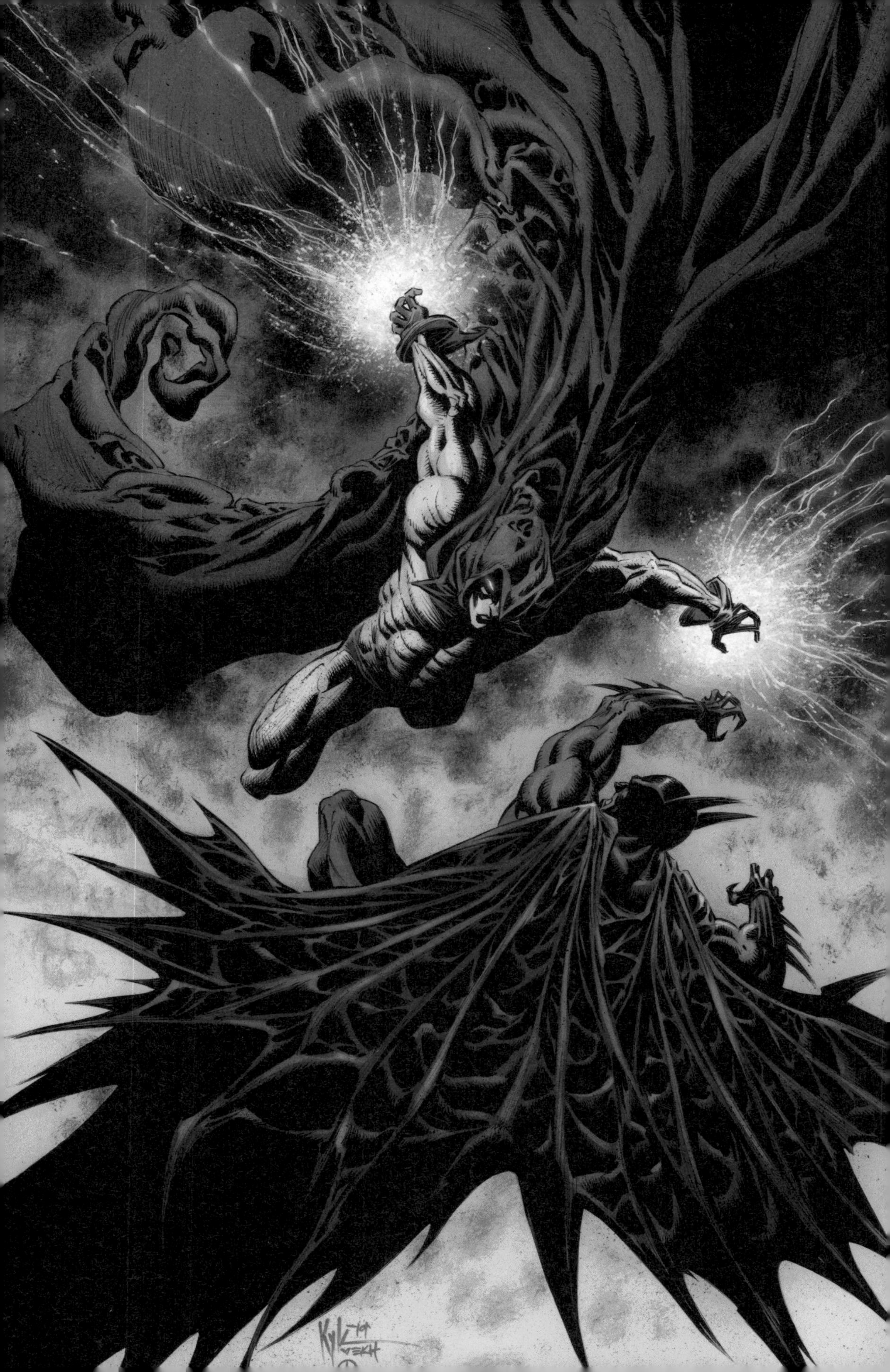

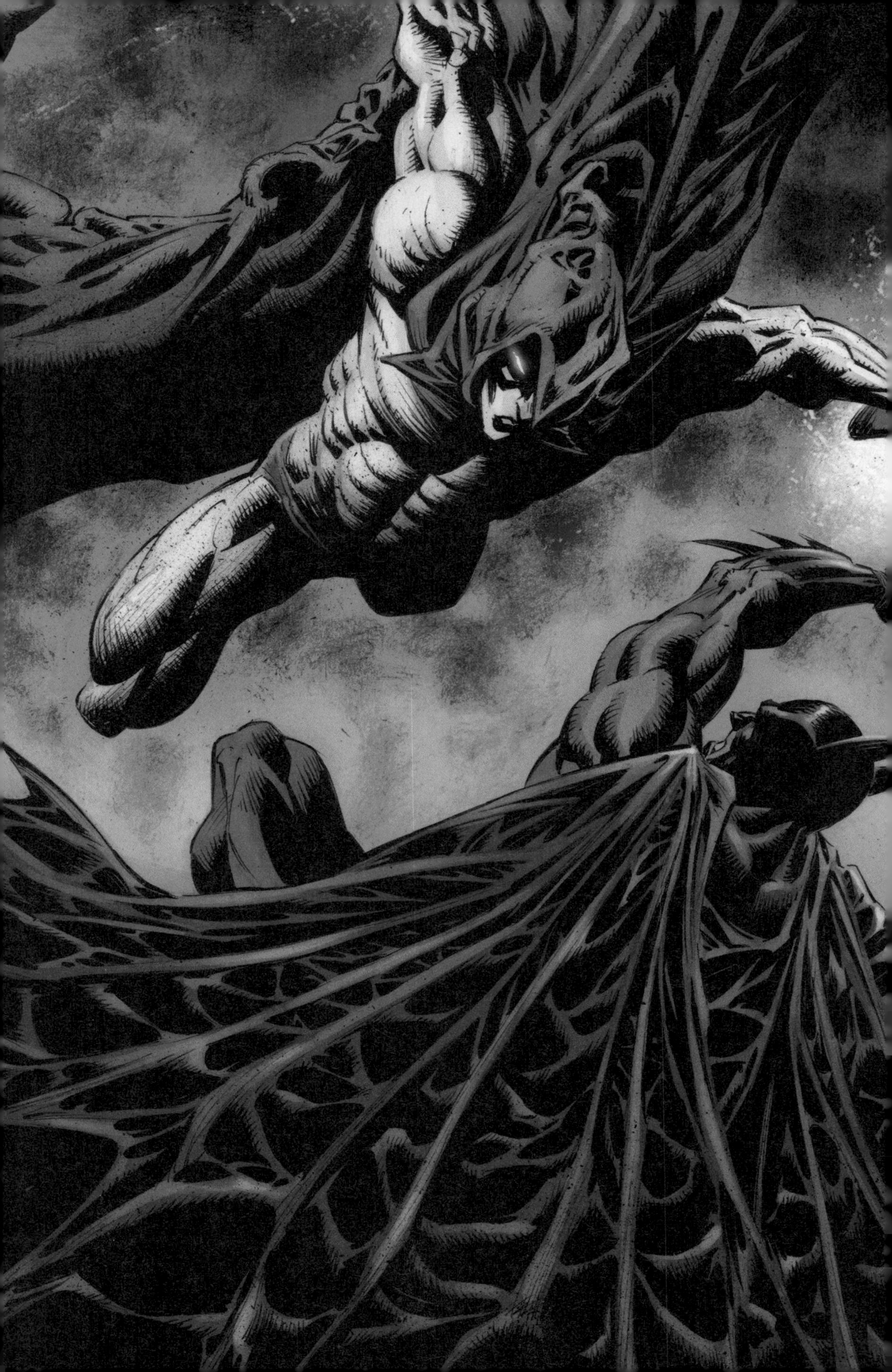

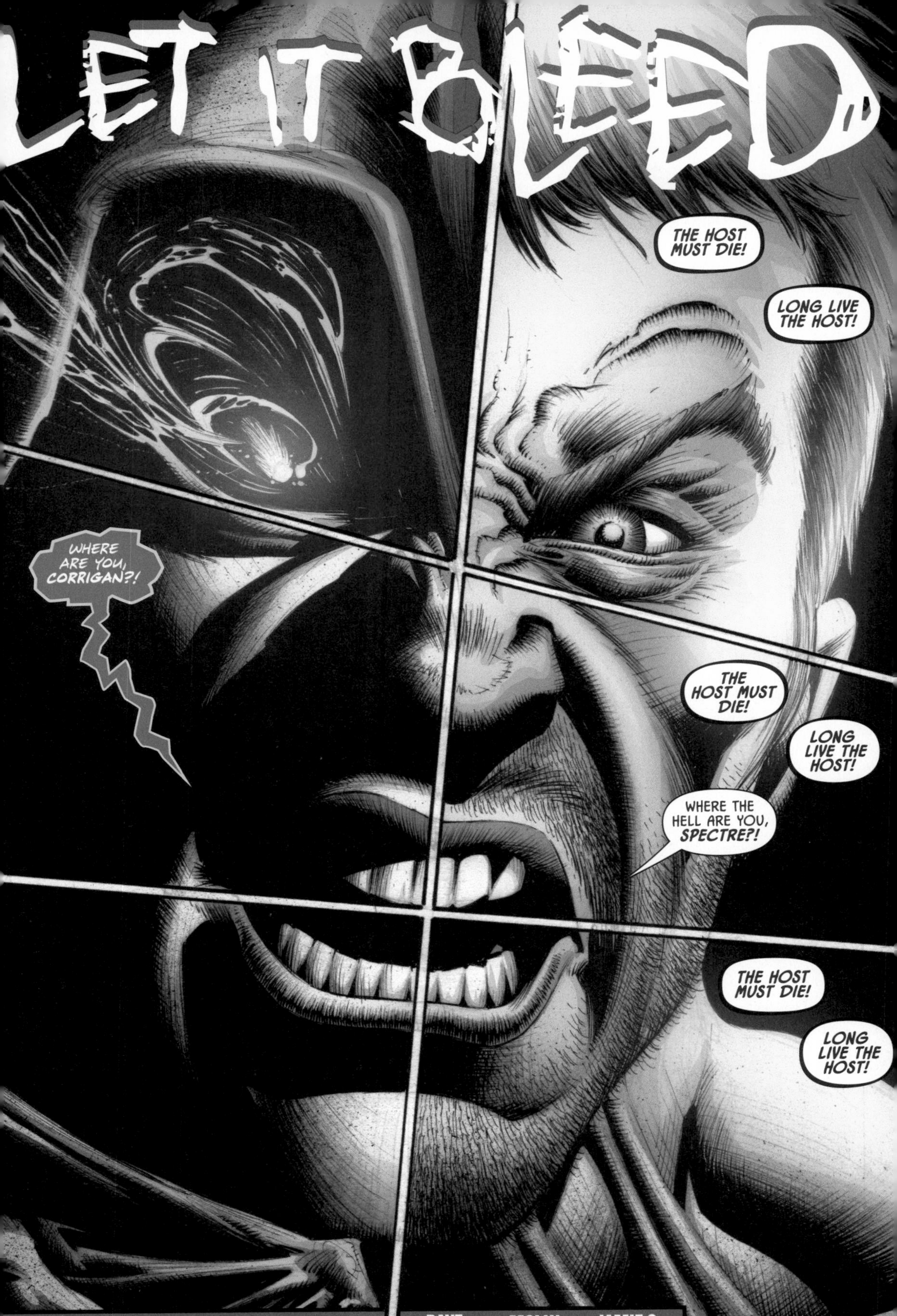
LET IT BLEED
THE HOST MUST DIE!
LONG LIVE THE HOST!
WHERE ARE YOU, CORRIGAN?!
THE HOST MUST DIE!
LONG LIVE THE HOST!
WHERE THE HELL ARE YOU, SPECTRE?!
THE HOST MUST DIE!
LONG LIVE THE HOST!

PETER J. TOMASI STORY & WORDS | KYLE HOTZ ARTIST | DAVID BARON COLORIST | ROB LEIGH LETTERER | KYLE HOTZ COVER | DAVE WIELGOSZ ASST. EDITOR | MOLLY MAHAN EDITOR | JAMIE S. RICH GROUP EDITOR

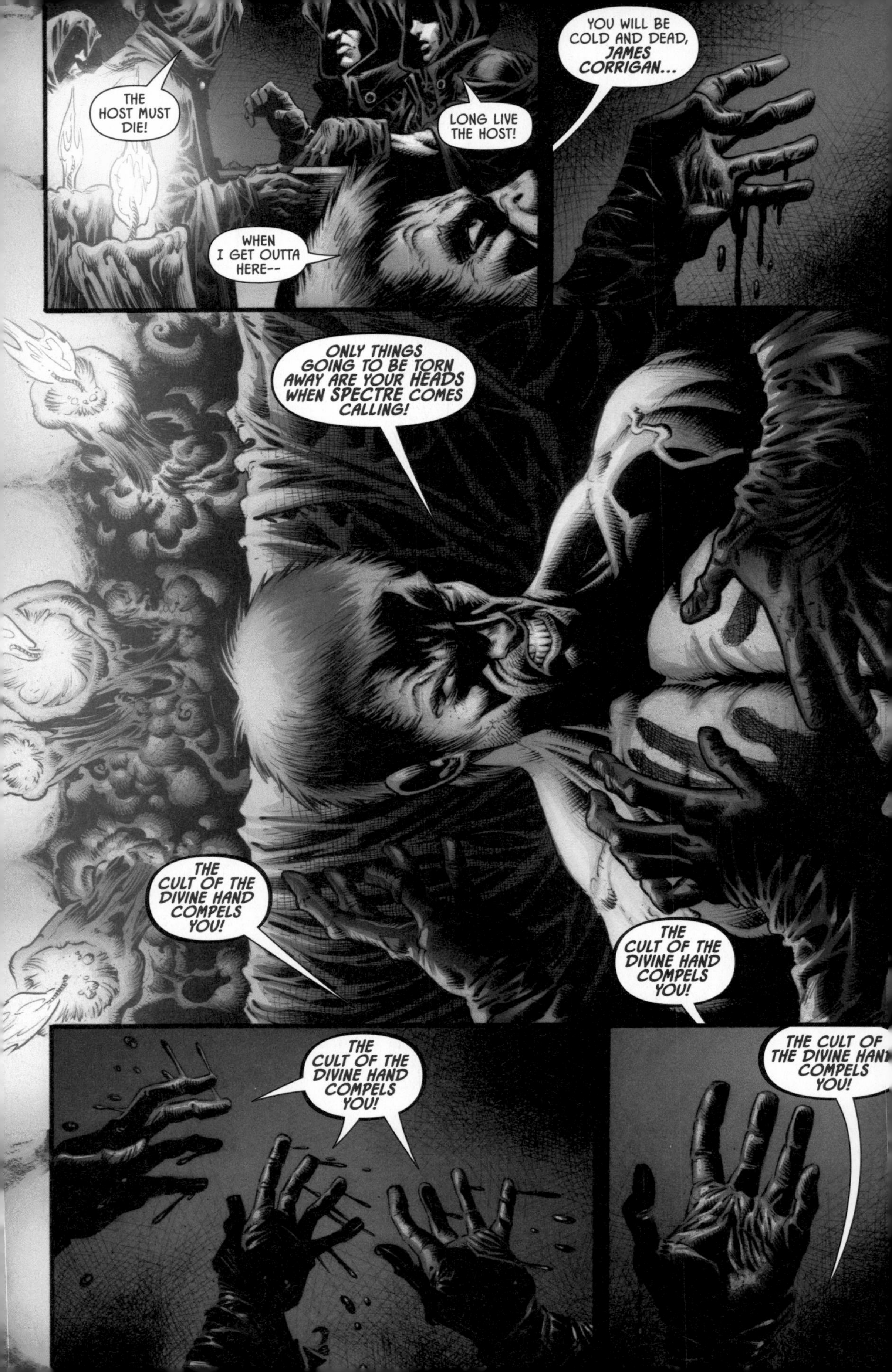
THE HOST MUST DIE!
LONG LIVE THE HOST!
WHEN I GET OUTTA HERE--
YOU WILL BE COLD AND DEAD, JAMES CORRIGAN...
ONLY THINGS GOING TO BE TORN AWAY ARE YOUR HEADS WHEN SPECTRE COMES CALLING!
THE CULT OF THE DIVINE HAND COMPELS YOU!
THE CULT OF THE DIVINE HAND COMPELS YOU!
THE CULT OF THE DIVINE HAND COMPELS YOU!
THE CULT OF THE DIVINE HAN COMPELS YOU!

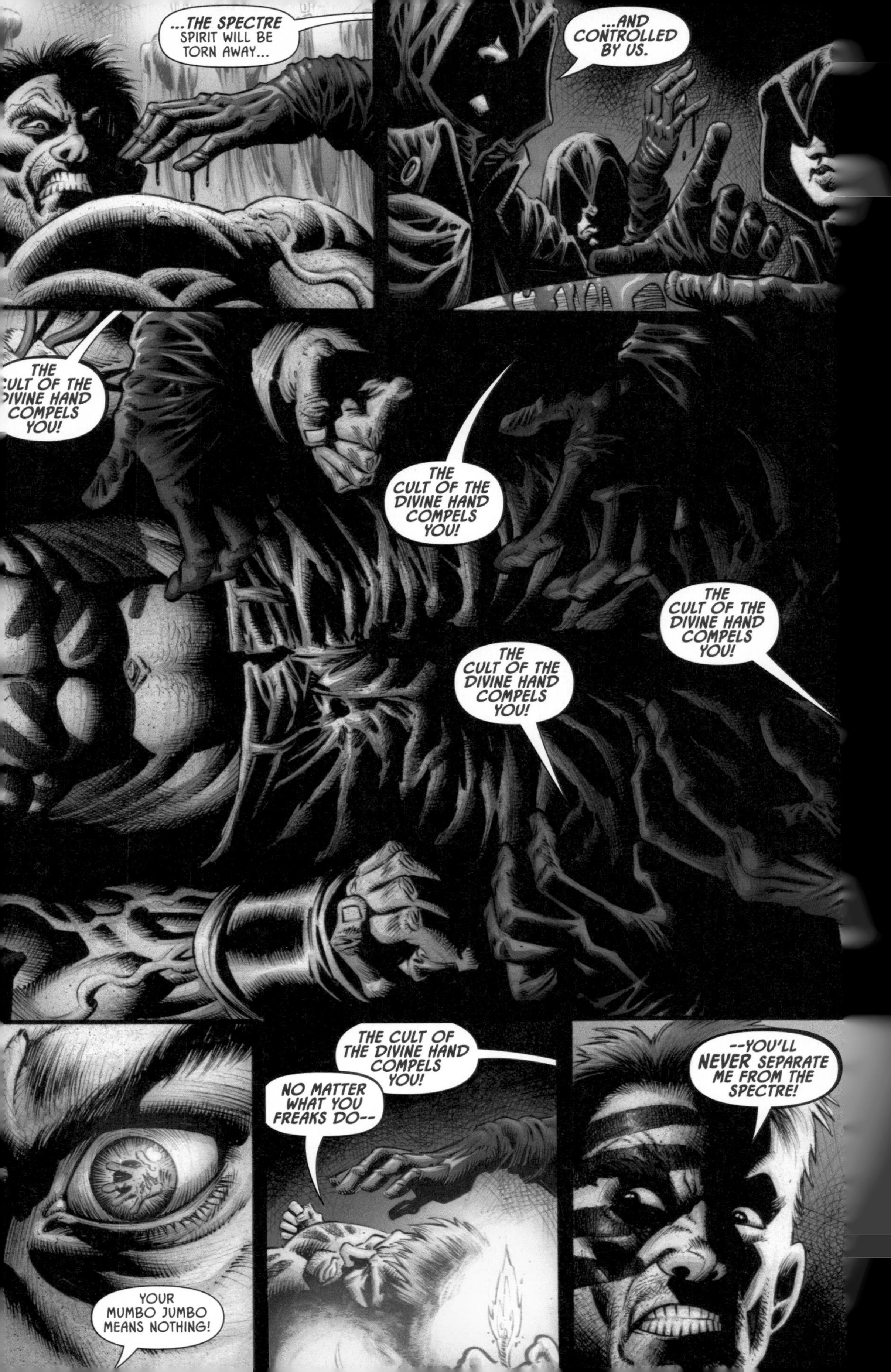
...THE SPECTRE SPIRIT WILL BE TORN AWAY...
...AND CONTROLLED BY US.
THE CULT OF THE DIVINE HAND COMPELS YOU!
THE CULT OF THE DIVINE HAND COMPELS YOU!
THE CULT OF THE DIVINE HAND COMPELS YOU!
THE CULT OF THE DIVINE HAND COMPELS YOU!
YOUR MUMBO JUMBO MEANS NOTHING!
THE CULT OF THE DIVINE HAND COMPELS YOU!
NO MATTER WHAT YOU FREAKS DO--
--YOU'LL NEVER SEPARATE ME FROM THE SPECTRE!

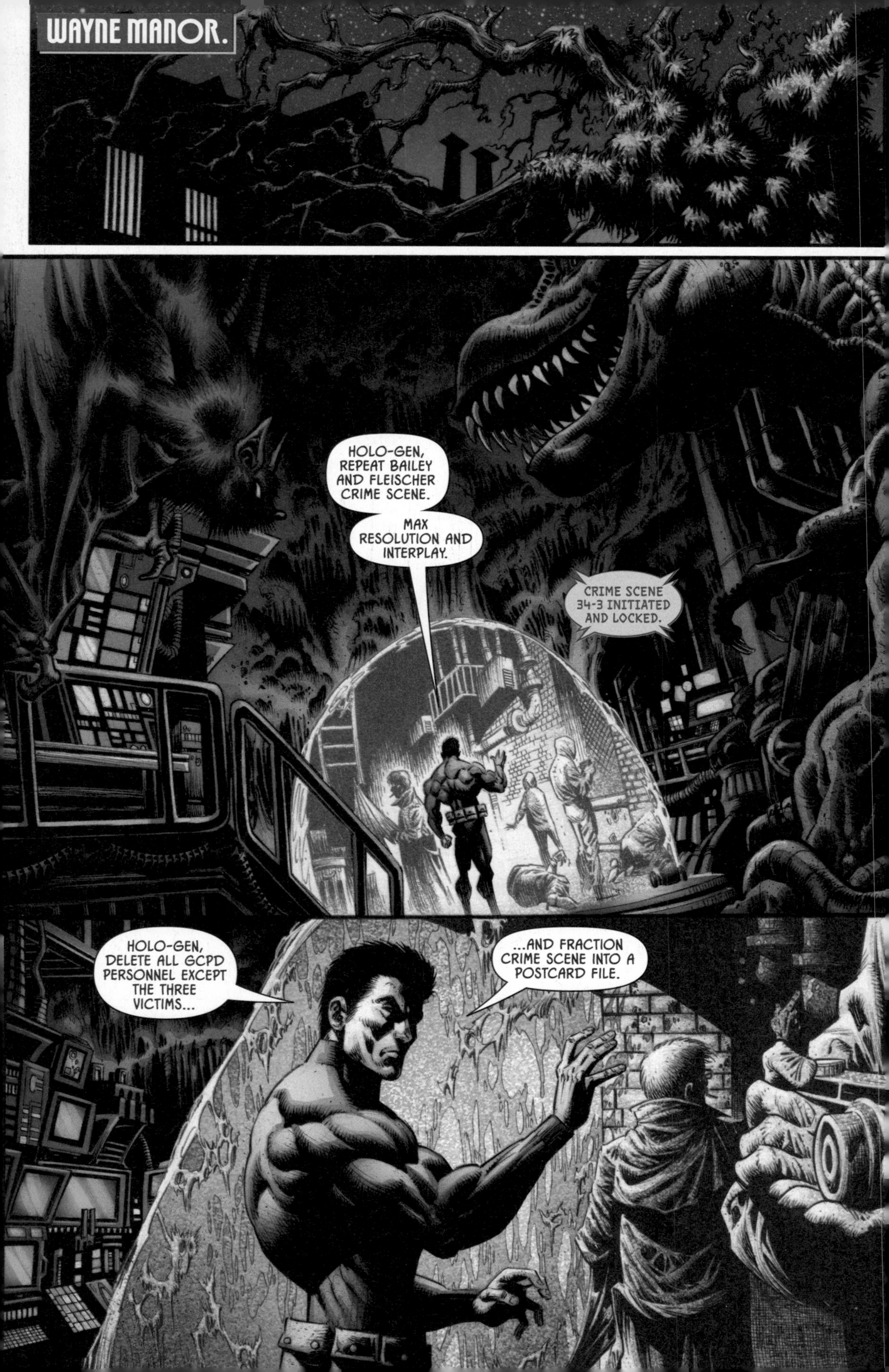
WAYNE MANOR.
HOLO-GEN, REPEAT BAILEY AND FLEISCHER CRIME SCENE.
MAX RESOLUTION AND INTERPLAY.
CRIME SCENE 34-3 INITIATED AND LOCKED.
HOLO-GEN, DELETE ALL GCPD PERSONNEL EXCEPT THE THREE VICTIMS...
...AND FRACTION CRIME SCENE INTO A POSTCARD FILE.

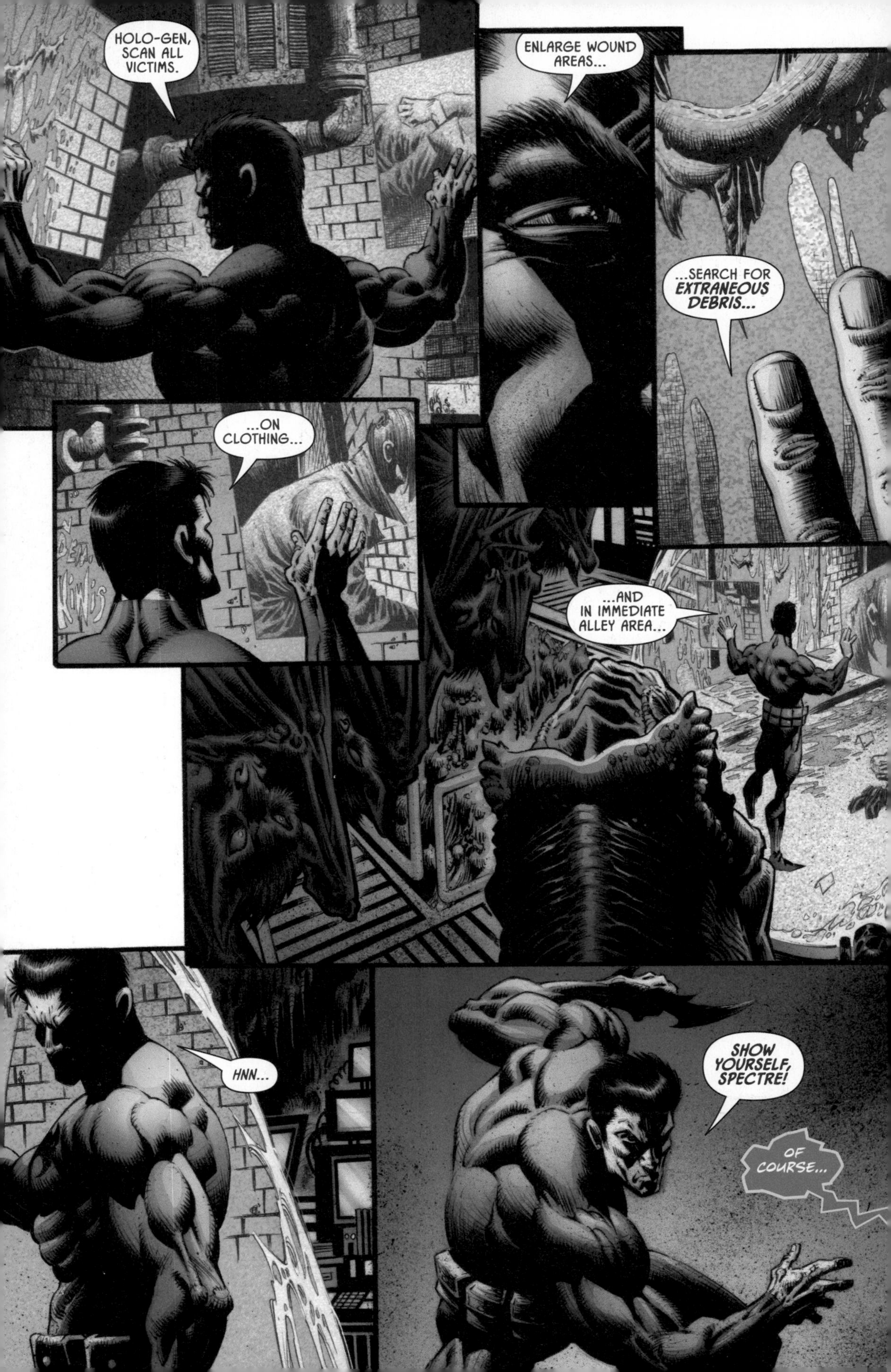
HOLO-GEN, SCAN ALL VICTIMS.
ENLARGE WOUND AREAS...
...SEARCH FOR EXTRANEOUS DEBRIS...
...ON CLOTHING...
...AND IN IMMEDIATE ALLEY AREA...
HNN...
SHOW YOURSELF, SPECTRE!
OF COURSE...

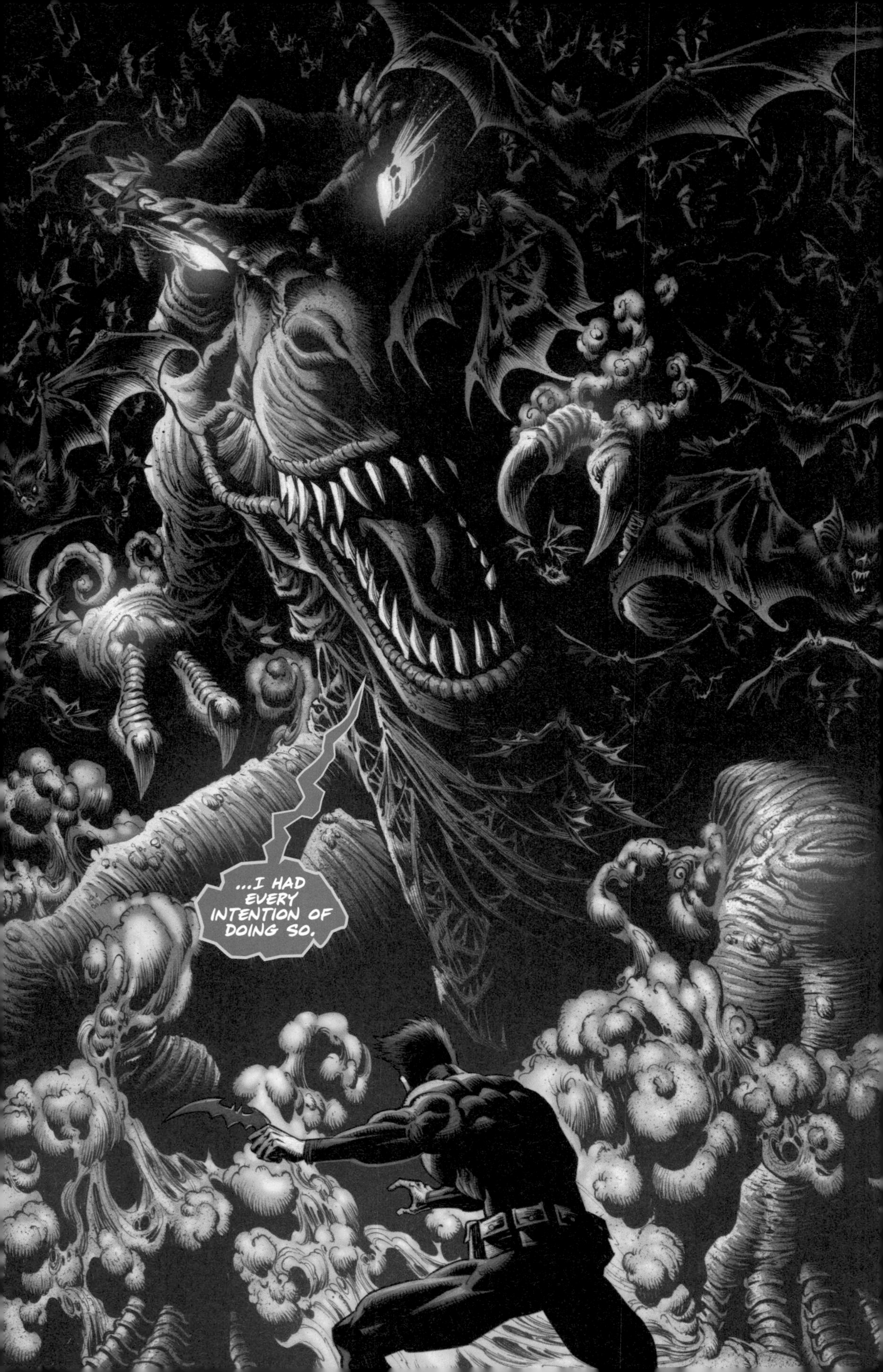
...I HAD EVERY INTENTION OF DOING SO.

REACHING FOR YOUR COWL IS A FUTILE GESTURE.

MASKS ARE USELESS.

THEY CONCEAL NOTHING FROM ME, BRUCE WAYNE.

MAYBE YOU WEAR YOUR COWL TO HIDE SOMETHING FROM YOURSELF.

HOW ABOUT YOU SHOW ME WHAT'S UNDER *YOUR* HOOD, SPECTRE?

DOES THIS RELIEVE ANY ANGST OF THE UNKNOWN?

DOES SEEING A HUMAN FACE ALLOW YOU TO RELATE TO ME BETTER?

WHAT'S YOUR CONNECTION? WHY IS CORRIGAN SO IMPORTANT TO YOU?

CORRIGAN AND I ARE ONE AND THE SAME.

I'M ALL EARS.

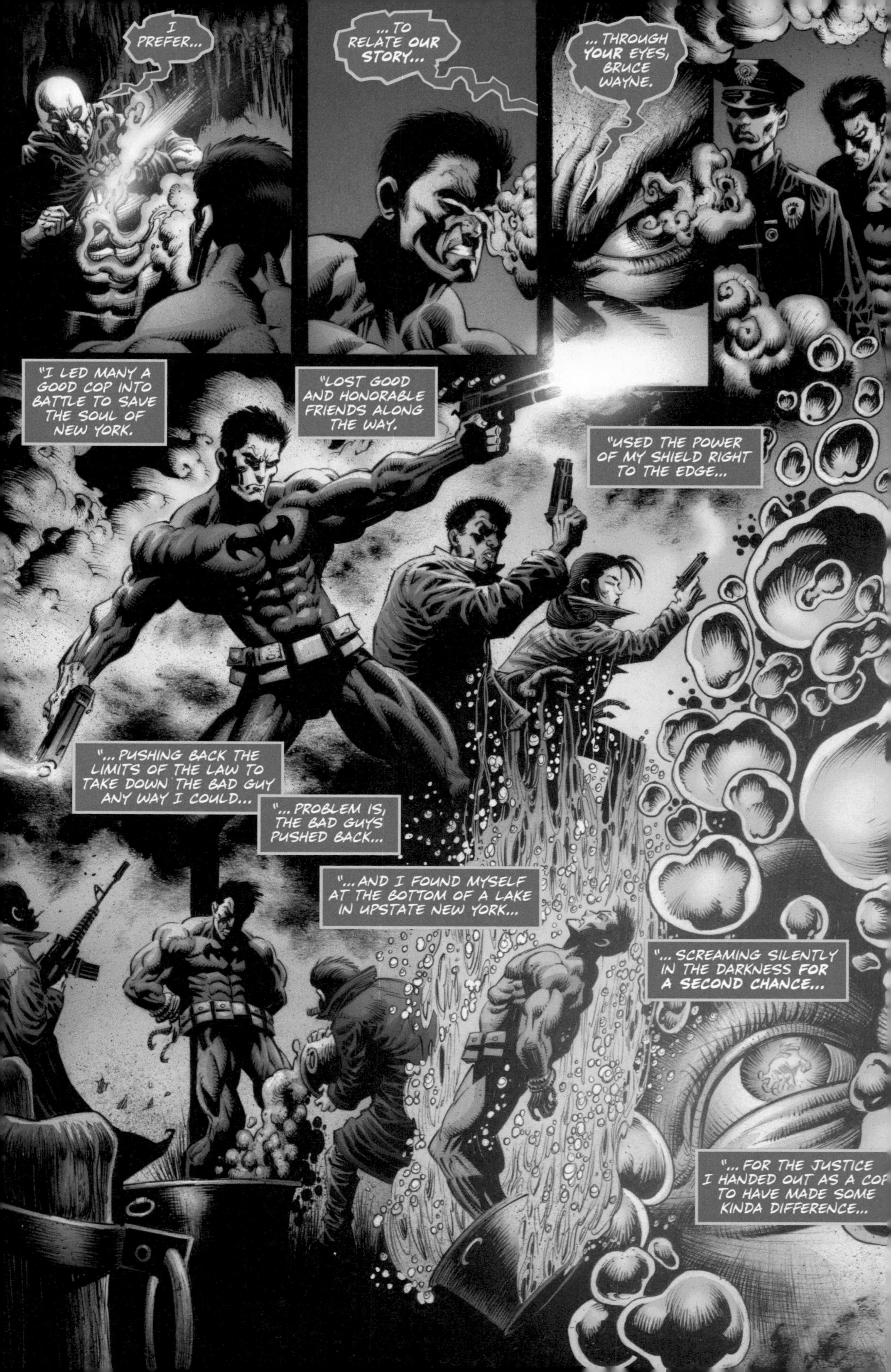
I PREFER...
...TO RELATE OUR STORY...
...THROUGH YOUR EYES, BRUCE WAYNE.
"I LED MANY A GOOD COP INTO BATTLE TO SAVE THE SOUL OF NEW YORK.
"LOST GOOD AND HONORABLE FRIENDS ALONG THE WAY.
"USED THE POWER OF MY SHIELD RIGHT TO THE EDGE...
"...PUSHING BACK THE LIMITS OF THE LAW TO TAKE DOWN THE BAD GUY ANY WAY I COULD...
"...PROBLEM IS, THE BAD GUYS PUSHED BACK...
"...AND I FOUND MYSELF AT THE BOTTOM OF A LAKE IN UPSTATE NEW YORK...
"...SCREAMING SILENTLY IN THE DARKNESS FOR A SECOND CHANCE...
"...FOR THE JUSTICE I HANDED OUT AS A COP TO HAVE MADE SOME KINDA DIFFERENCE...

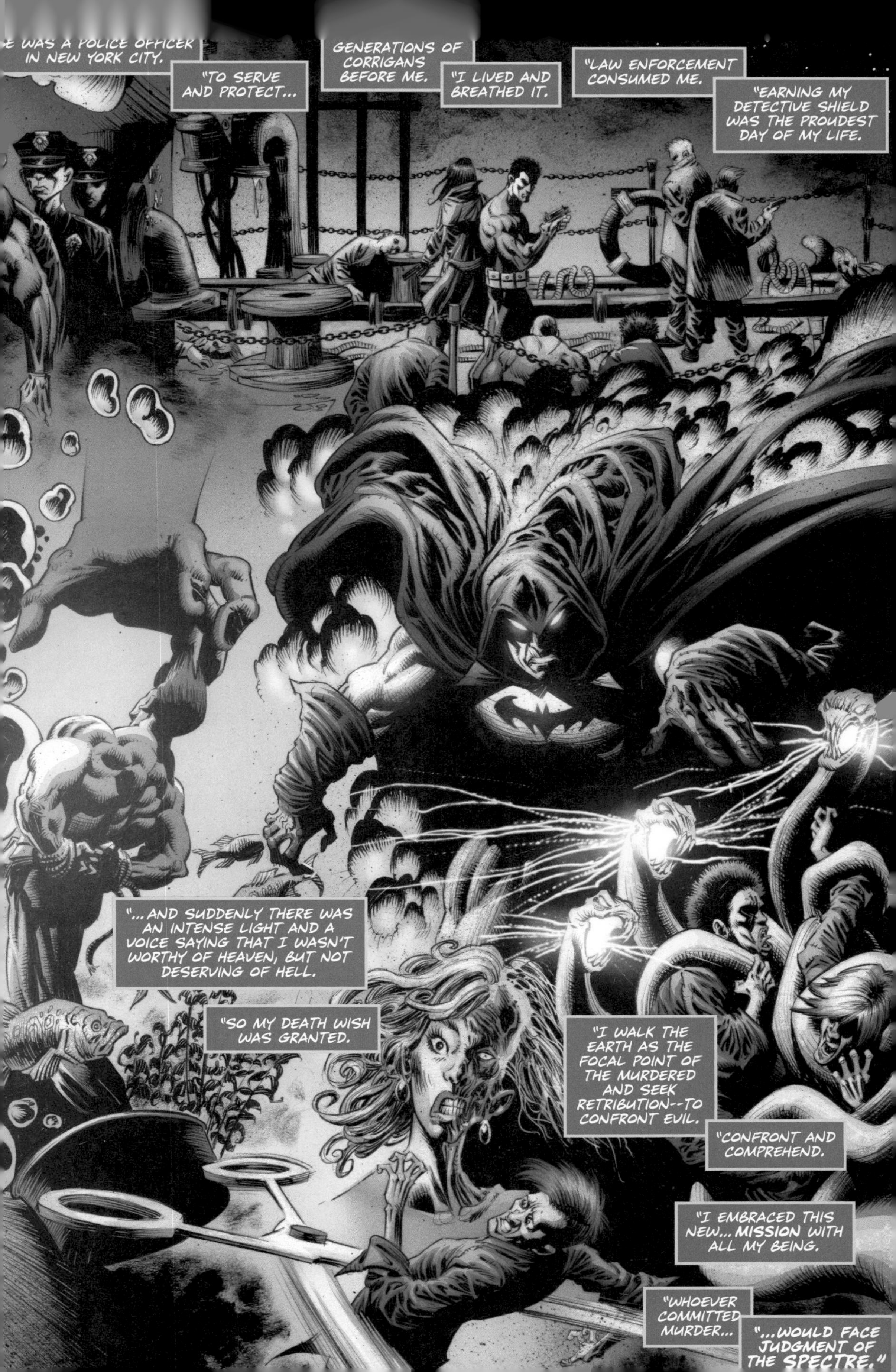
E WAS A POLICE OFFICER IN NEW YORK CITY.
"TO SERVE AND PROTECT...
GENERATIONS OF CORRIGANS BEFORE ME.
"I LIVED AND BREATHED IT.
"LAW ENFORCEMENT CONSUMED ME.
"EARNING MY DETECTIVE SHIELD WAS THE PROUDEST DAY OF MY LIFE.
"...AND SUDDENLY THERE WAS AN INTENSE LIGHT AND A VOICE SAYING THAT I WASN'T WORTHY OF HEAVEN, BUT NOT DESERVING OF HELL.
"SO MY DEATH WISH WAS GRANTED.
"I WALK THE EARTH AS THE FOCAL POINT OF THE MURDERED AND SEEK RETRIBUTION--TO CONFRONT EVIL.
"CONFRONT AND COMPREHEND.
"I EMBRACED THIS NEW...MISSION WITH ALL MY BEING.
"WHOEVER COMMITTED MURDER...
"...WOULD FACE JUDGMENT OF THE SPECTRE."

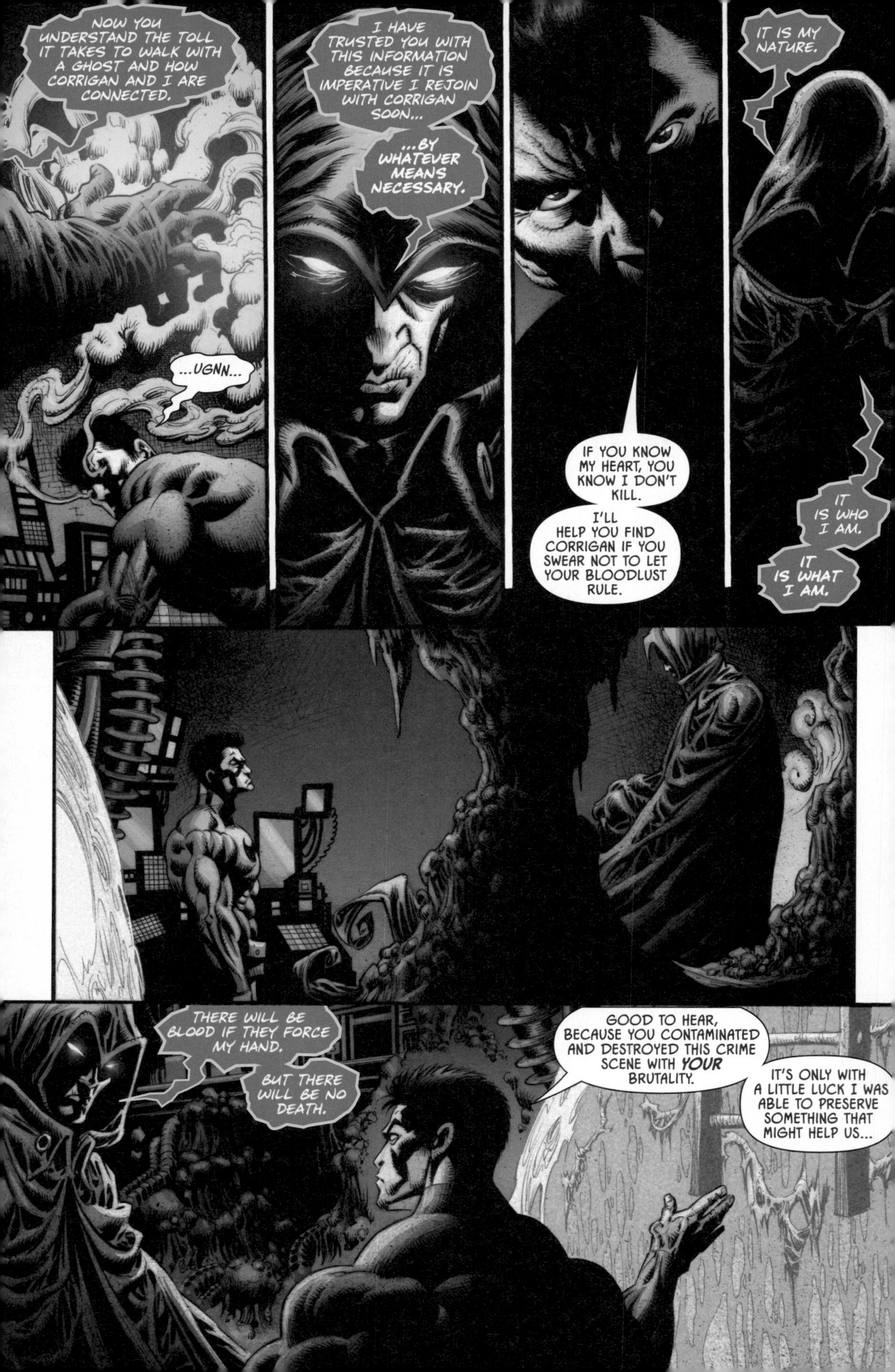
NOW YOU UNDERSTAND THE TOLL IT TAKES TO WALK WITH A GHOST AND HOW CORRIGAN AND I ARE CONNECTED.
...UGNN...
I HAVE TRUSTED YOU WITH THIS INFORMATION BECAUSE IT IS IMPERATIVE I REJOIN WITH CORRIGAN SOON...
...BY WHATEVER MEANS NECESSARY.
IF YOU KNOW MY HEART, YOU KNOW I DON'T KILL.
I'LL HELP YOU FIND CORRIGAN IF YOU SWEAR NOT TO LET YOUR BLOODLUST RULE.
IT IS MY NATURE.
IT IS WHO I AM.
IT IS WHAT I AM.
THERE WILL BE BLOOD IF THEY FORCE MY HAND.
BUT THERE WILL BE NO DEATH.
GOOD TO HEAR, BECAUSE YOU CONTAMINATED AND DESTROYED THIS CRIME SCENE WITH YOUR BRUTALITY.
IT'S ONLY WITH A LITTLE LUCK I WAS ABLE TO PRESERVE SOMETHING THAT MIGHT HELP US...

I FOUND THIS SMALL PIECE OF FABRIC IN THE BLOODY ALLEY...

...APPLY A LITTLE SCIENCE, TIME AND LEGWORK, AND A MURDERER CAN BE BROUGHT TO JUSTICE...

...WITHOUT SPRAYING THEIR ORGANS AND BRAIN MATTER ALL ACROSS THE WALLS.

OKAY, WE'VE GOT A NARROW FIELD OF MANUFACTURERS OF THAT SPECIFIC FABRIC...

...ALONG WITH WHAT APPEARS TO BE THE TIP OF A FINGER SEARED INTO IT.

COMPUTER, CROSS-REFERENCE FINGERPRINT WHORL, LOOP AND ARCH PATTERNS AGAINST ALL CASES IN THE GCPD...

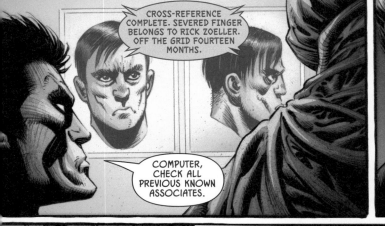

CROSS-REFERENCE COMPLETE. SEVERED FINGER BELONGS TO RICK ZOELLER. OFF THE GRID FOURTEEN MONTHS.

COMPUTER, CHECK ALL PREVIOUS KNOWN ASSOCIATES.

LIST OF ZOELLER, RICK, KNOWN ASSOCIATES.

WELL, THAT'S WHAT I CALL...

"...A TRUE CASE OF SERENDIPITY."

I NEED MEDICAL ATTENTION...MY ARM IS BROKEN...

BE, TOO. BATMAN BROKE BY NOBE...

I WANT MY PHONE CALL AND A LAWYER!

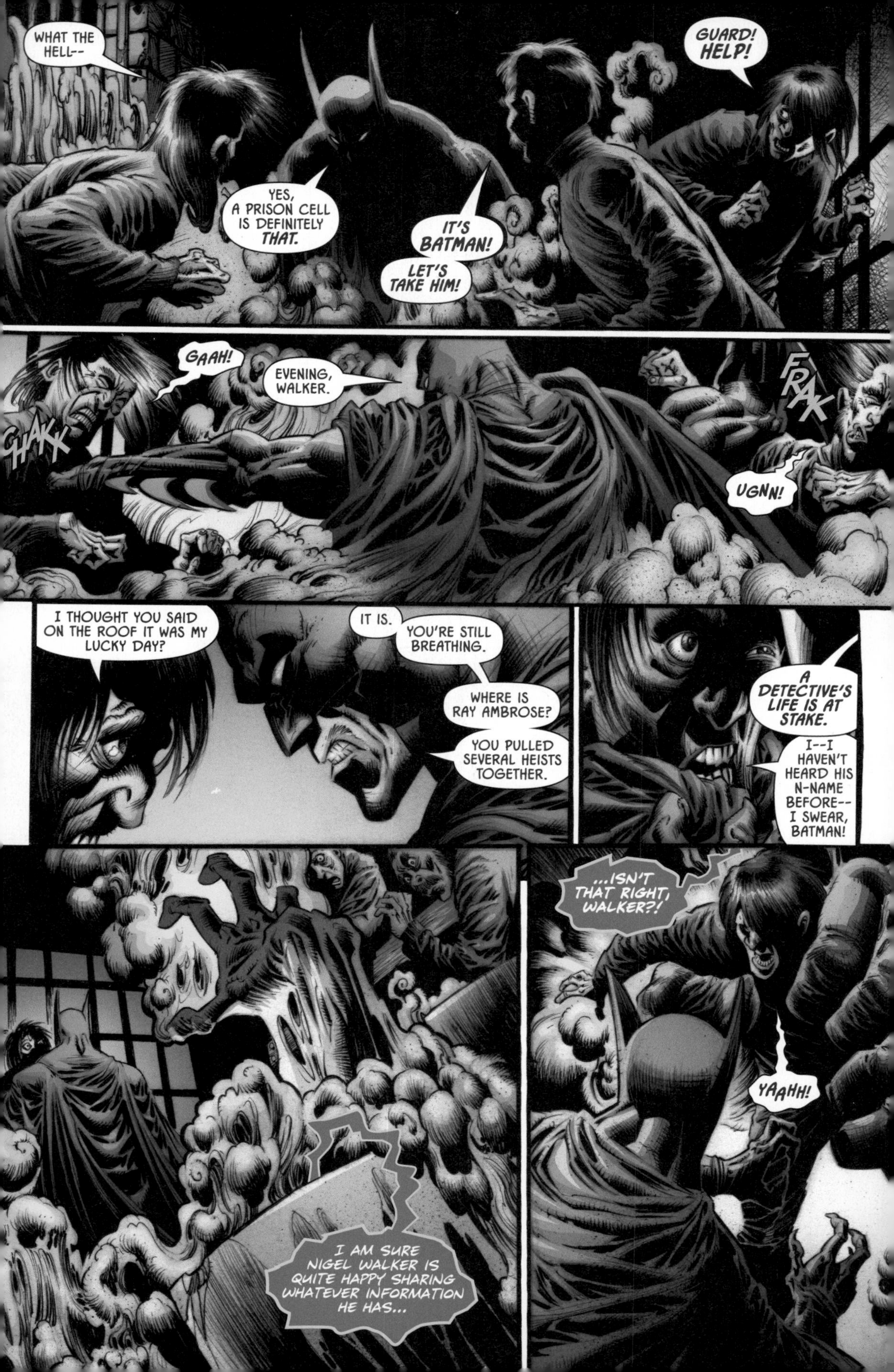
WHAT THE HELL--
YES, A PRISON CELL IS DEFINITELY THAT.
IT'S BATMAN!
LET'S TAKE HIM!
GUARD! HELP!
GAAH!
EVENING, WALKER.
CHAKK
FRAK
UGNN!
I THOUGHT YOU SAID ON THE ROOF IT WAS MY LUCKY DAY?
IT IS.
YOU'RE STILL BREATHING.
WHERE IS RAY AMBROSE?
YOU PULLED SEVERAL HEISTS TOGETHER.
A DETECTIVE'S LIFE IS AT STAKE.
I--I HAVEN'T HEARD HIS N-NAME BEFORE-- I SWEAR, BATMAN!
I AM SURE NIGEL WALKER IS QUITE HAPPY SHARING WHATEVER INFORMATION HE HAS...
...ISN'T THAT RIGHT, WALKER?!
YAAHH!

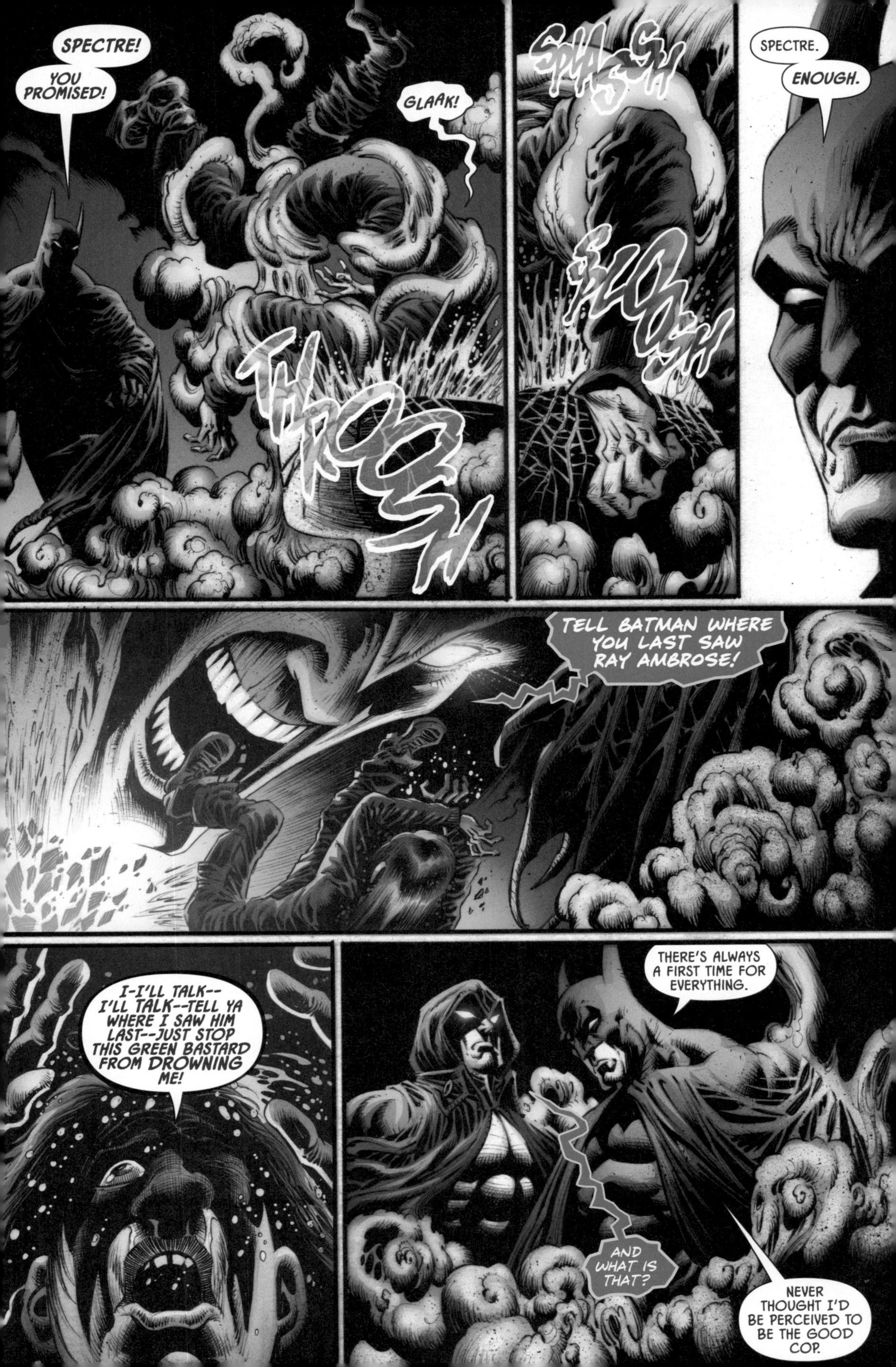

SPECTRE!
YOU PROMISED!
GLAAK!
THOOOSH
SPLASSH
FLOOSH
SPECTRE.
ENOUGH.
TELL BATMAN WHERE YOU LAST SAW RAY AMBROSE!
I-I'LL TALK-- I'LL TALK--TELL YA WHERE I SAW HIM LAST--JUST STOP THIS GREEN BASTARD FROM DROWNING ME!
THERE'S ALWAYS A FIRST TIME FOR EVERYTHING.
AND WHAT IS THAT?
NEVER THOUGHT I'D BE PERCEIVED TO BE THE GOOD COP.

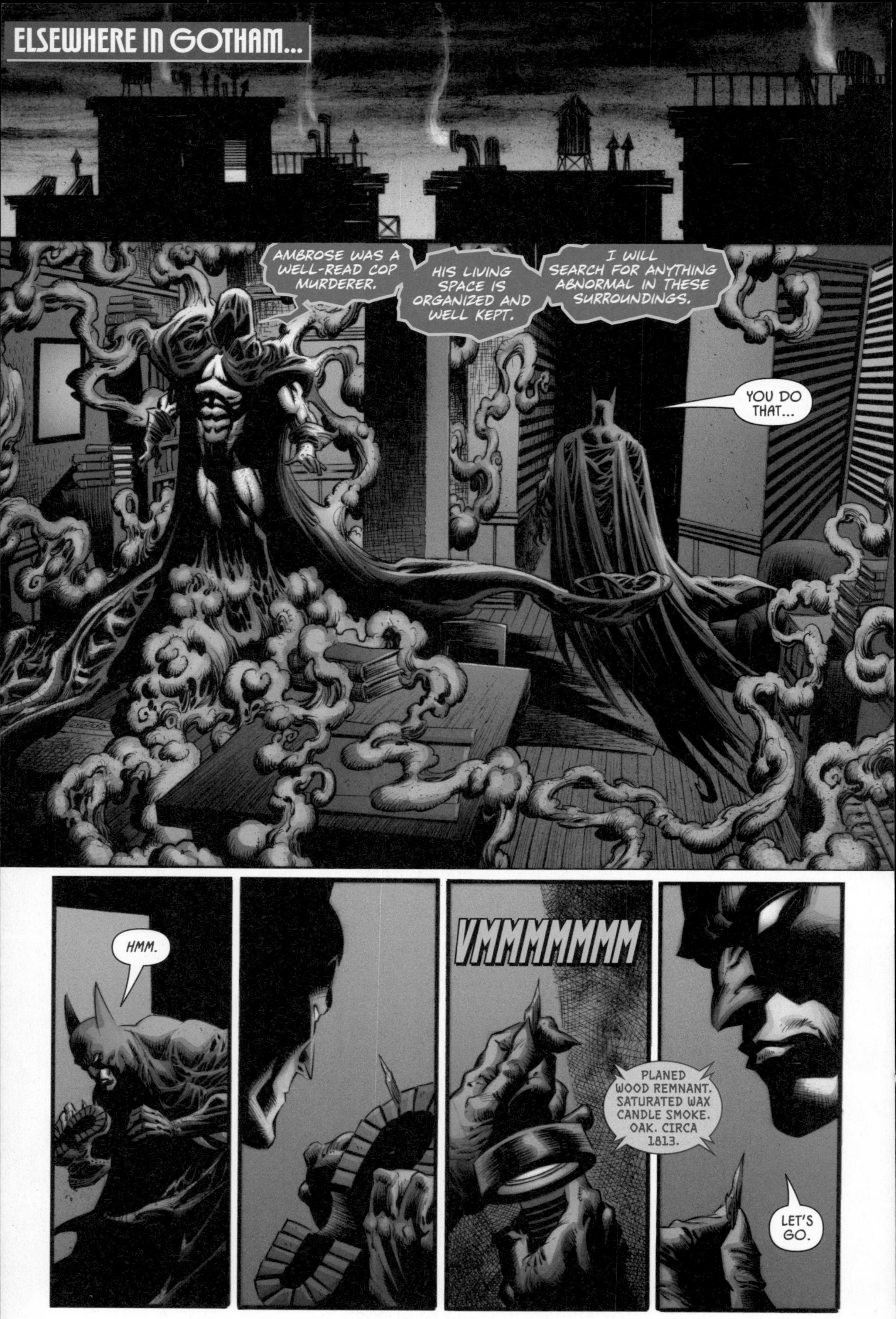
ELSEWHERE IN GOTHAM...
AMBROSE WAS A WELL-READ COP MURDERER.
HIS LIVING SPACE IS ORGANIZED AND WELL KEPT.
I WILL SEARCH FOR ANYTHING ABNORMAL IN THESE SURROUNDINGS.
YOU DO THAT...
HMM.
VMMMMMMM
PLANED WOOD REMNANT. SATURATED WAX CANDLE SMOKE. OAK. CIRCA 1813.
LET'S GO.

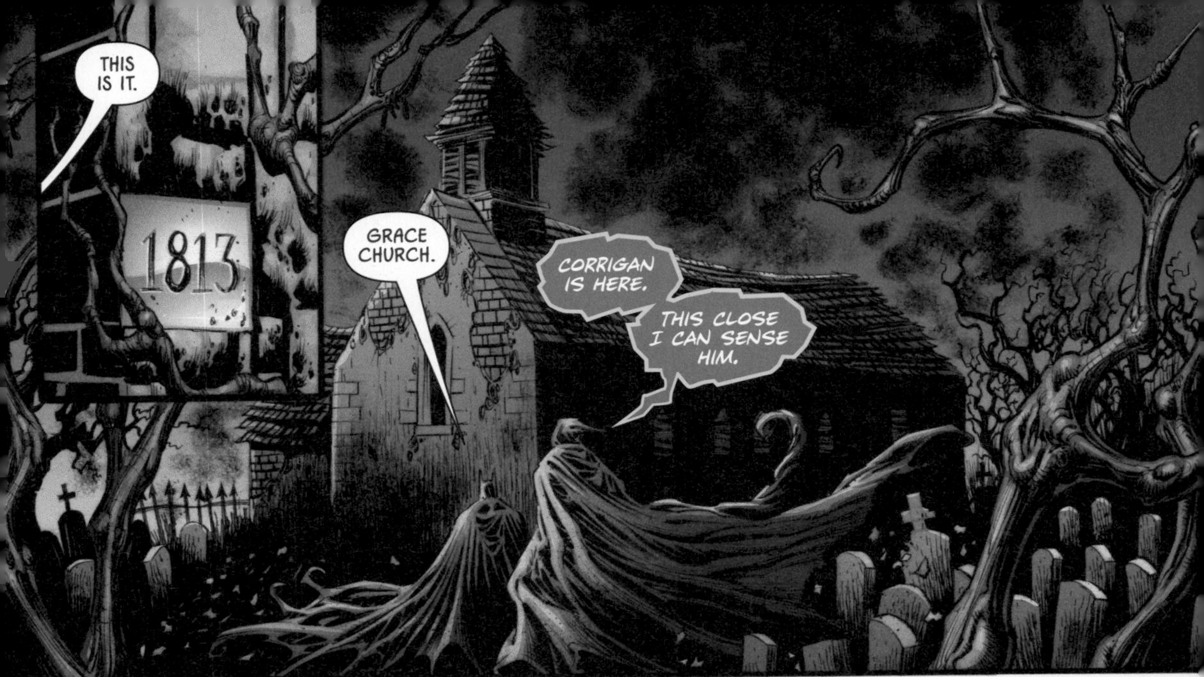
THIS IS IT.
1813
GRACE CHURCH.
CORRIGAN IS HERE.
THIS CLOSE I CAN SENSE HIM.

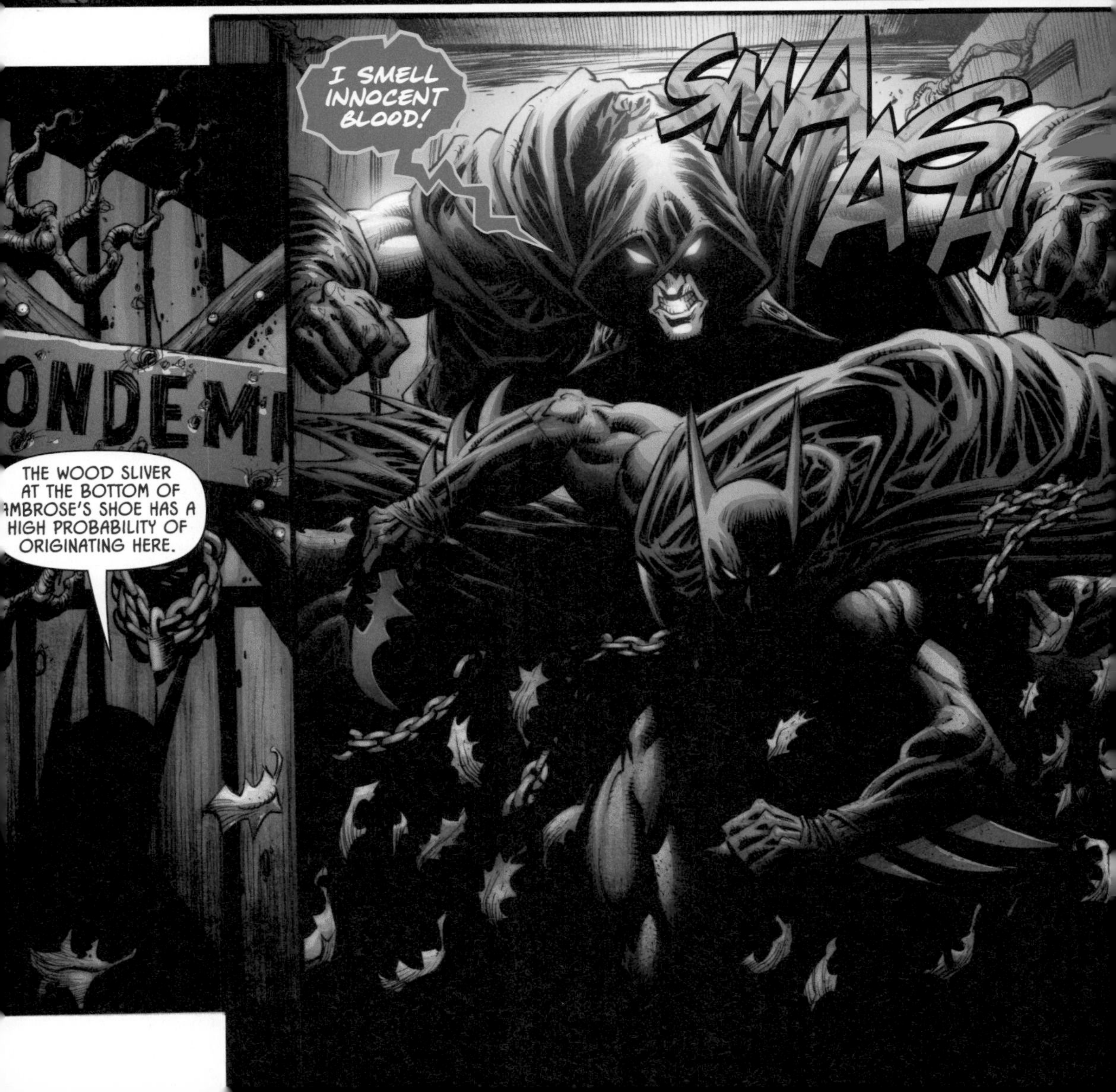
THE WOOD SLIVER AT THE BOTTOM OF AMBROSE'S SHOE HAS A HIGH PROBABILITY OF ORIGINATING HERE.
I SMELL INNOCENT BLOOD!
SMASH!

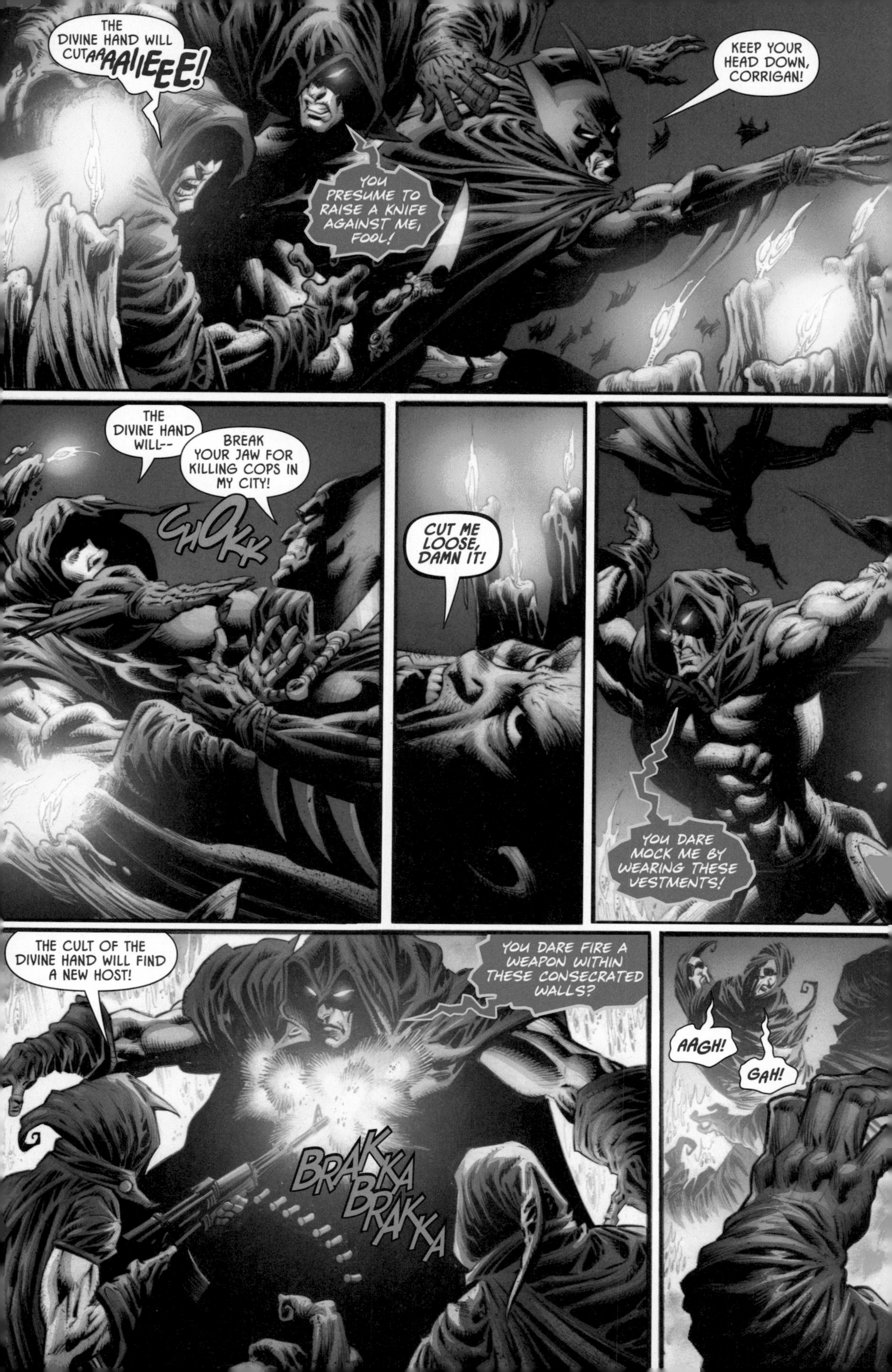
THE DIVINE HAND WILL CUTAAAAIIEEE!
KEEP YOUR HEAD DOWN, CORRIGAN!
YOU PRESUME TO RAISE A KNIFE AGAINST ME, FOOL!
THE DIVINE HAND WILL--
BREAK YOUR JAW FOR KILLING COPS IN MY CITY!
CHOKK
CUT ME LOOSE, DAMN IT!
YOU DARE MOCK ME BY WEARING THESE VESTMENTS!
THE CULT OF THE DIVINE HAND WILL FIND A NEW HOST!
YOU DARE FIRE A WEAPON WITHIN THESE CONSECRATED WALLS?
BRAKKA BRAKKA
AAGH!
GAH!

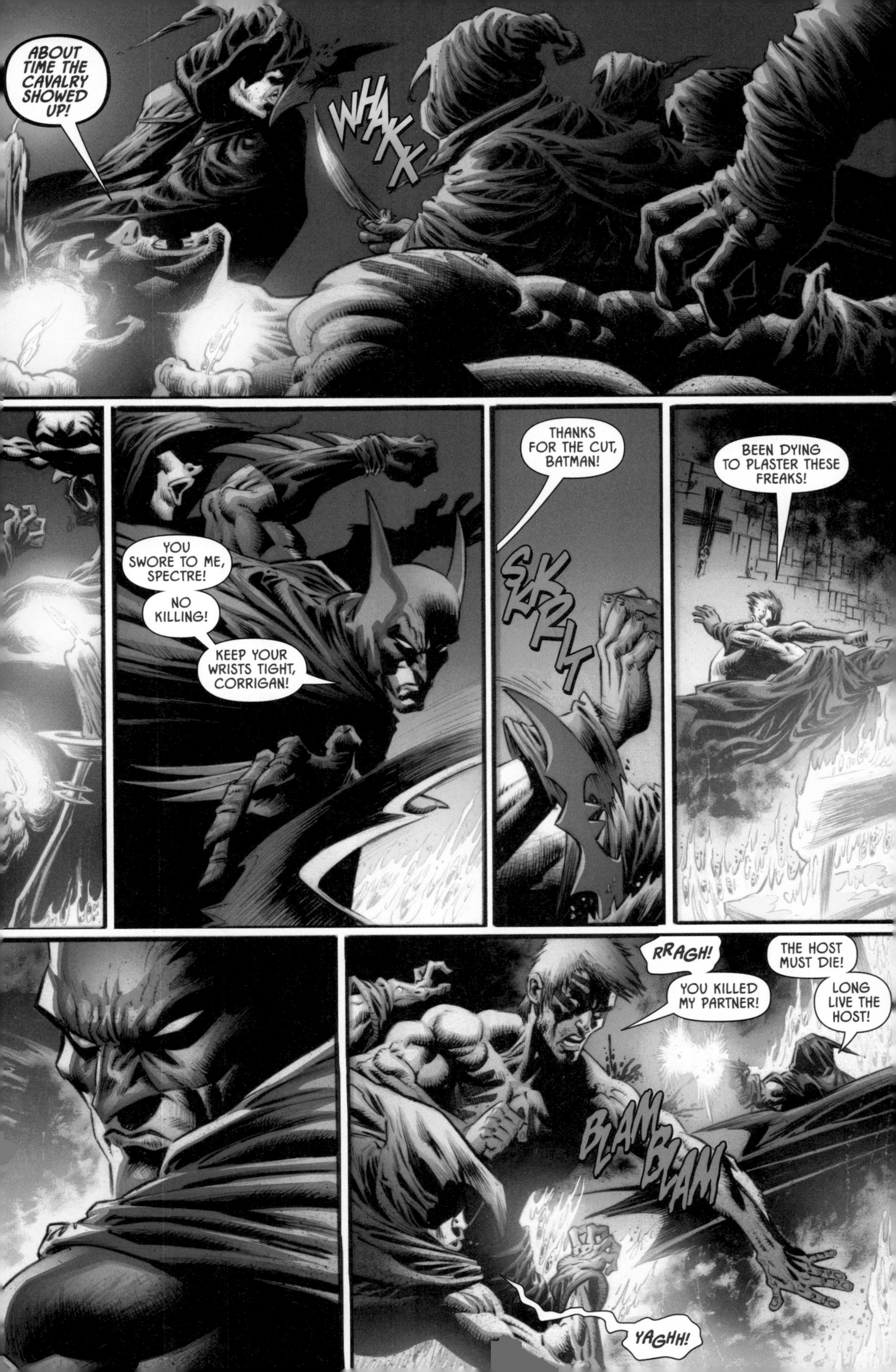
ABOUT TIME THE CAVALRY SHOWED UP!
WHAKK
YOU SWORE TO ME, SPECTRE!
NO KILLING!
KEEP YOUR WRISTS TIGHT, CORRIGAN!
THANKS FOR THE CUT, BATMAN!
SKRRK
BEEN DYING TO PLASTER THESE FREAKS!
RRAGH!
YOU KILLED MY PARTNER!
THE HOST MUST DIE!
LONG LIVE THE HOST!
BLAM BLAM
YAGHH!

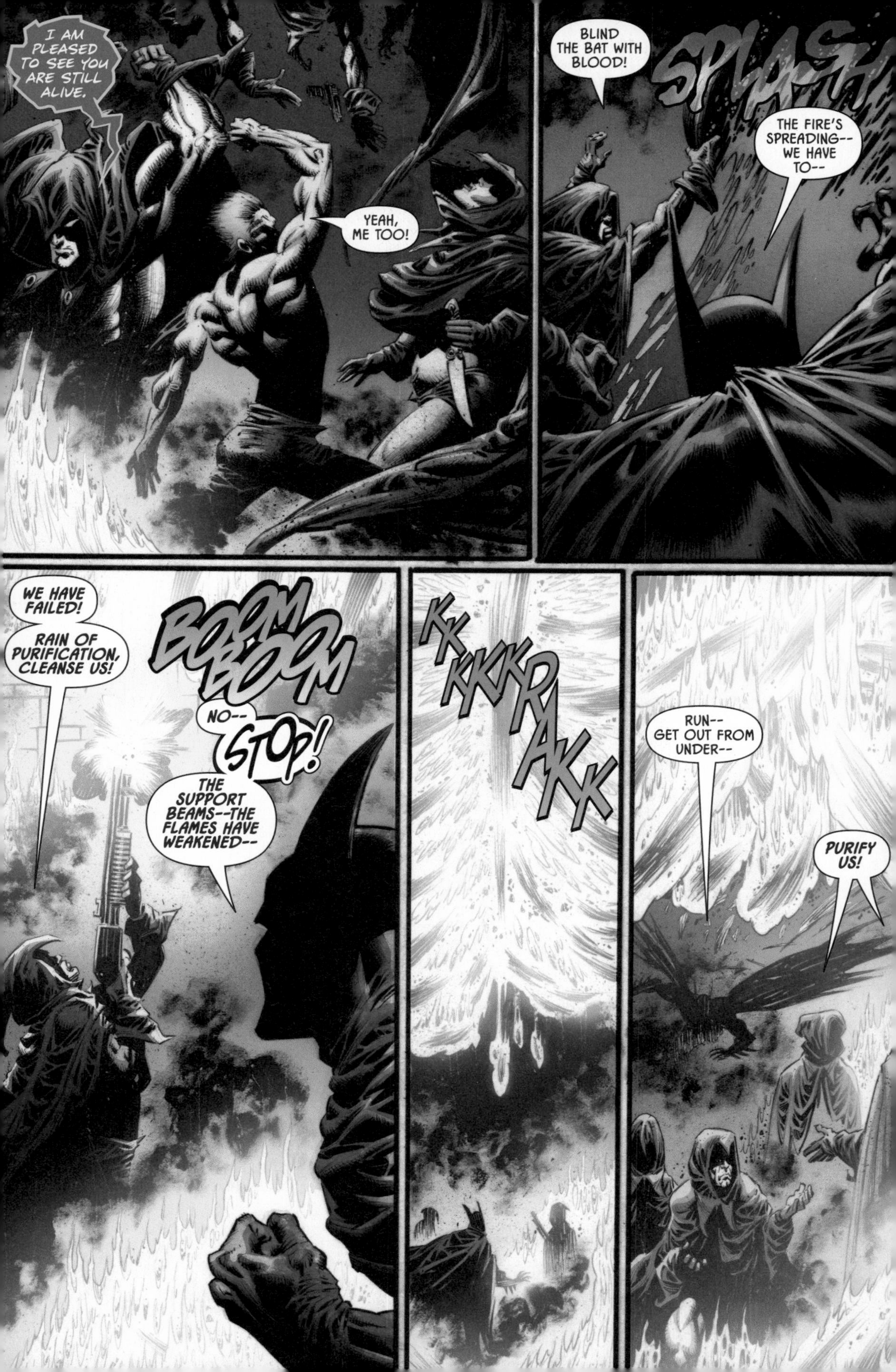
I AM PLEASED TO SEE YOU ARE STILL ALIVE.
YEAH, ME TOO!
BLIND THE BAT WITH BLOOD!
SPLASH
THE FIRE'S SPREADING-- WE HAVE TO--
WE HAVE FAILED!
RAIN OF PURIFICATION, CLEANSE US!
BOOM BOOM
NO--
STOP!
THE SUPPORT BEAMS--THE FLAMES HAVE WEAKENED--
KKKKKRAKK
RUN-- GET OUT FROM UNDER--
PURIFY US!

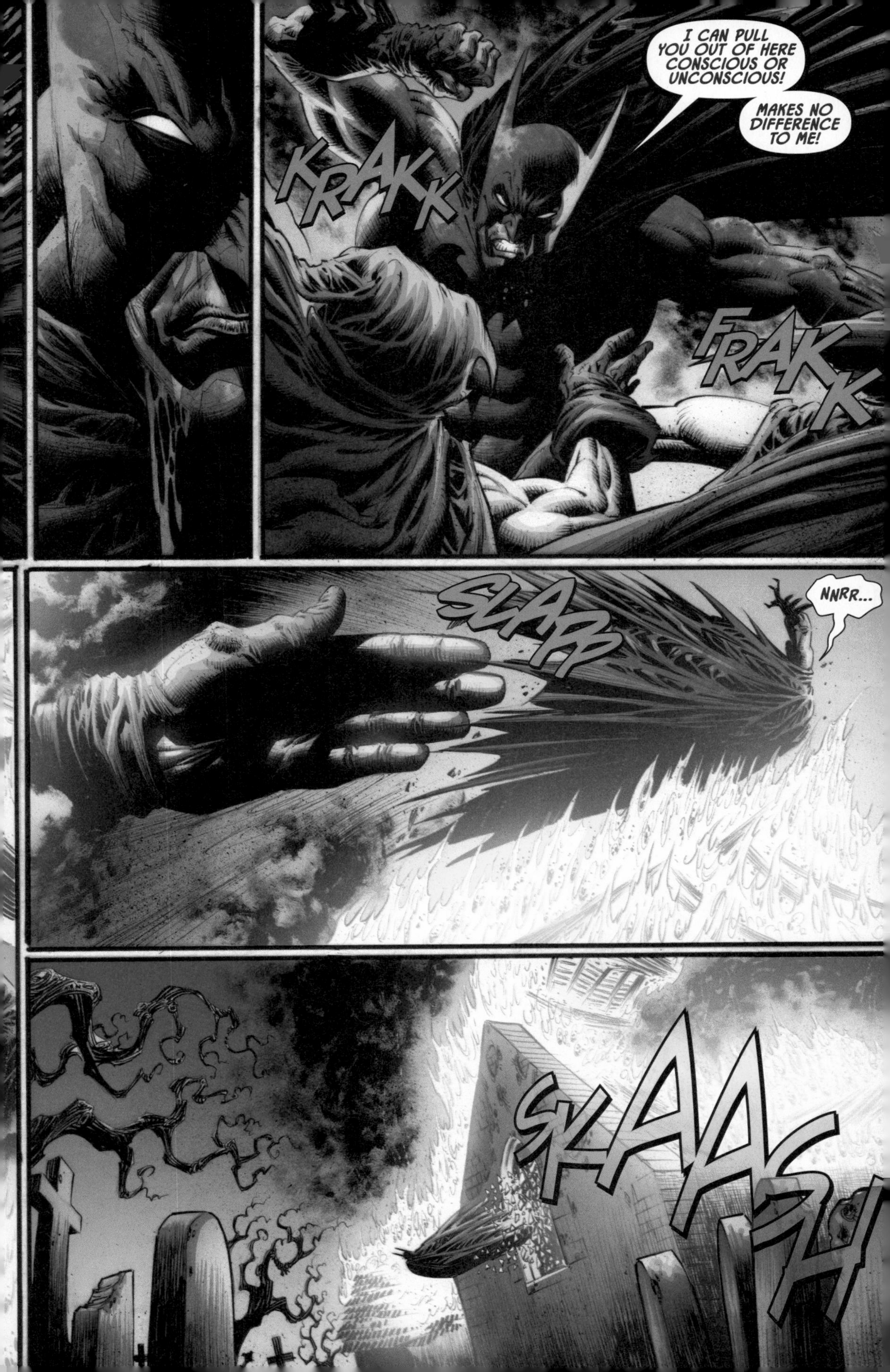

I CAN PULL YOU OUT OF HERE CONSCIOUS OR UNCONSCIOUS!
MAKES NO DIFFERENCE TO ME!
KRAKK
FRAKK
SLAPP
NNRR...
SKAASH

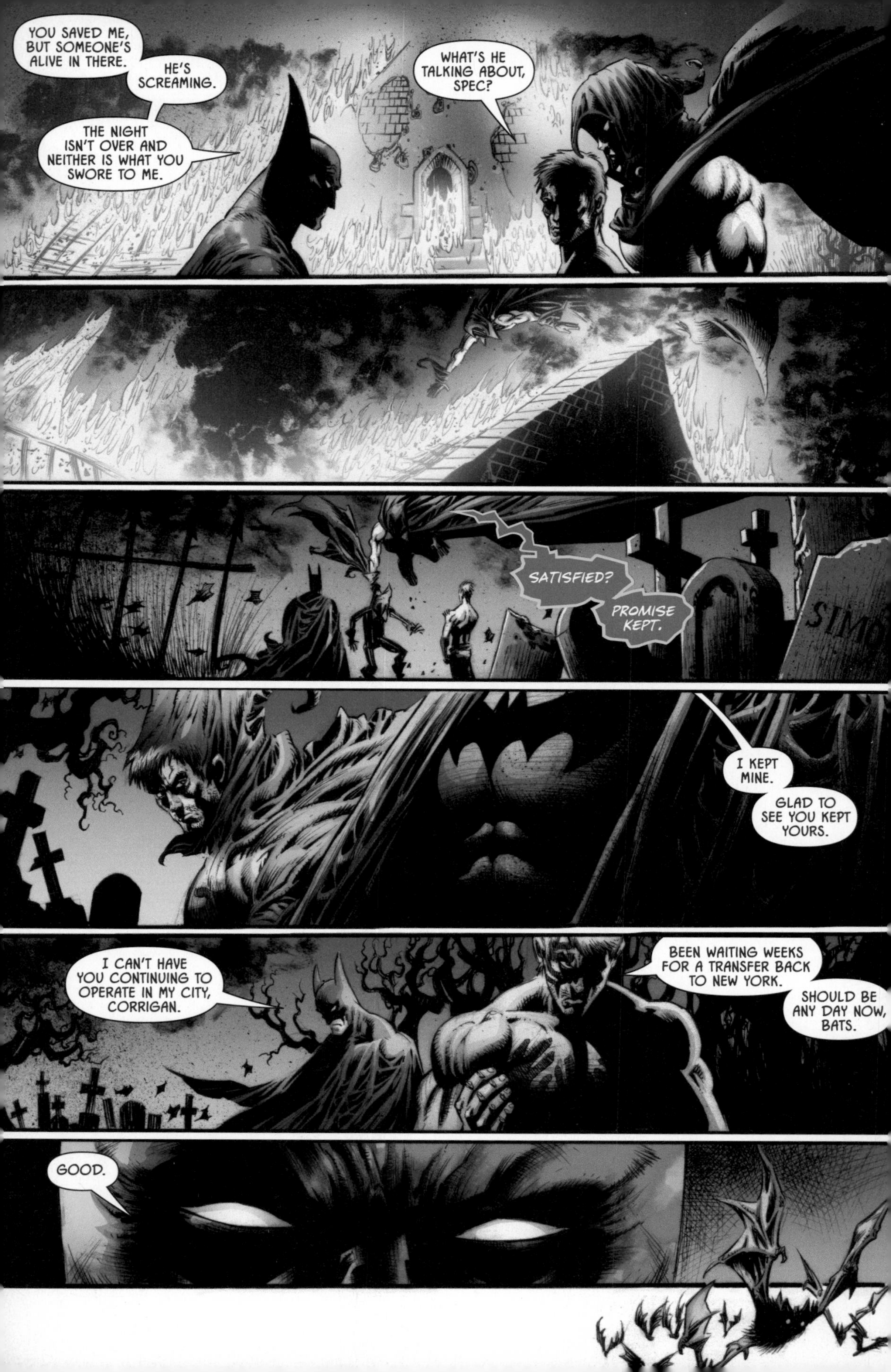
YOU SAVED ME, BUT SOMEONE'S ALIVE IN THERE.
HE'S SCREAMING.
THE NIGHT ISN'T OVER AND NEITHER IS WHAT YOU SWORE TO ME.
WHAT'S HE TALKING ABOUT, SPEC?
SATISFIED?
PROMISE KEPT.
I KEPT MINE.
GLAD TO SEE YOU KEPT YOURS.
I CAN'T HAVE YOU CONTINUING TO OPERATE IN MY CITY, CORRIGAN.
BEEN WAITING WEEKS FOR A TRANSFER BACK TO NEW YORK.
SHOULD BE ANY DAY NOW, BATS.
GOOD.

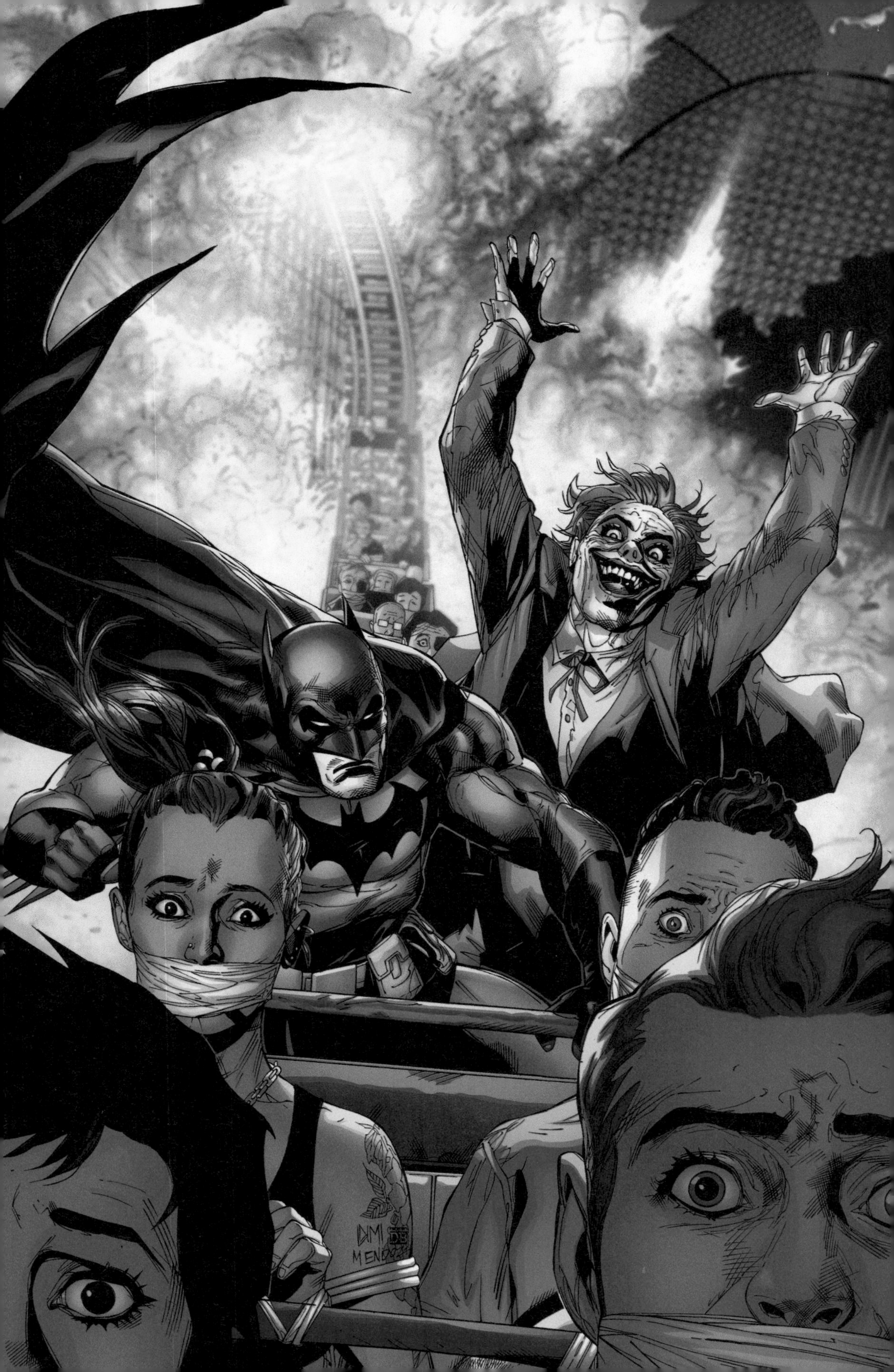

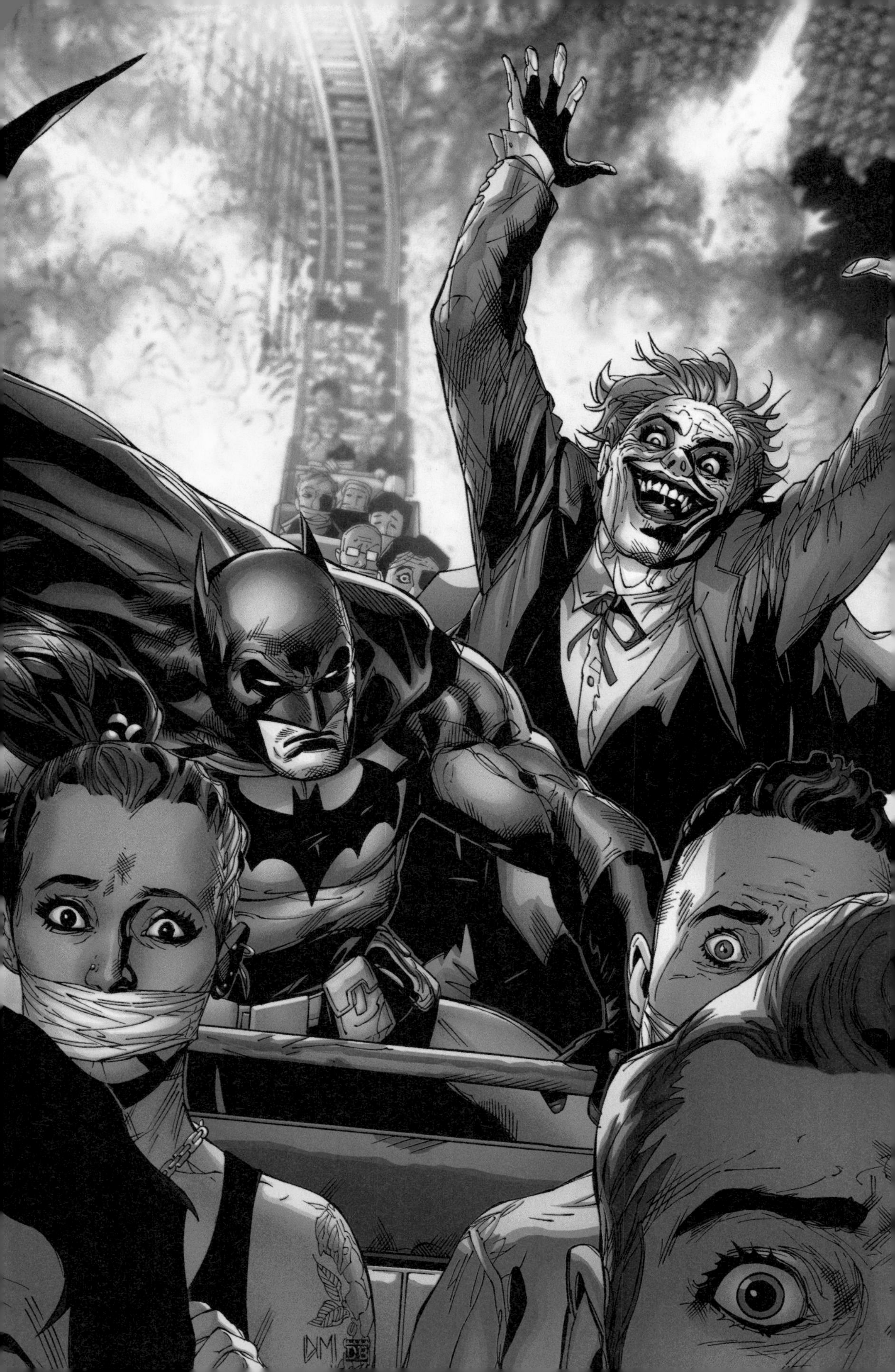

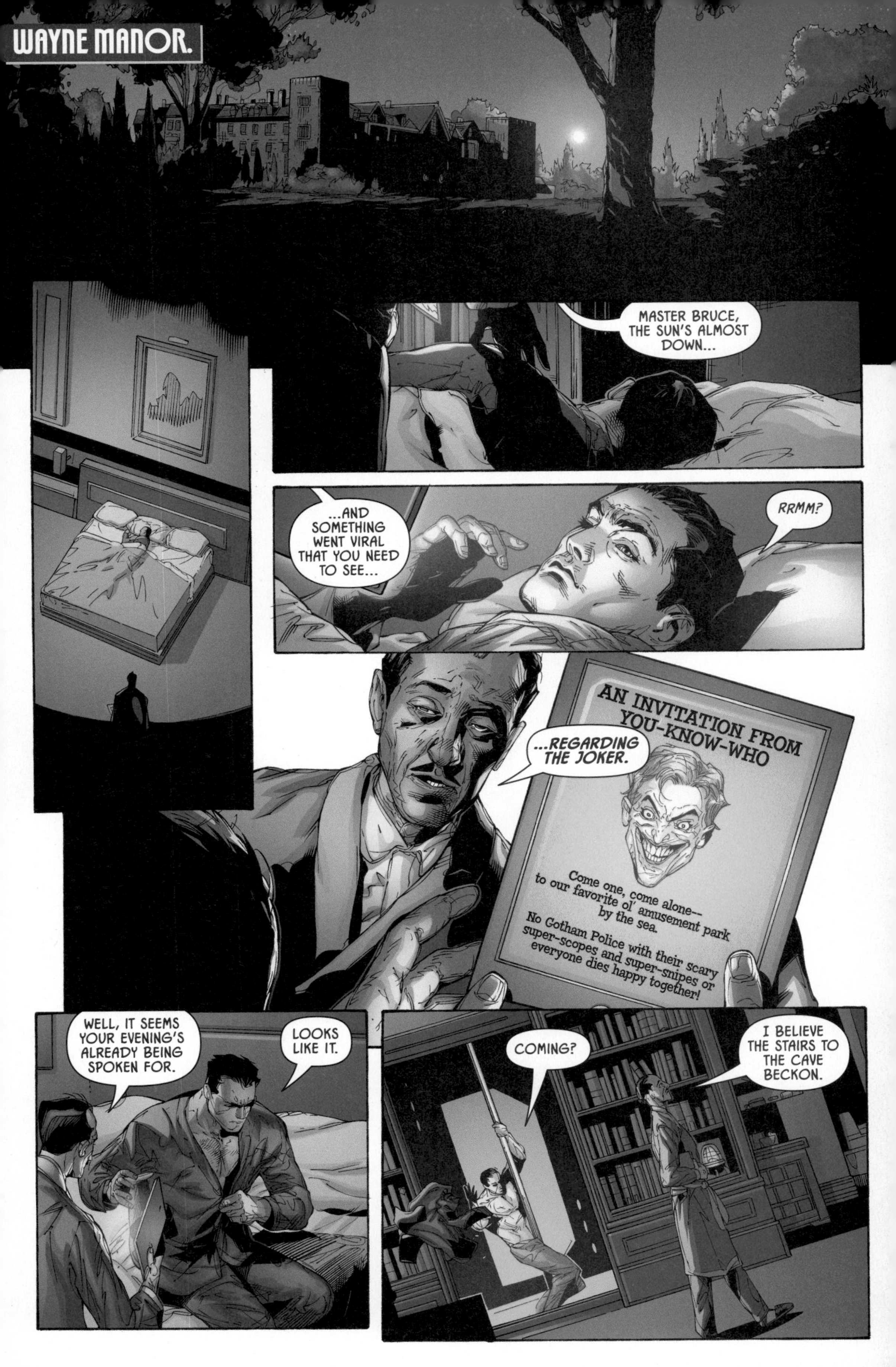
WAYNE MANOR.
MASTER BRUCE, THE SUN'S ALMOST DOWN...
...AND SOMETHING WENT VIRAL THAT YOU NEED TO SEE...
RRMM?
...REGARDING THE JOKER.
AN INVITATION FROM YOU-KNOW-WHO
Come one, come alone-- to our favorite ol' amusement park by the sea.
No Gotham Police with their scary super-scopes and super-snipes or everyone dies happy together!
WELL, IT SEEMS YOUR EVENING'S ALREADY BEING SPOKEN FOR.
LOOKS LIKE IT.
COMING?
I BELIEVE THE STAIRS TO THE CAVE BECKON.

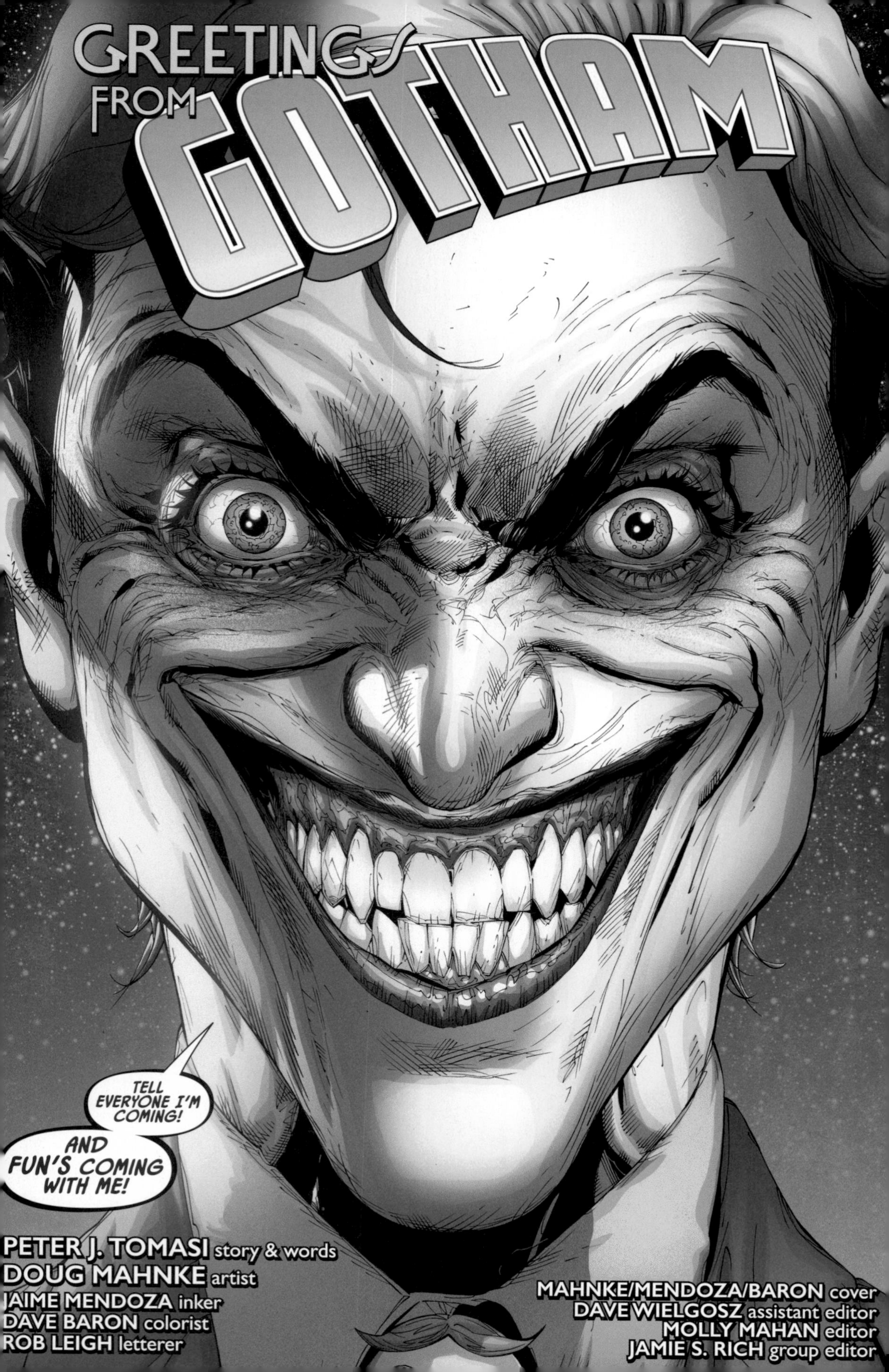
GREETINGS FROM GOTHAM
TELL EVERYONE I'M COMING!
AND FUN'S COMING WITH ME!
PETER J. TOMASI story & words
DOUG MAHNKE artist
JAIME MENDOZA inker
DAVE BARON colorist
ROB LEIGH letterer
MAHNKE/MENDOZA/BARON cover
DAVE WIELGOSZ assistant editor
MOLLY MAHAN editor
JAMIE S. RICH group editor

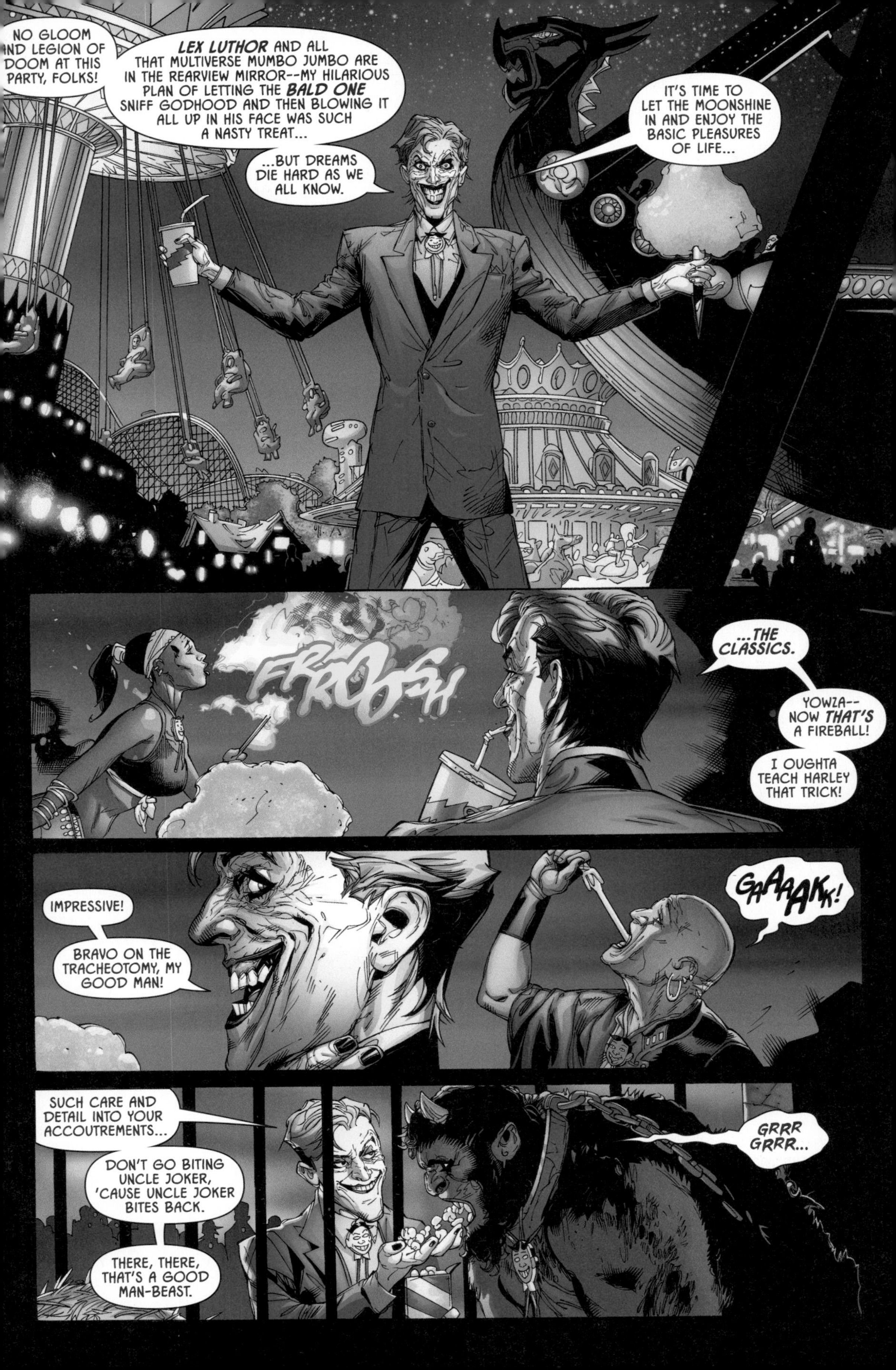

NO GLOOM AND LEGION OF DOOM AT THIS PARTY, FOLKS!
LEX LUTHOR AND ALL THAT MULTIVERSE MUMBO JUMBO ARE IN THE REARVIEW MIRROR--MY HILARIOUS PLAN OF LETTING THE BALD ONE SNIFF GODHOOD AND THEN BLOWING IT ALL UP IN HIS FACE WAS SUCH A NASTY TREAT...
...BUT DREAMS DIE HARD AS WE ALL KNOW.
IT'S TIME TO LET THE MOONSHINE IN AND ENJOY THE BASIC PLEASURES OF LIFE...
FRROOSH
...THE CLASSICS.
YOWZA-- NOW THAT'S A FIREBALL!
I OUGHTA TEACH HARLEY THAT TRICK!
IMPRESSIVE!
BRAVO ON THE TRACHEOTOMY, MY GOOD MAN!
GAAAAKK!
SUCH CARE AND DETAIL INTO YOUR ACCOUTREMENTS...
DON'T GO BITING UNCLE JOKER, 'CAUSE UNCLE JOKER BITES BACK.
THERE, THERE, THAT'S A GOOD MAN-BEAST.
GRRR GRRR...

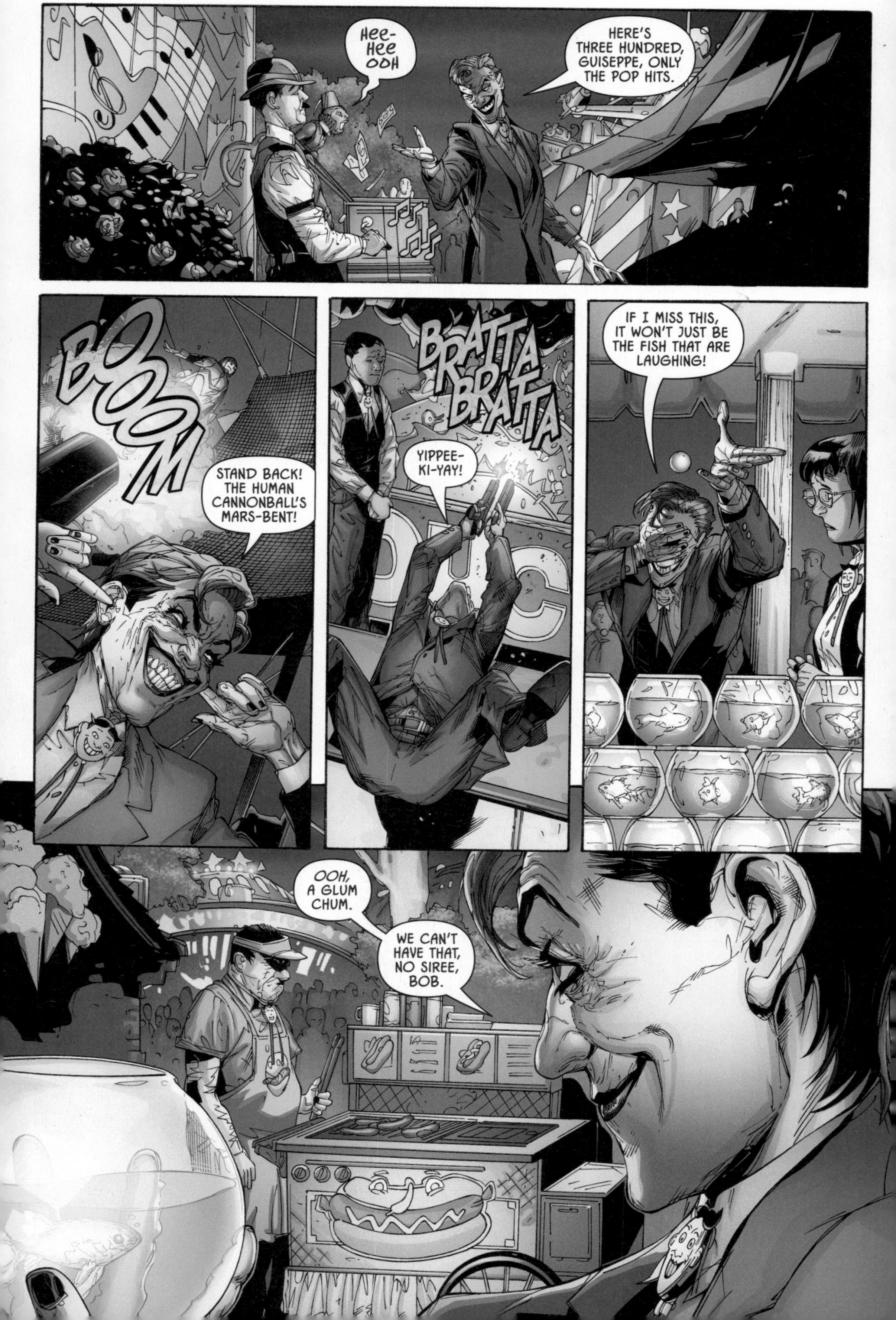
HEE-HEE OOH
HERE'S THREE HUNDRED, GUISEPPE, ONLY THE POP HITS.
BOOOOM
STAND BACK! THE HUMAN CANNONBALL'S MARS-BENT!
BRATTA BRATTA
YIPPEE-KI-YAY!
IF I MISS THIS, IT WON'T JUST BE THE FISH THAT ARE LAUGHING!
OOH, A GLUM CHUM.
WE CAN'T HAVE THAT, NO SIREE, BOB.

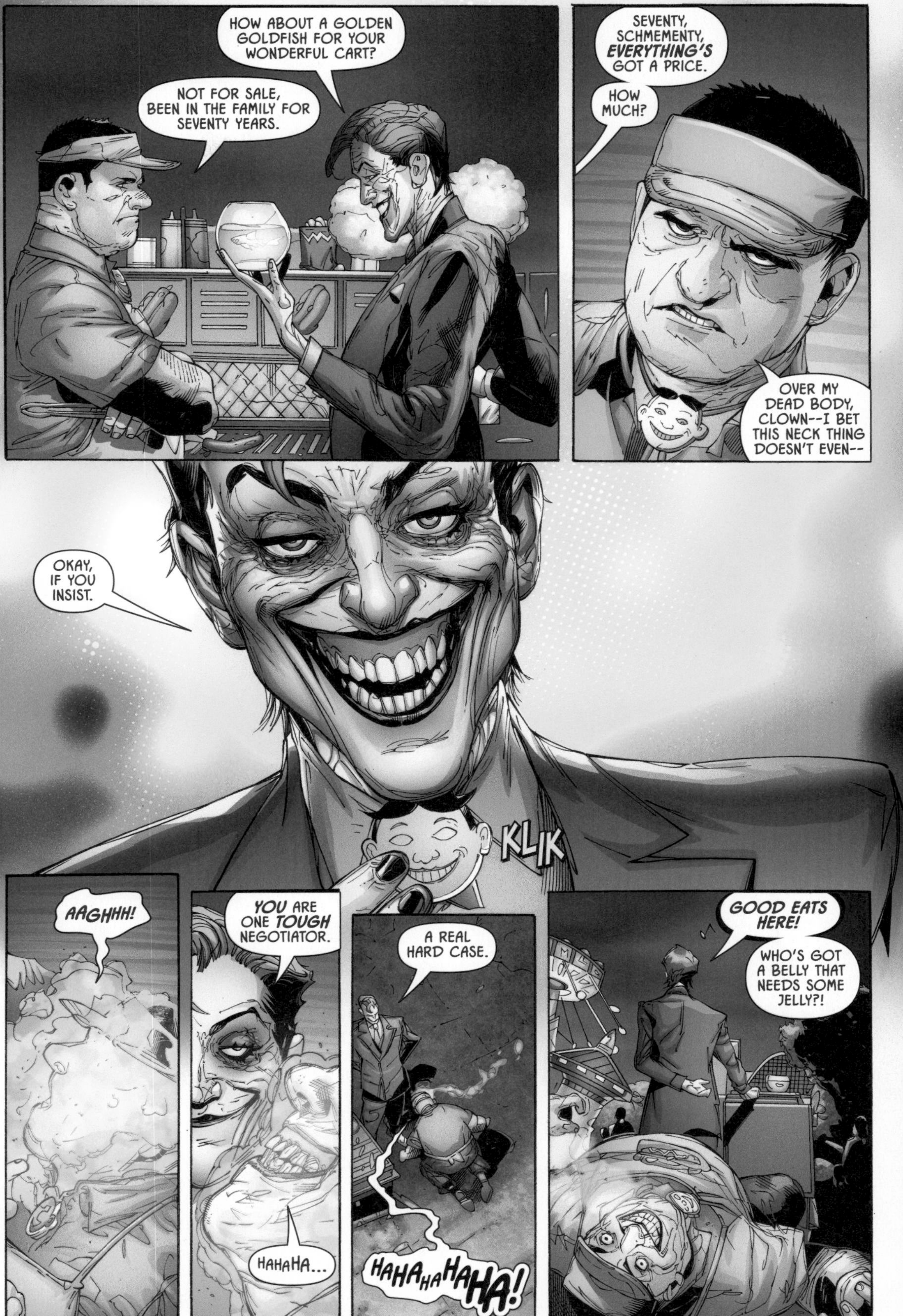
HOW ABOUT A GOLDEN GOLDFISH FOR YOUR WONDERFUL CART?
NOT FOR SALE, BEEN IN THE FAMILY FOR SEVENTY YEARS.
SEVENTY, SCHMEMENTY, EVERYTHING'S GOT A PRICE.
HOW MUCH?
OVER MY DEAD BODY, CLOWN--I BET THIS NECK THING DOESN'T EVEN--
OKAY, IF YOU INSIST.
KLIK
AAGHHH!
YOU ARE ONE TOUGH NEGOTIATOR.
HAHAHA...
A REAL HARD CASE.
HAHAHAHAHA!
GOOD EATS HERE!
WHO'S GOT A BELLY THAT NEEDS SOME JELLY?!

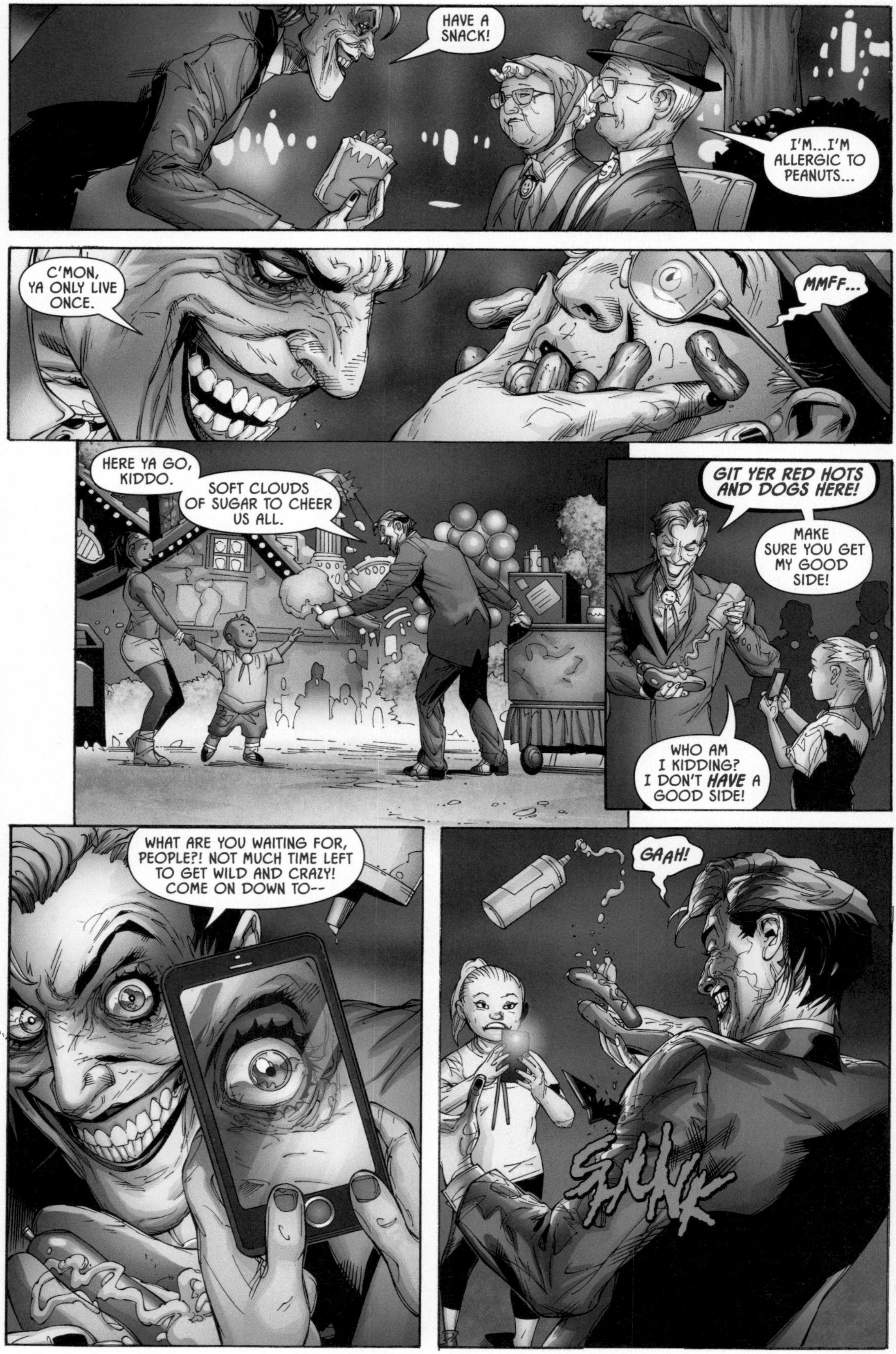
HAVE A SNACK!
I'M...I'M ALLERGIC TO PEANUTS...
C'MON, YA ONLY LIVE ONCE.
MMFF...
HERE YA GO, KIDDO.
SOFT CLOUDS OF SUGAR TO CHEER US ALL.
GIT YER RED HOTS AND DOGS HERE!
MAKE SURE YOU GET MY GOOD SIDE!
WHO AM I KIDDING? I DON'T HAVE A GOOD SIDE!
WHAT ARE YOU WAITING FOR, PEOPLE?! NOT MUCH TIME LEFT TO GET WILD AND CRAZY! COME ON DOWN TO--
GAAH!
SHUNK

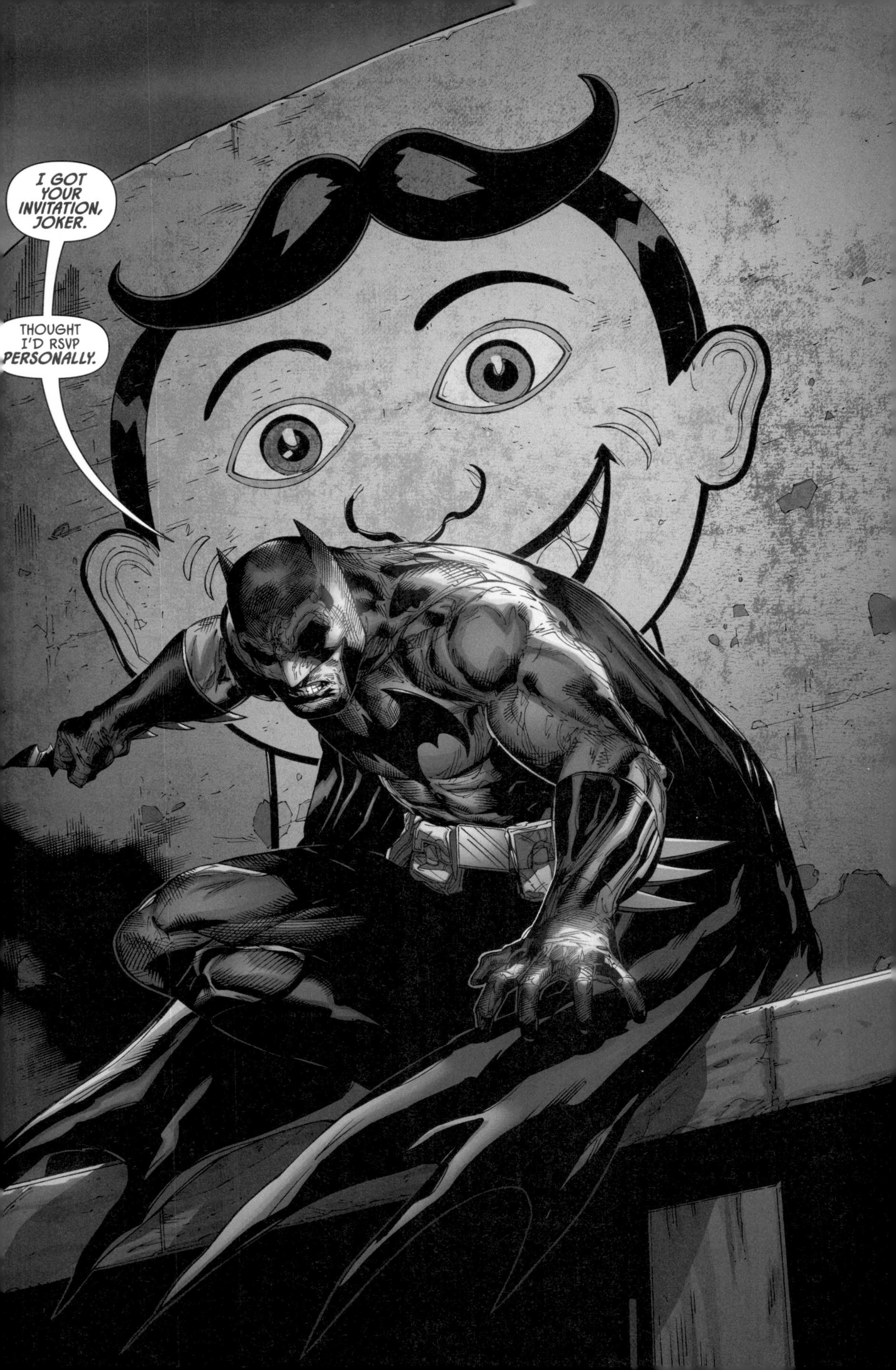
I GOT YOUR INVITATION, JOKER.
THOUGHT I'D RSVP PERSONALLY.

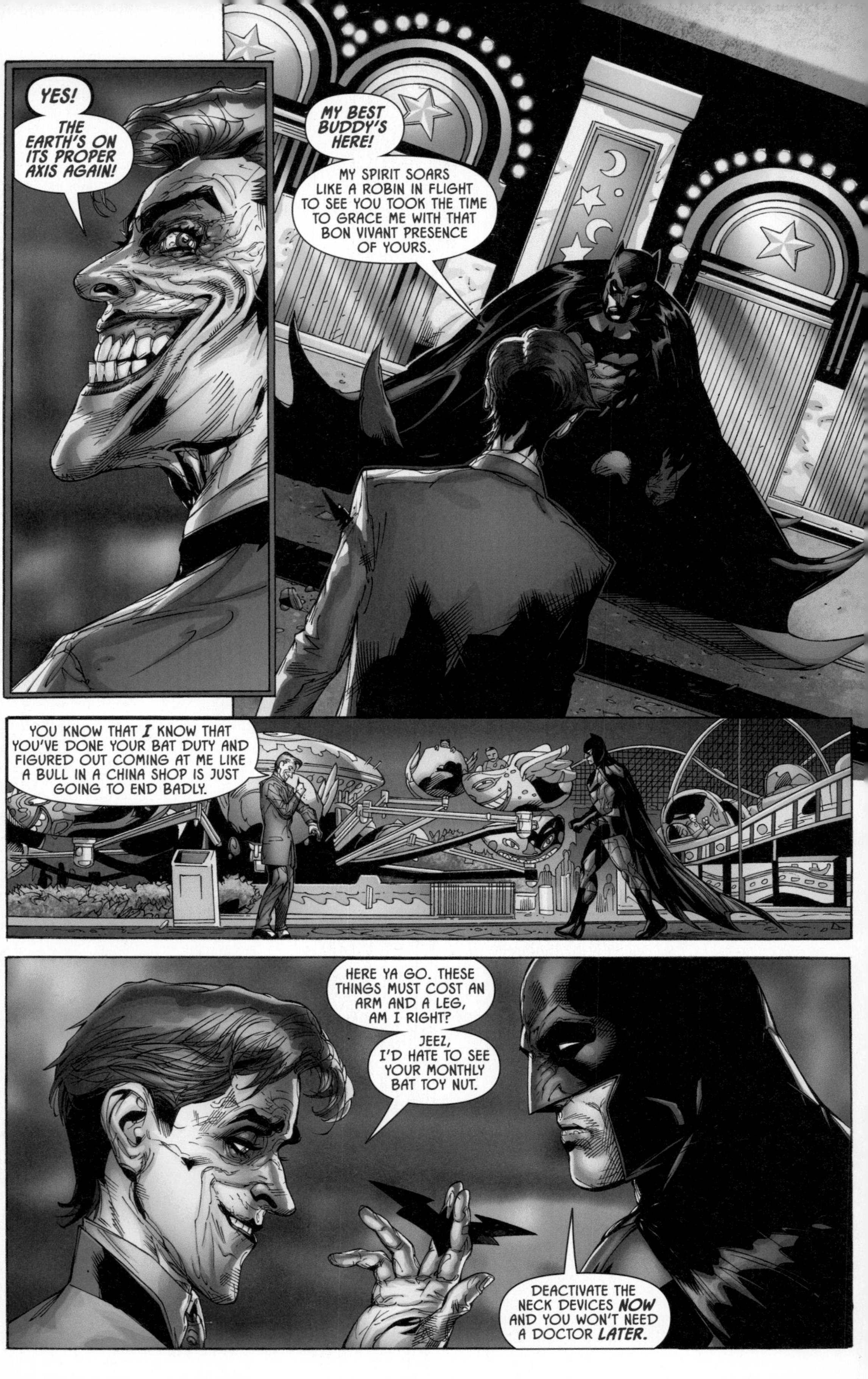
YES!
THE EARTH'S ON ITS PROPER AXIS AGAIN!
MY BEST BUDDY'S HERE!
MY SPIRIT SOARS LIKE A ROBIN IN FLIGHT TO SEE YOU TOOK THE TIME TO GRACE ME WITH THAT BON VIVANT PRESENCE OF YOURS.
YOU KNOW THAT I KNOW THAT YOU'VE DONE YOUR BAT DUTY AND FIGURED OUT COMING AT ME LIKE A BULL IN A CHINA SHOP IS JUST GOING TO END BADLY.
HERE YA GO. THESE THINGS MUST COST AN ARM AND A LEG, AM I RIGHT?
JEEZ, I'D HATE TO SEE YOUR MONTHLY BAT TOY NUT.
DEACTIVATE THE NECK DEVICES NOW AND YOU WON'T NEED A DOCTOR LATER.

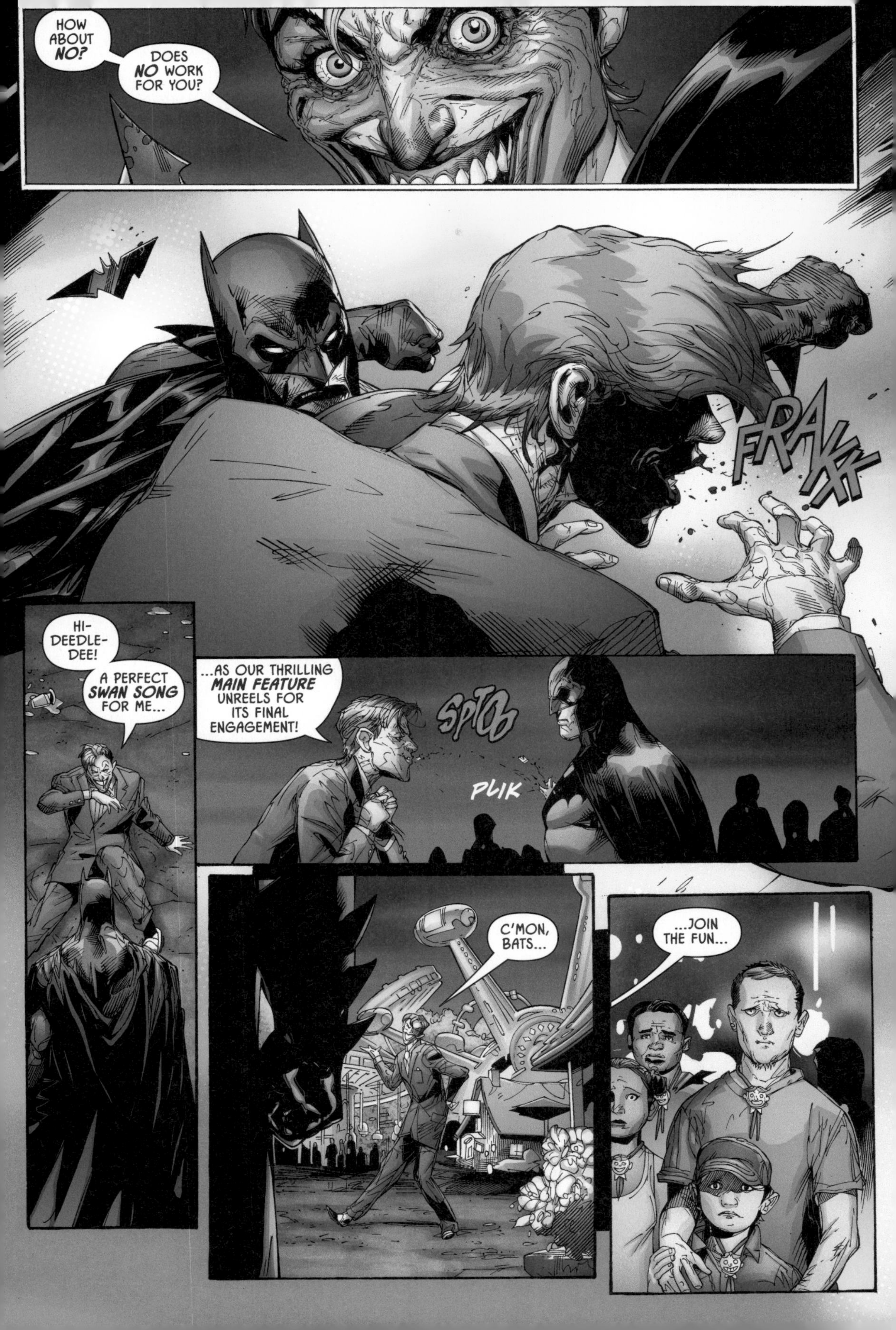
HOW ABOUT NO?
DOES NO WORK FOR YOU?
FRAKK!!
HI-DEEDLE-DEE!
A PERFECT SWAN SONG FOR ME...
...AS OUR THRILLING MAIN FEATURE UNREELS FOR ITS FINAL ENGAGEMENT!
SPTOO
PLIK
C'MON, BATS...
...JOIN THE FUN...

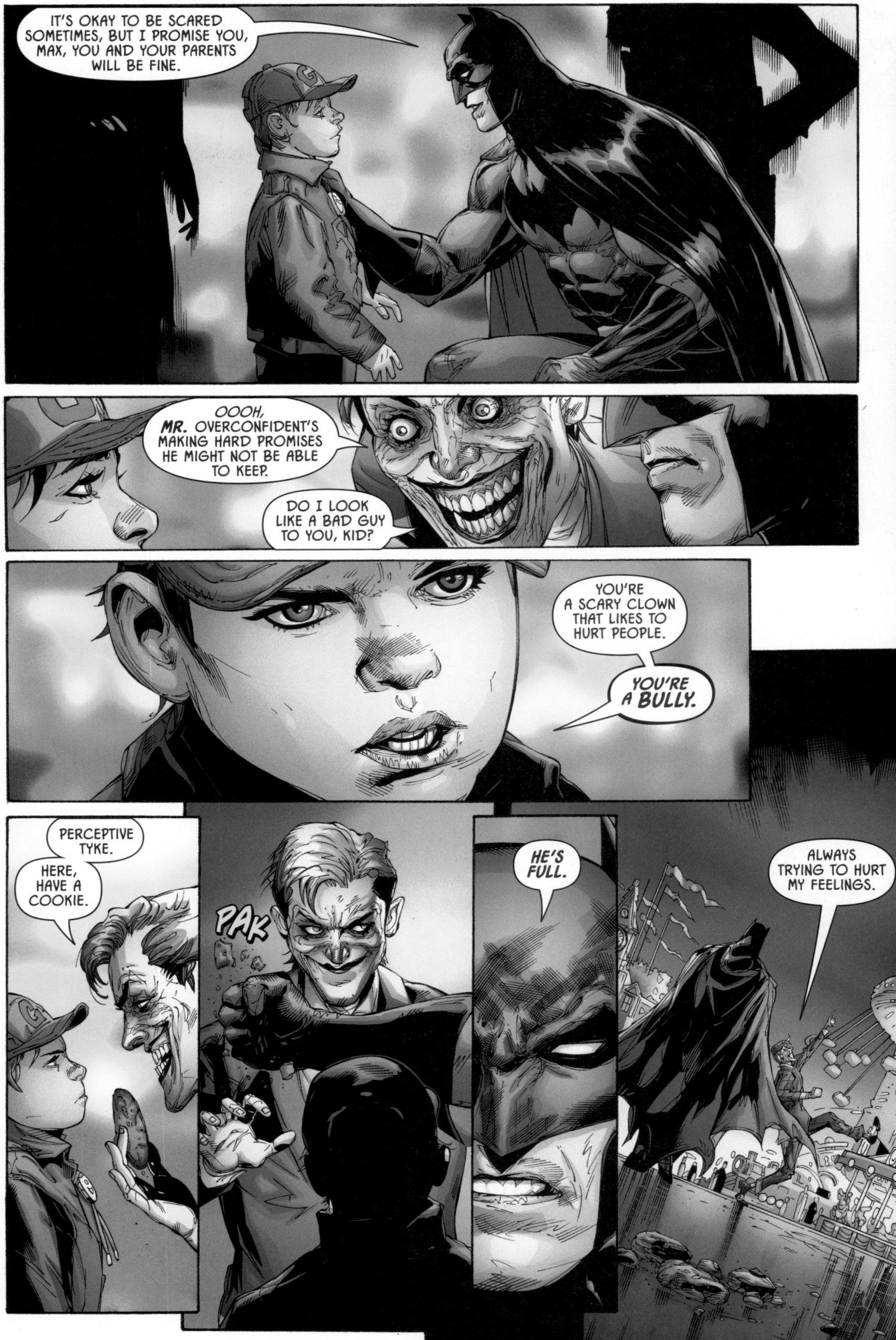
IT'S OKAY TO BE SCARED SOMETIMES, BUT I PROMISE YOU, MAX, YOU AND YOUR PARENTS WILL BE FINE.
OOOH, MR. OVERCONFIDENT'S MAKING HARD PROMISES HE MIGHT NOT BE ABLE TO KEEP.
DO I LOOK LIKE A BAD GUY TO YOU, KID?
YOU'RE A SCARY CLOWN THAT LIKES TO HURT PEOPLE.
YOU'RE A BULLY.
PERCEPTIVE TYKE.
HERE, HAVE A COOKIE.
PAK
HE'S FULL.
ALWAYS TRYING TO HURT MY FEELINGS.

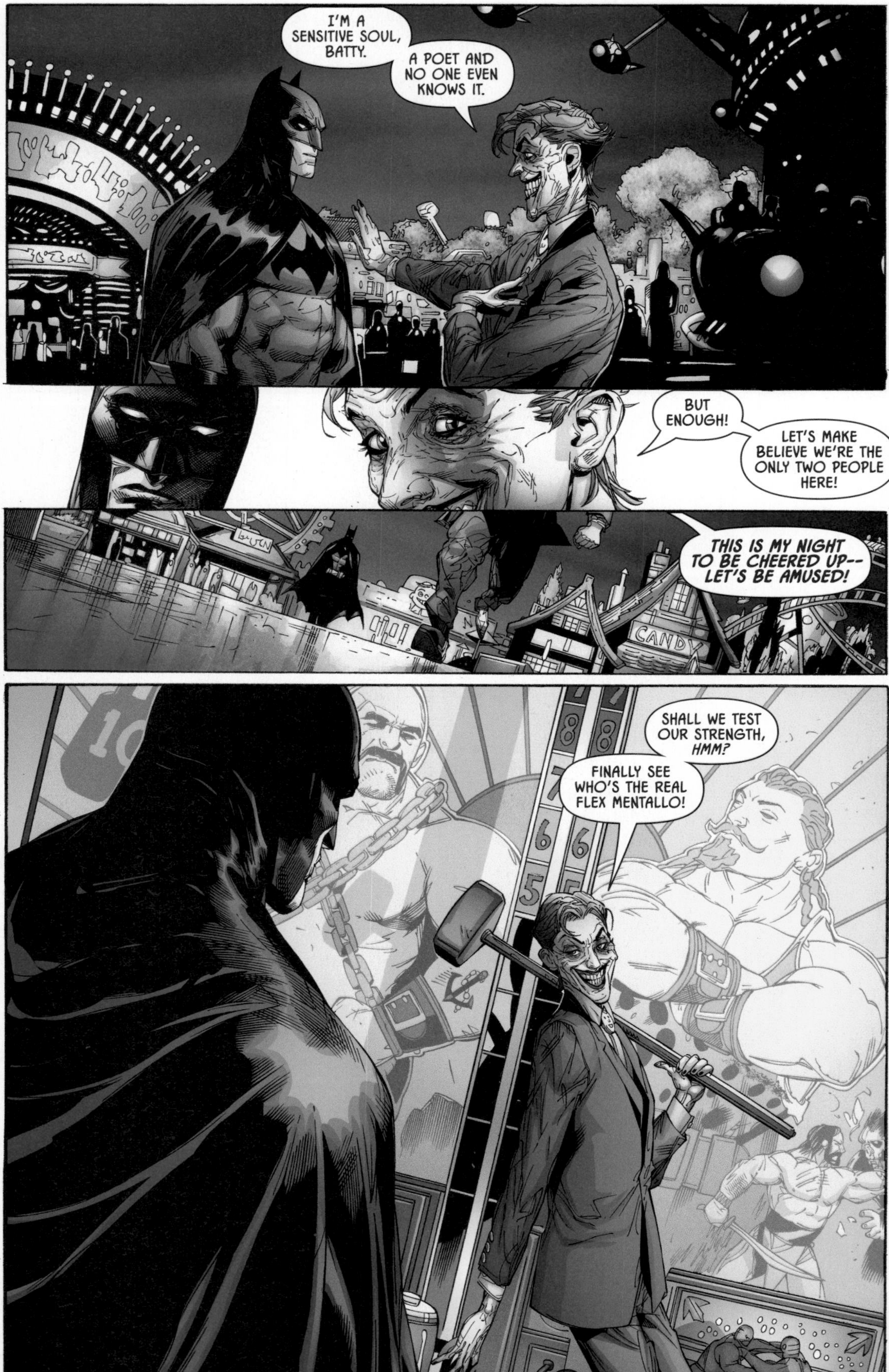
I'M A SENSITIVE SOUL, BATTY.
A POET AND NO ONE EVEN KNOWS IT.
BUT ENOUGH!
LET'S MAKE BELIEVE WE'RE THE ONLY TWO PEOPLE HERE!
THIS IS MY NIGHT TO BE CHEERED UP-- LET'S BE AMUSED!
CANDY
SHALL WE TEST OUR STRENGTH, HMM?
FINALLY SEE WHO'S THE REAL FLEX MENTALLO!

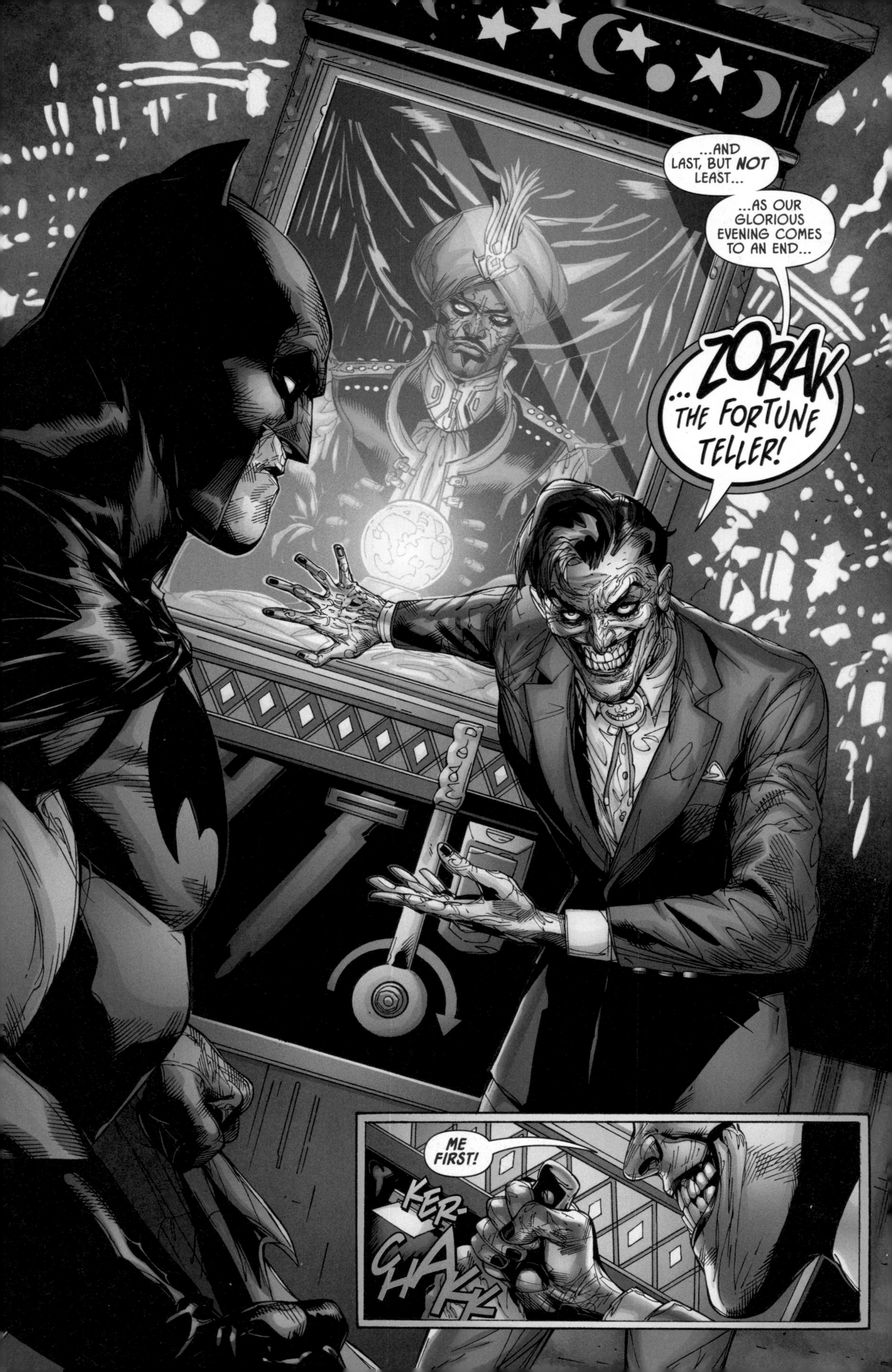
...AND LAST, BUT NOT LEAST...
...AS OUR GLORIOUS EVENING COMES TO AN END...
...ZORAK THE FORTUNE TELLER!
ME FIRST!
KER-CHAKK

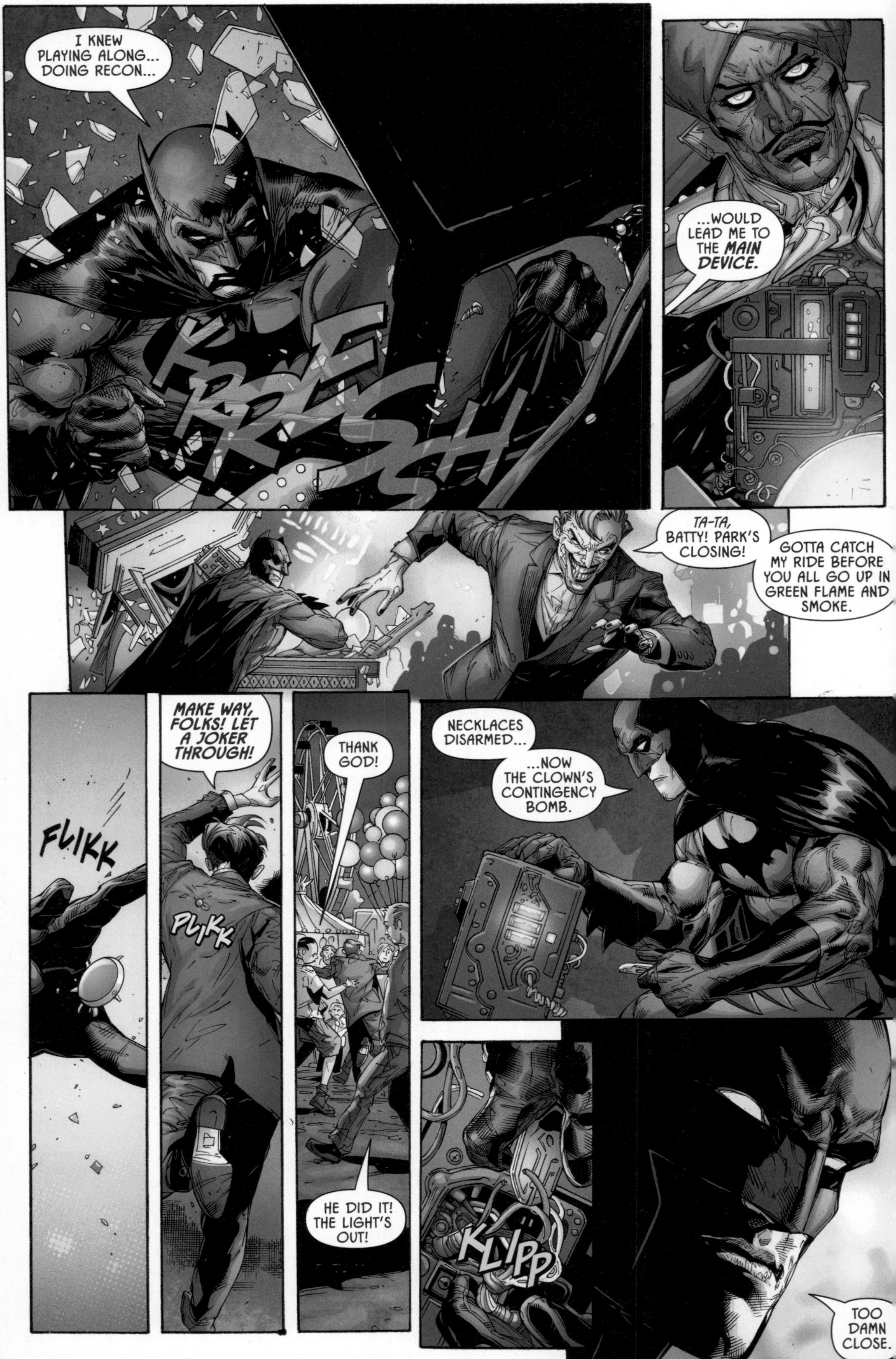

I KNEW PLAYING ALONG... DOING RECON...
KRRAASH
...WOULD LEAD ME TO THE MAIN DEVICE.
TA-TA, BATTY! PARK'S CLOSING!
GOTTA CATCH MY RIDE BEFORE YOU ALL GO UP IN GREEN FLAME AND SMOKE.
FLIKK
MAKE WAY, FOLKS! LET A JOKER THROUGH!
PLIKK
THANK GOD!
HE DID IT! THE LIGHT'S OUT!
NECKLACES DISARMED...
...NOW THE CLOWN'S CONTINGENCY BOMB.
KLIPP
TOO DAMN CLOSE.

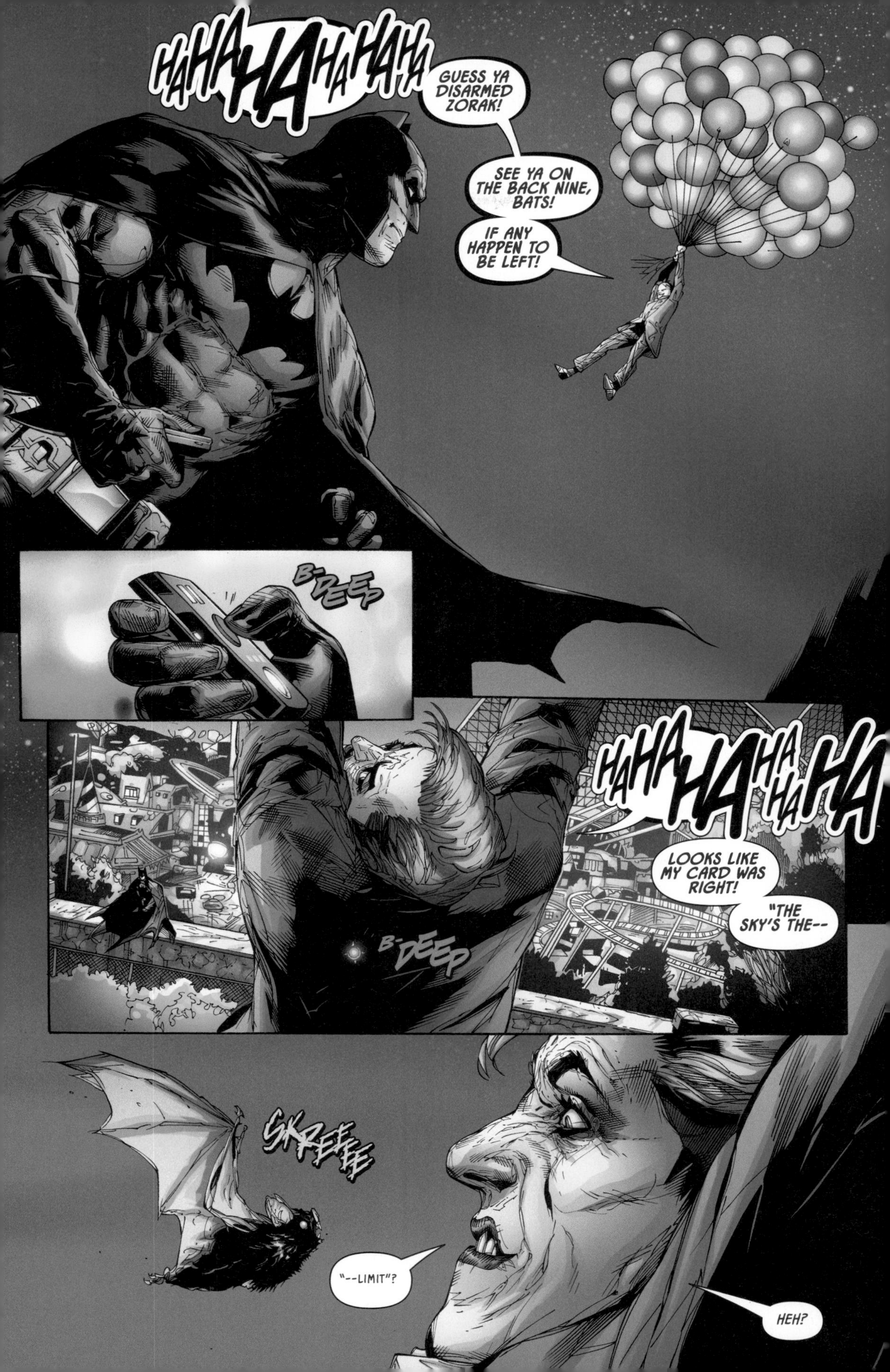
HAHAHAHAHAHAHA
GUESS YA DISARMED ZORAK!
SEE YA ON THE BACK NINE, BATS!
IF ANY HAPPEN TO BE LEFT!
B-DEEP
HAHAHAHAHAHAHA
LOOKS LIKE MY CARD WAS RIGHT!
"THE SKY'S THE--
B-DEEP
SKREEEE
"--LIMIT"?
HEH?

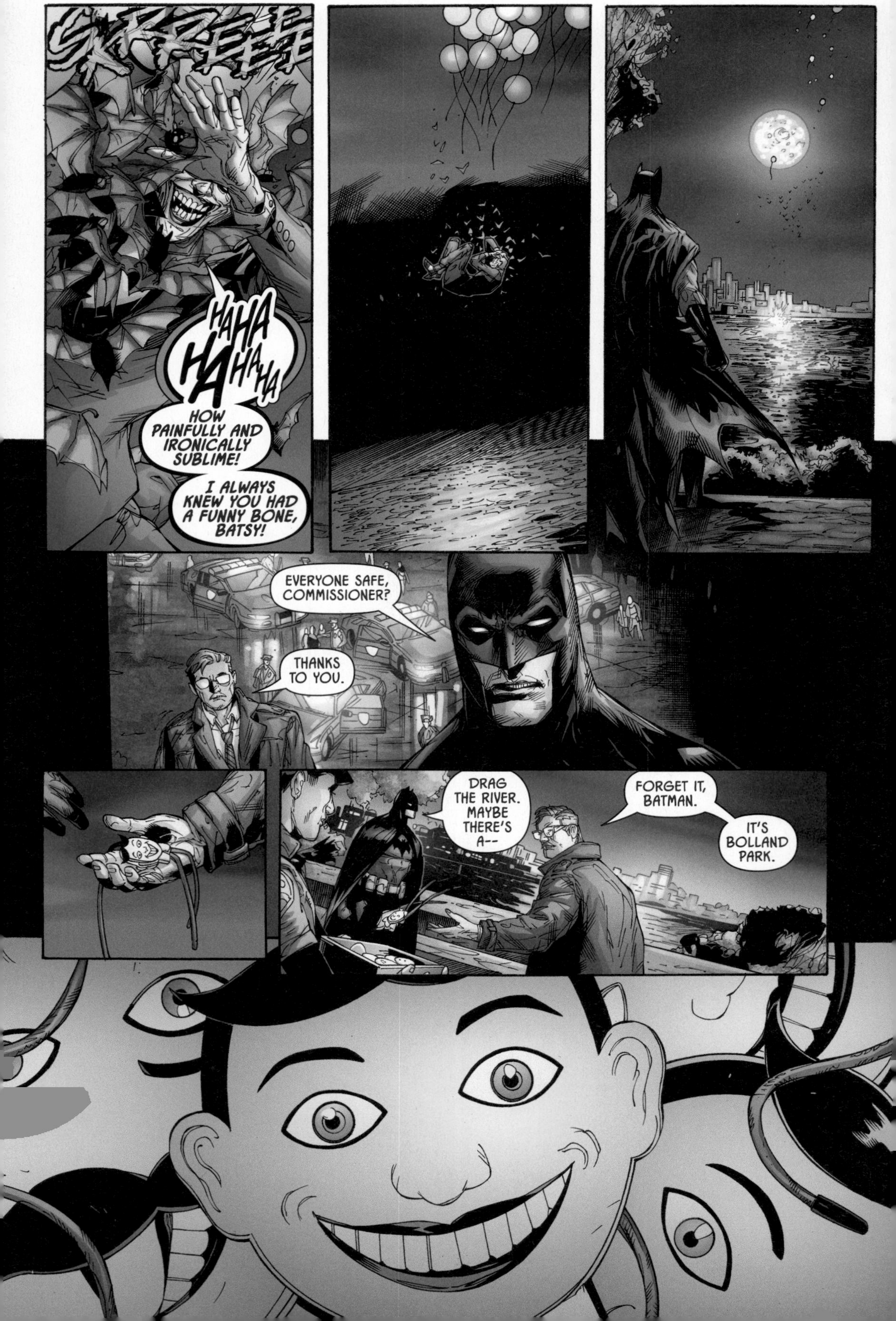
HAHAHA HAHAHA
HOW PAINFULLY AND IRONICALLY SUBLIME!
I ALWAYS KNEW YOU HAD A FUNNY BONE, BATSY!
EVERYONE SAFE, COMMISSIONER?
THANKS TO YOU.
DRAG THE RIVER. MAYBE THERE'S A--
FORGET IT, BATMAN.
IT'S BOLLAND PARK.

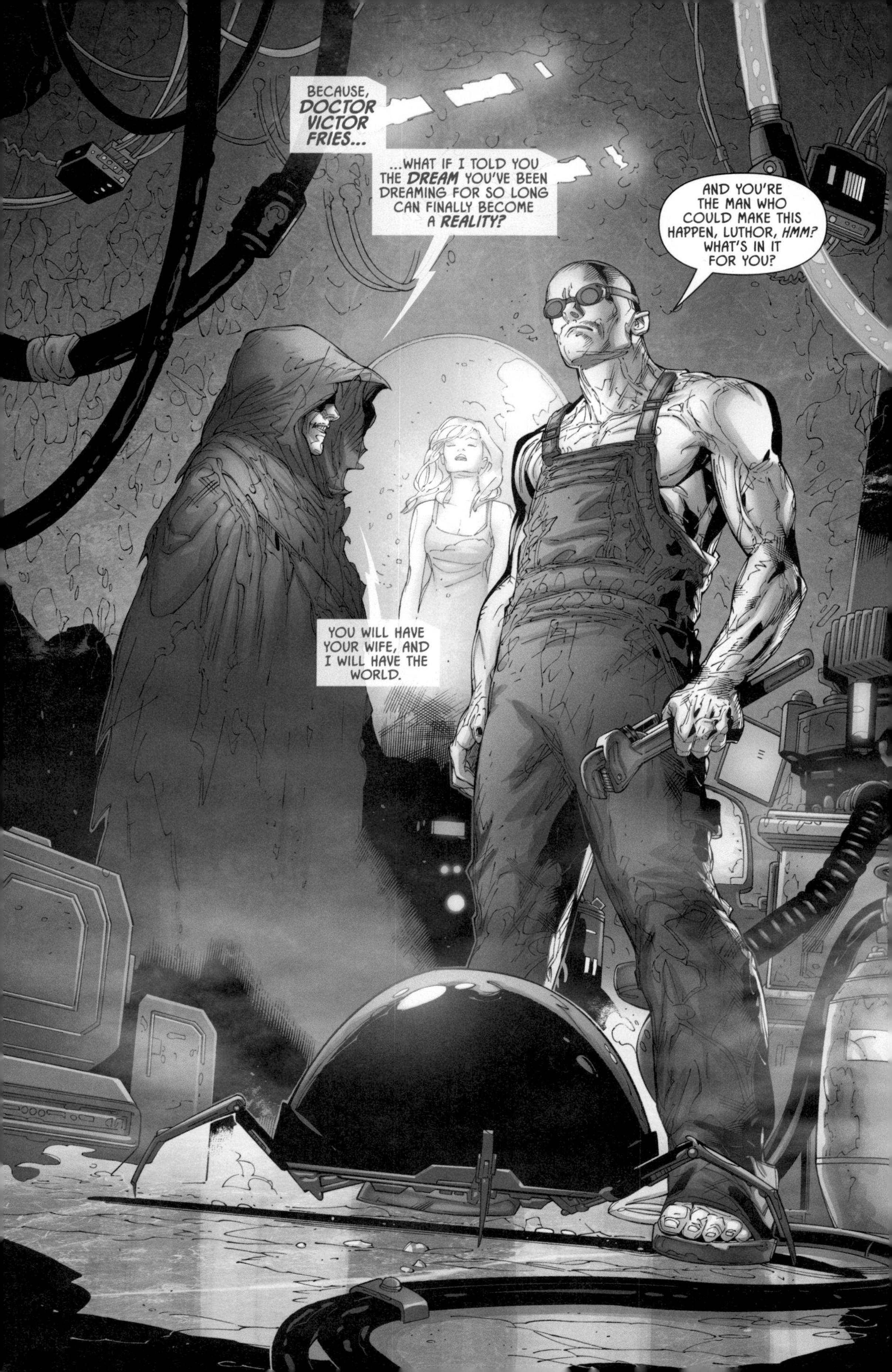
BECAUSE, DOCTOR VICTOR FRIES...
...WHAT IF I TOLD YOU THE DREAM YOU'VE BEEN DREAMING FOR SO LONG CAN FINALLY BECOME A REALITY?
AND YOU'RE THE MAN WHO COULD MAKE THIS HAPPEN, LUTHOR, HMM? WHAT'S IN IT FOR YOU?
YOU WILL HAVE YOUR WIFE, AND I WILL HAVE THE WORLD.

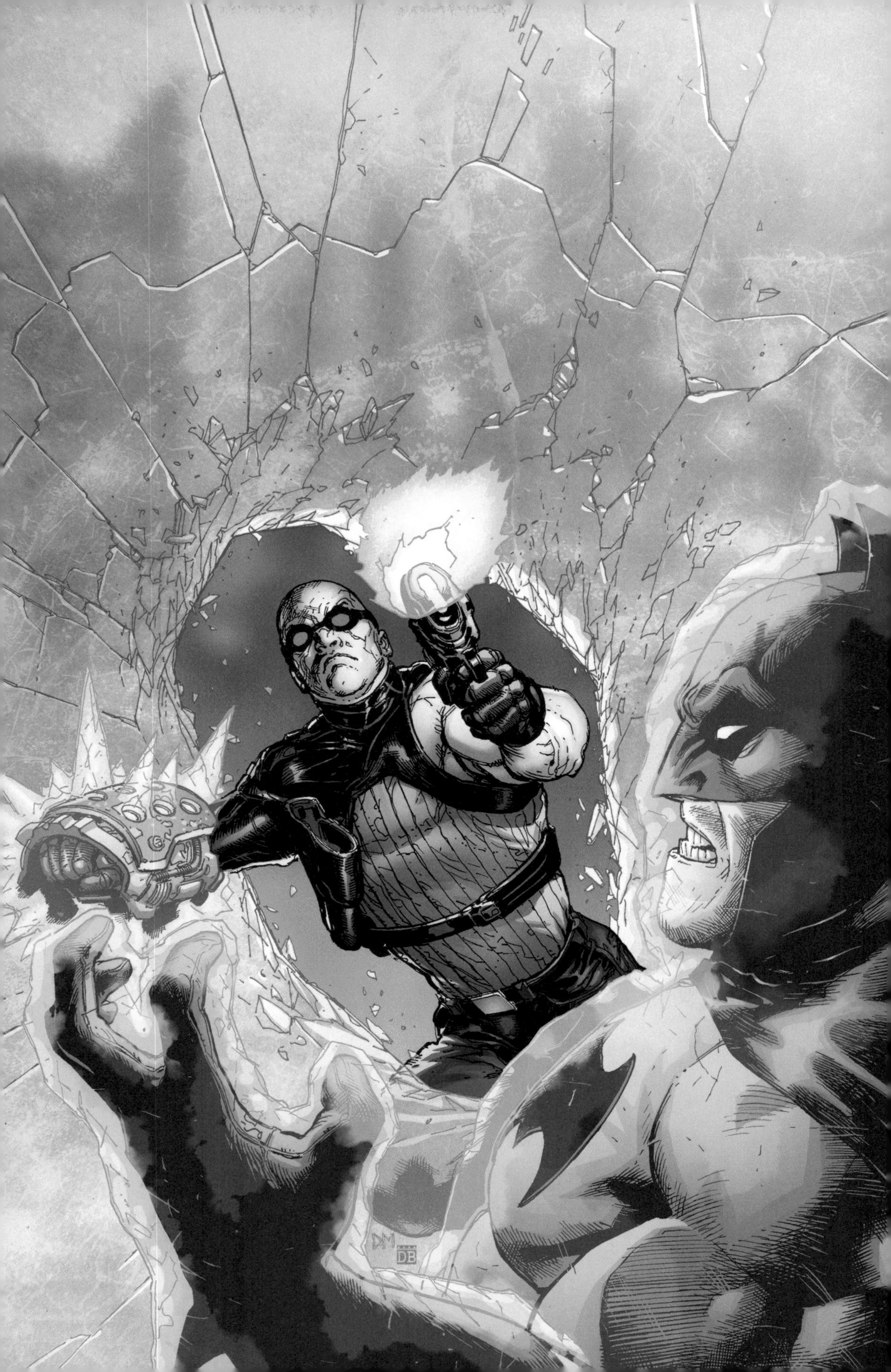

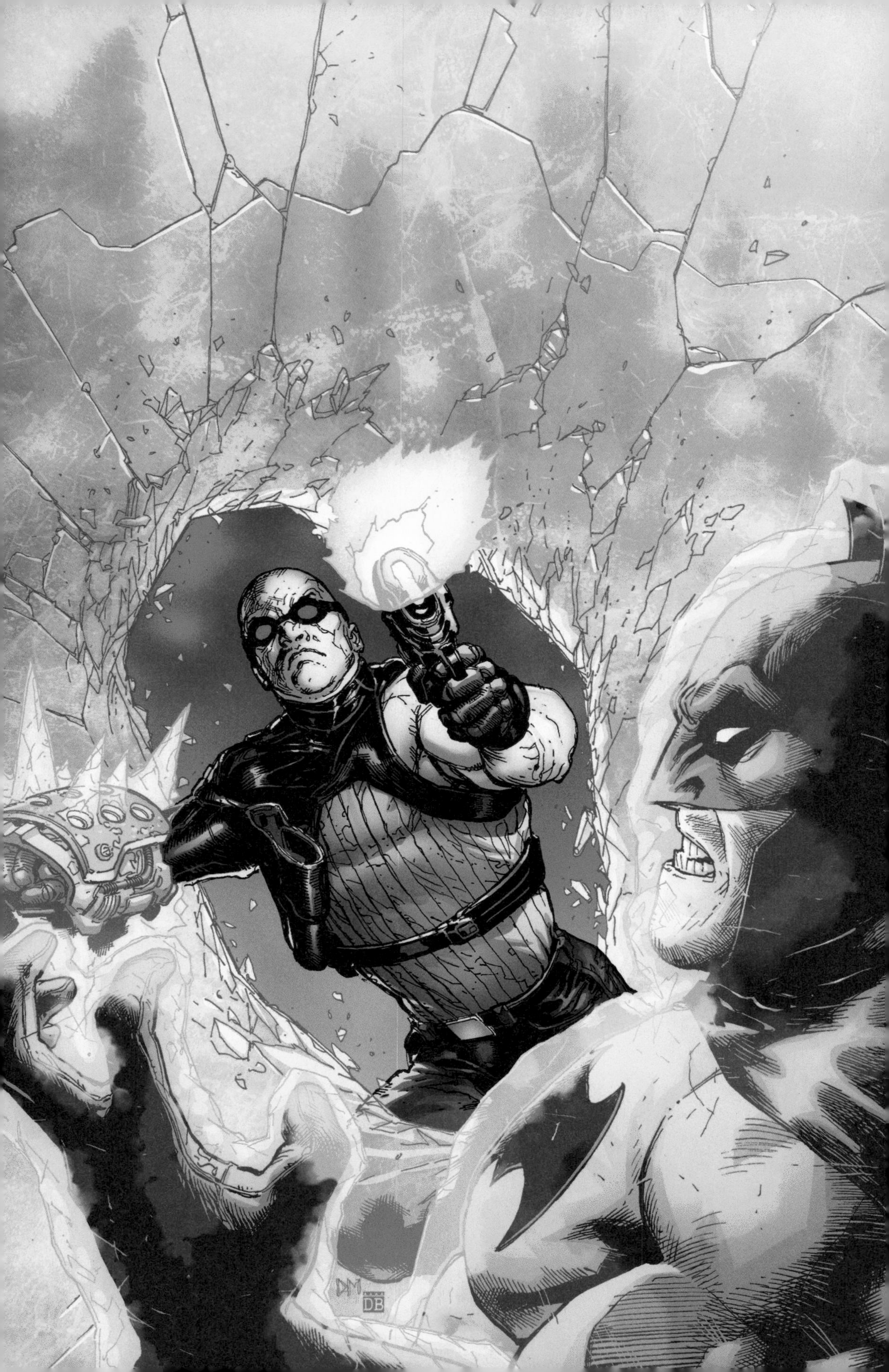

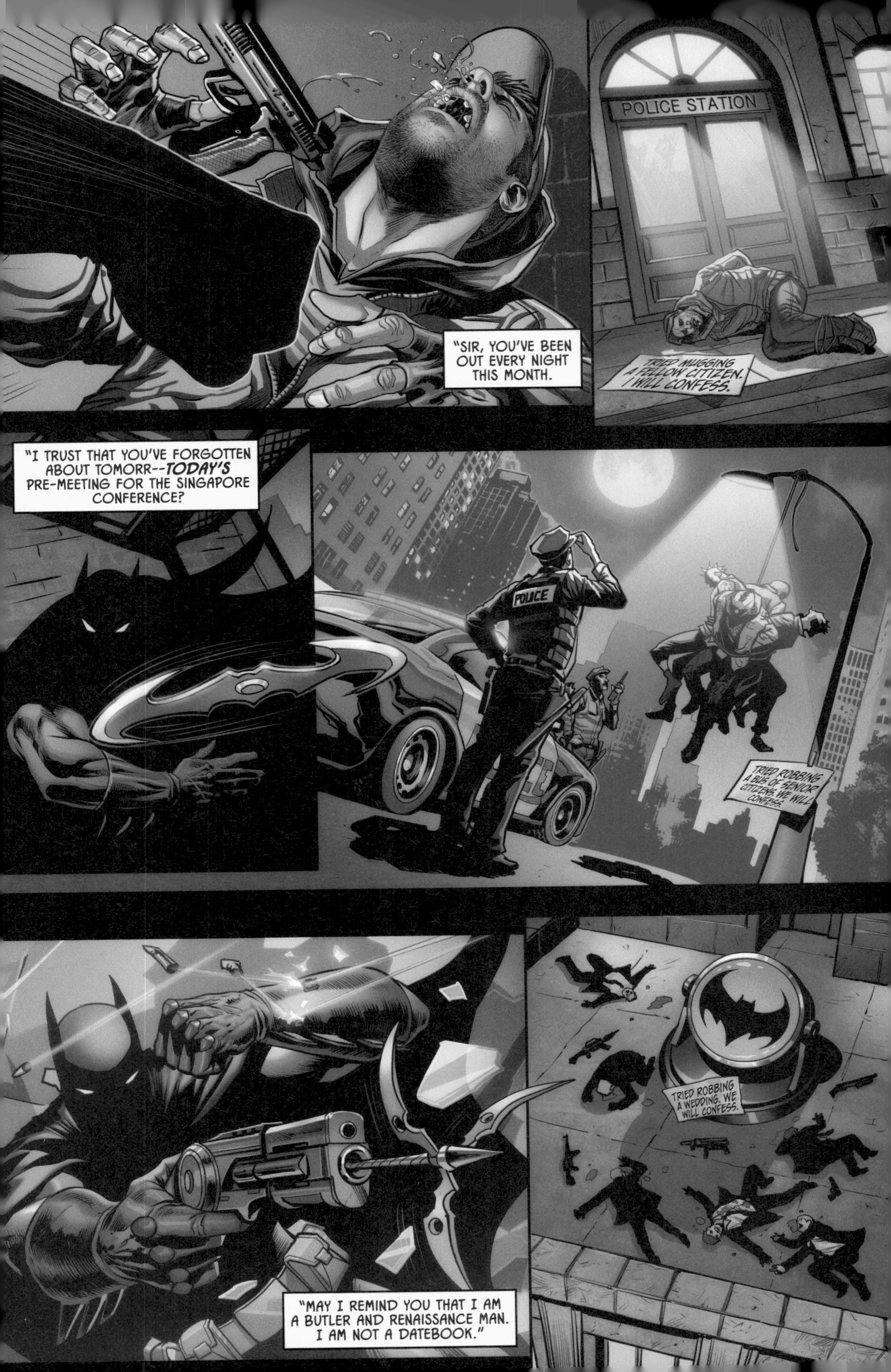
"SIR, YOU'VE BEEN OUT EVERY NIGHT THIS MONTH.
POLICE STATION
TRIED MUGGING A FELLOW CITIZEN. I WILL CONFESS.
"I TRUST THAT YOU'VE FORGOTTEN ABOUT TOMORR--TODAY'S PRE-MEETING FOR THE SINGAPORE CONFERENCE?
POLICE
TRIED ROBBING A BUS OF SENIOR CITIZENS. WE WILL CONFESS.
"MAY I REMIND YOU THAT I AM A BUTLER AND RENAISSANCE MAN. I AM NOT A DATEBOOK."
TRIED ROBBING A WEDDING. WE WILL CONFESS.

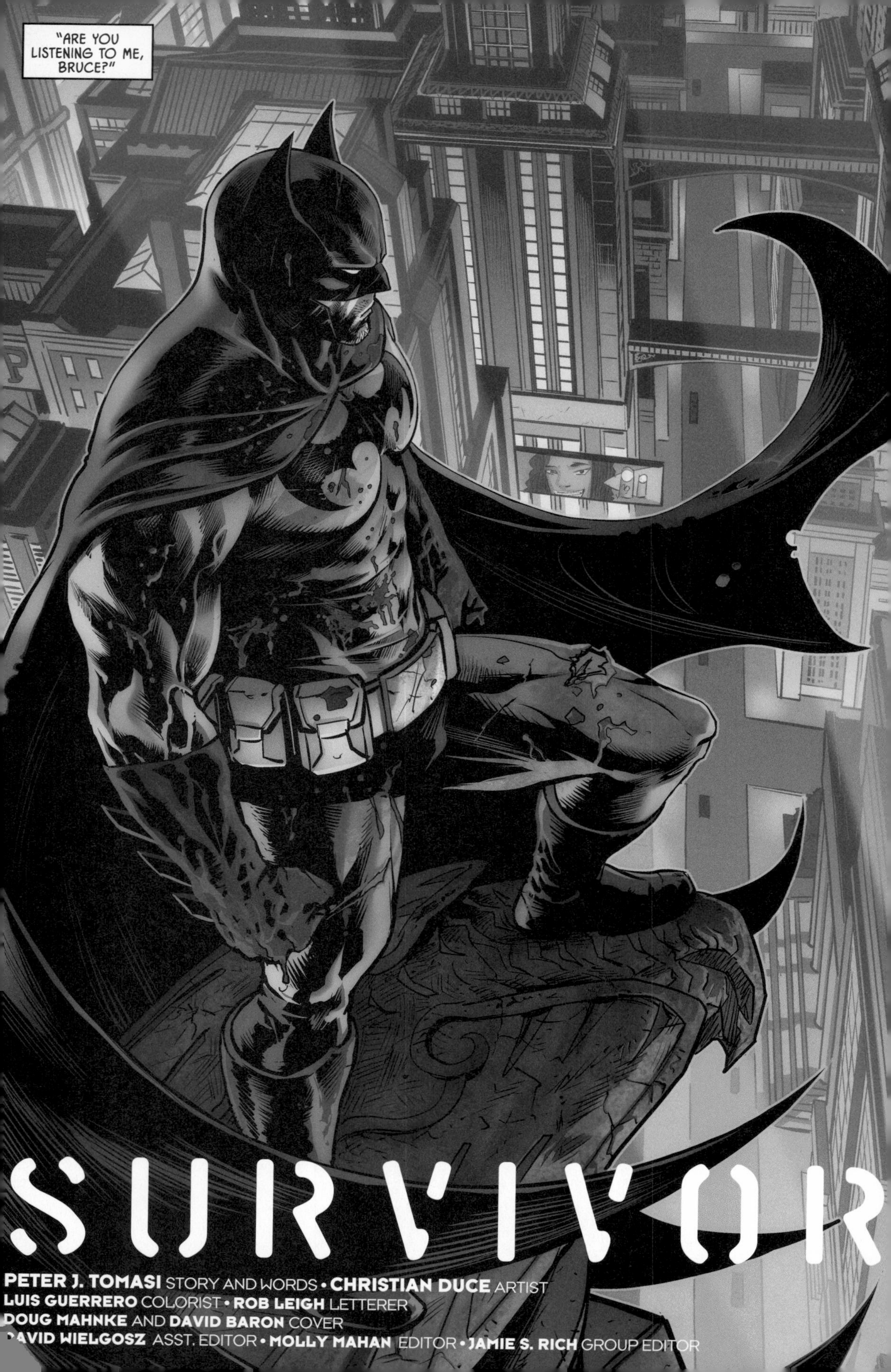
"ARE YOU LISTENING TO ME, BRUCE?"
SURVIVOR
PETER J. TOMASI STORY AND WORDS • CHRISTIAN DUCE ARTIST
LUIS GUERRERO COLORIST • ROB LEIGH LETTERER
DOUG MAHNKE AND DAVID BARON COVER
DAVID WIELGOSZ ASST. EDITOR • MOLLY MAHAN EDITOR • JAMIE S. RICH GROUP EDITOR

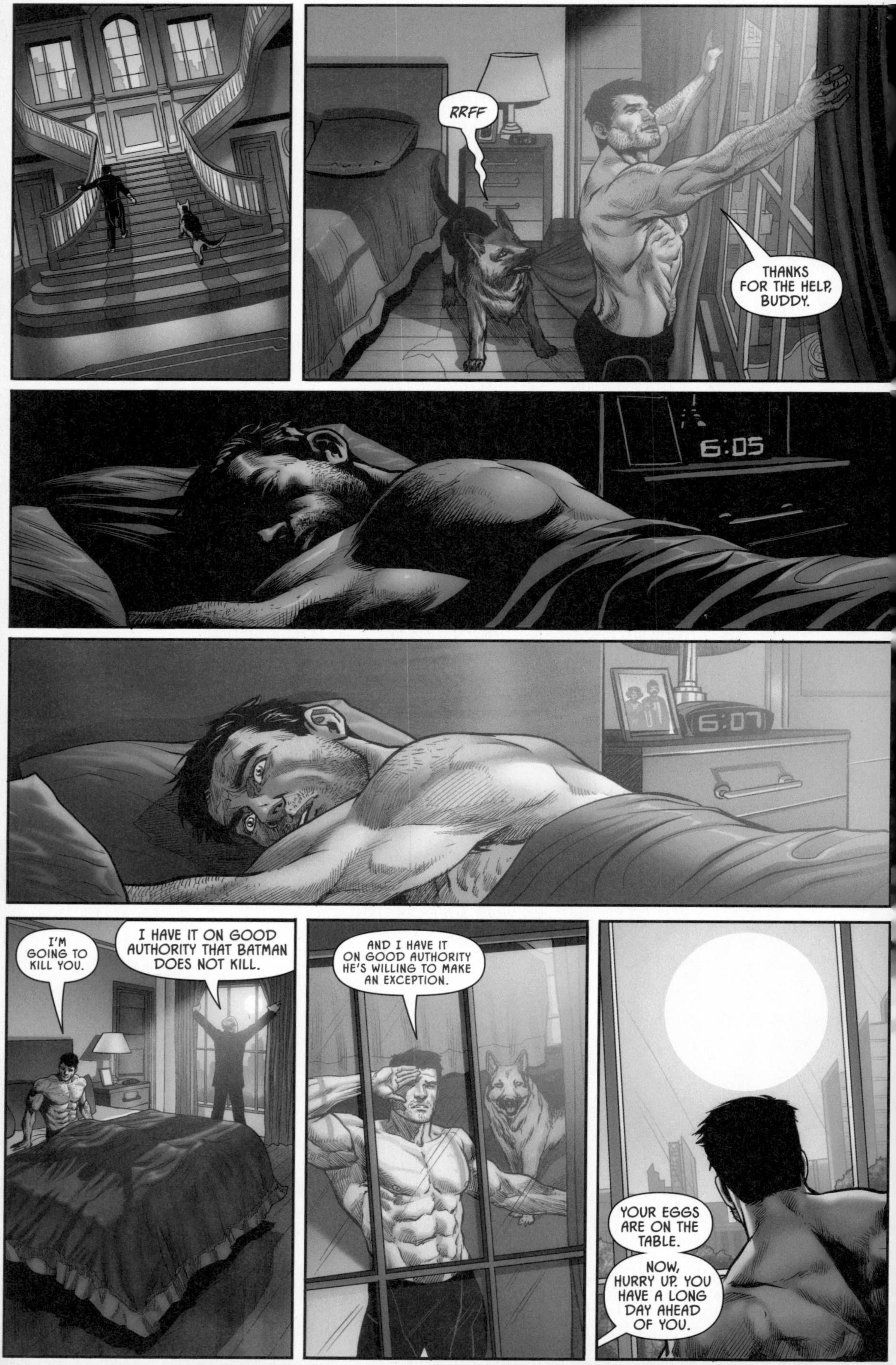
RRFF
THANKS FOR THE HELP, BUDDY.
6:05
6:07
I'M GOING TO KILL YOU.
I HAVE IT ON GOOD AUTHORITY THAT BATMAN DOES NOT KILL.
AND I HAVE IT ON GOOD AUTHORITY HE'S WILLING TO MAKE AN EXCEPTION.
YOUR EGGS ARE ON THE TABLE.
NOW, HURRY UP. YOU HAVE A LONG DAY AHEAD OF YOU.

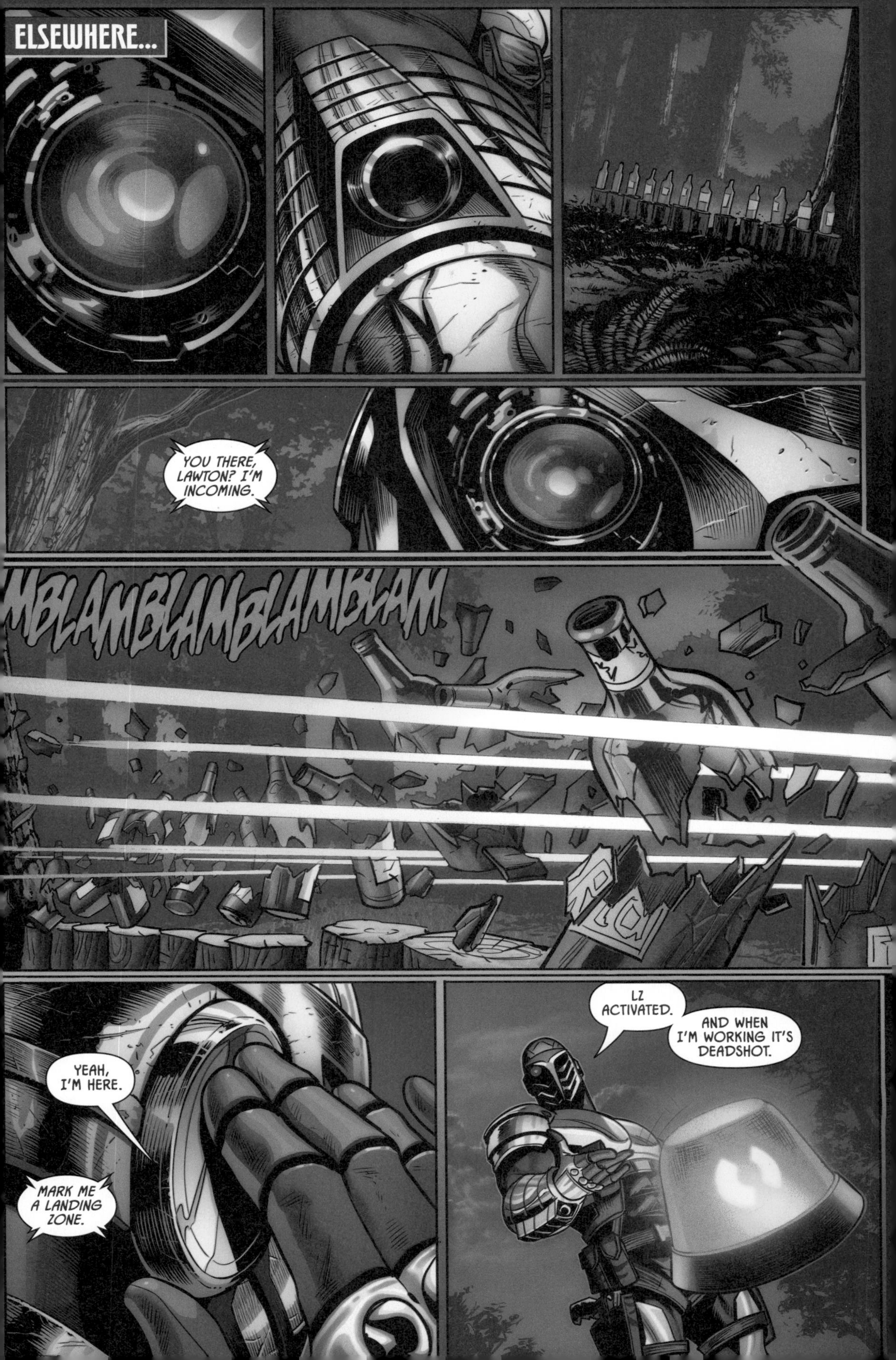
ELSEWHERE...
YOU THERE, LAWTON? I'M INCOMING.
MBLAMBLAMBLAMBLAMBLAM
YEAH, I'M HERE.
MARK ME A LANDING ZONE.
LZ ACTIVATED.
AND WHEN I'M WORKING IT'S DEADSHOT.

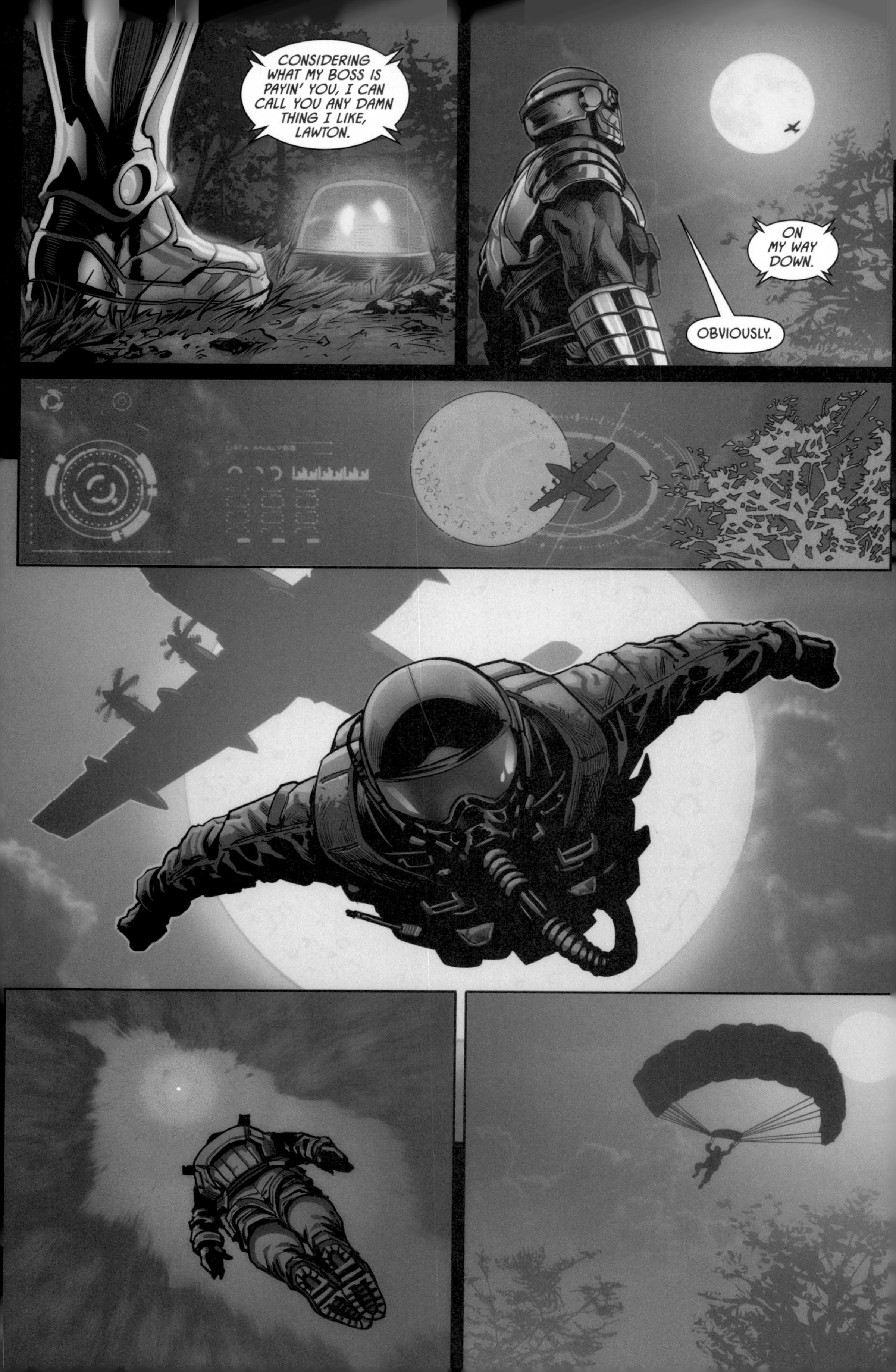
CONSIDERING WHAT MY BOSS IS PAYIN' YOU, I CAN CALL YOU ANY DAMN THING I LIKE, LAWTON.
ON MY WAY DOWN.
OBVIOUSLY.

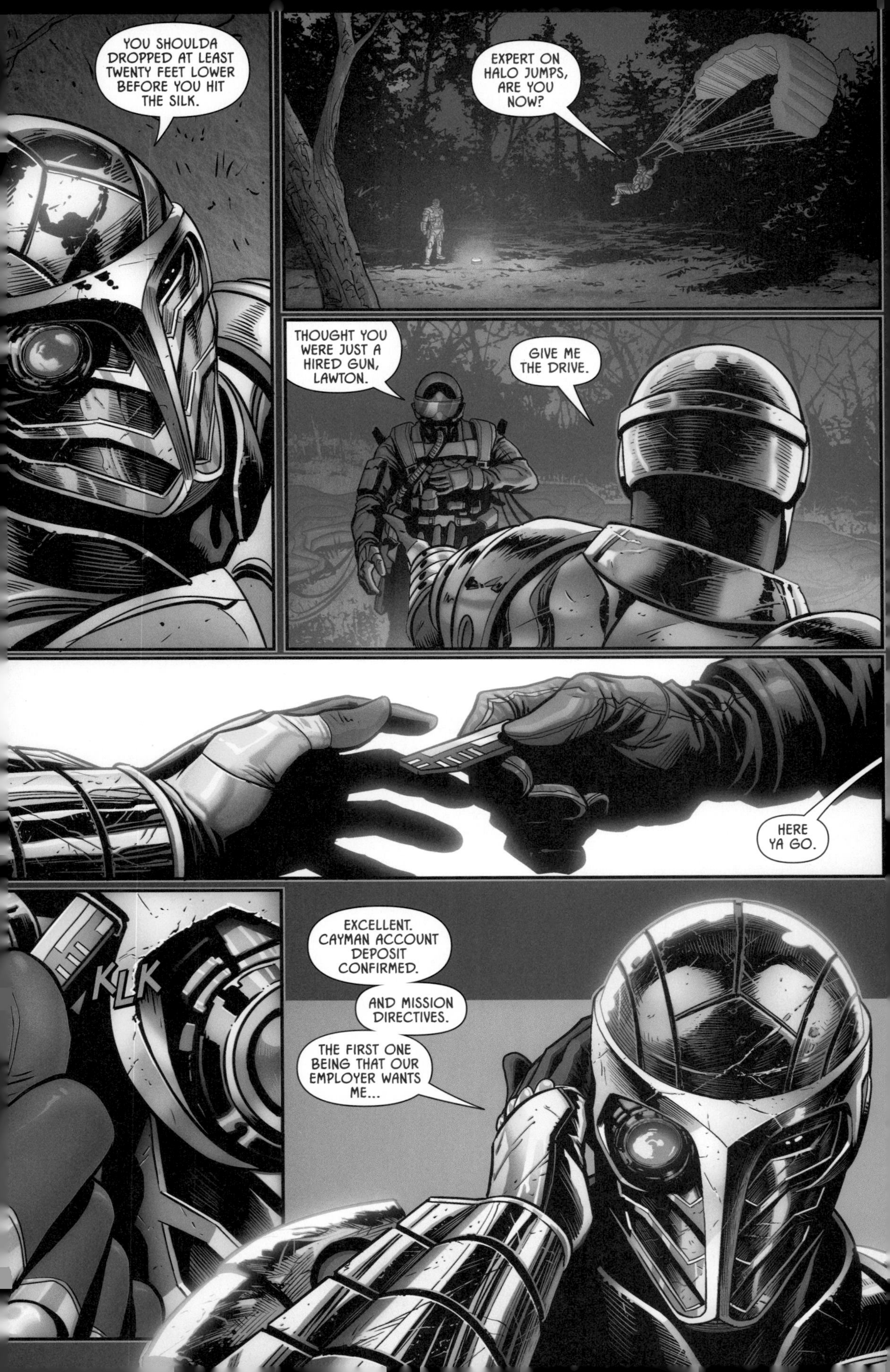
YOU SHOULDA DROPPED AT LEAST TWENTY FEET LOWER BEFORE YOU HIT THE SILK.
EXPERT ON HALO JUMPS, ARE YOU NOW?
THOUGHT YOU WERE JUST A HIRED GUN, LAWTON.
GIVE ME THE DRIVE.
HERE YA GO.
KLK
EXCELLENT. CAYMAN ACCOUNT DEPOSIT CONFIRMED.
AND MISSION DIRECTIVES.
THE FIRST ONE BEING THAT OUR EMPLOYER WANTS ME...

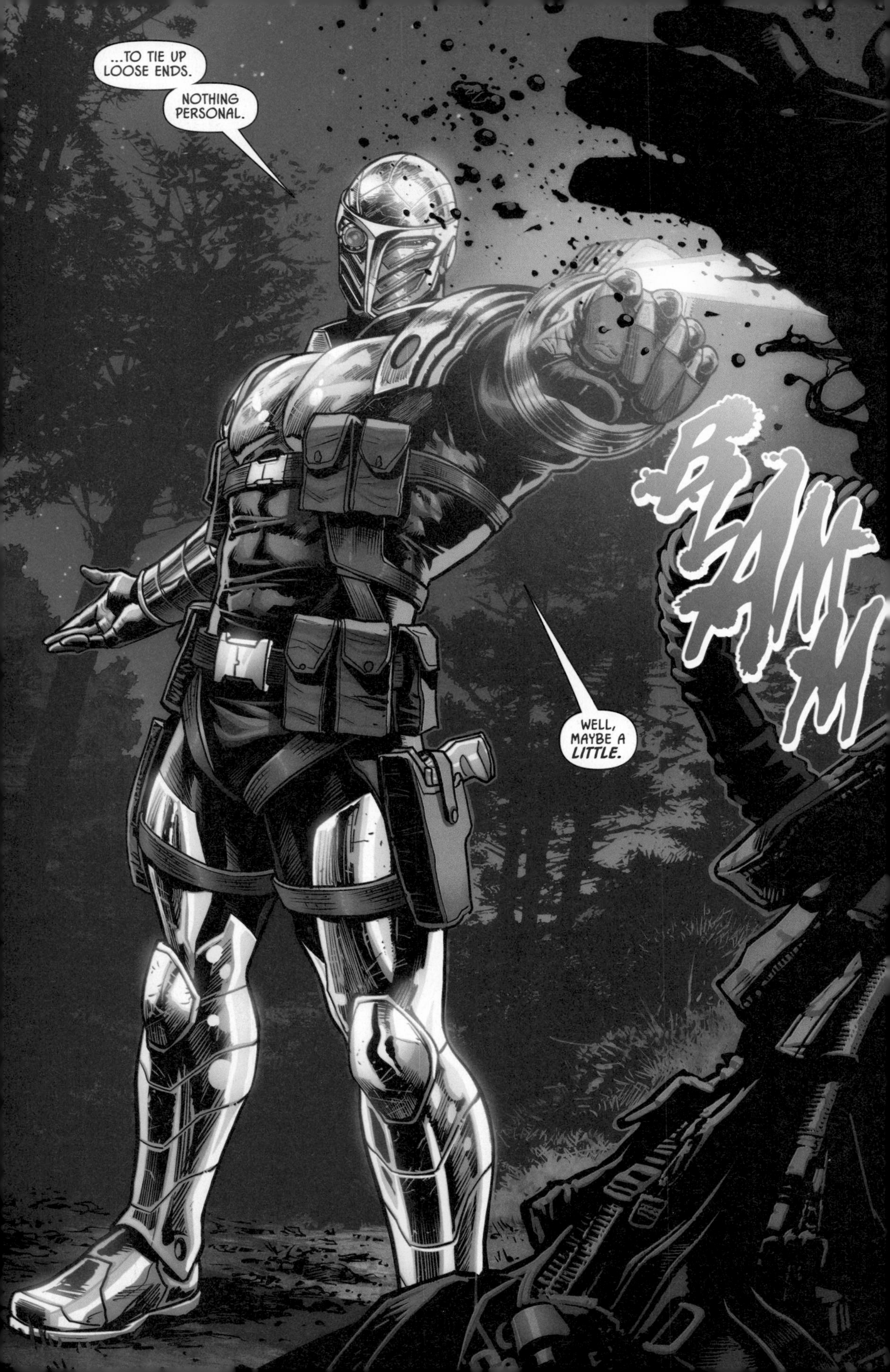
...TO TIE UP LOOSE ENDS.
NOTHING PERSONAL.
WELL, MAYBE A LITTLE.
BLAMM

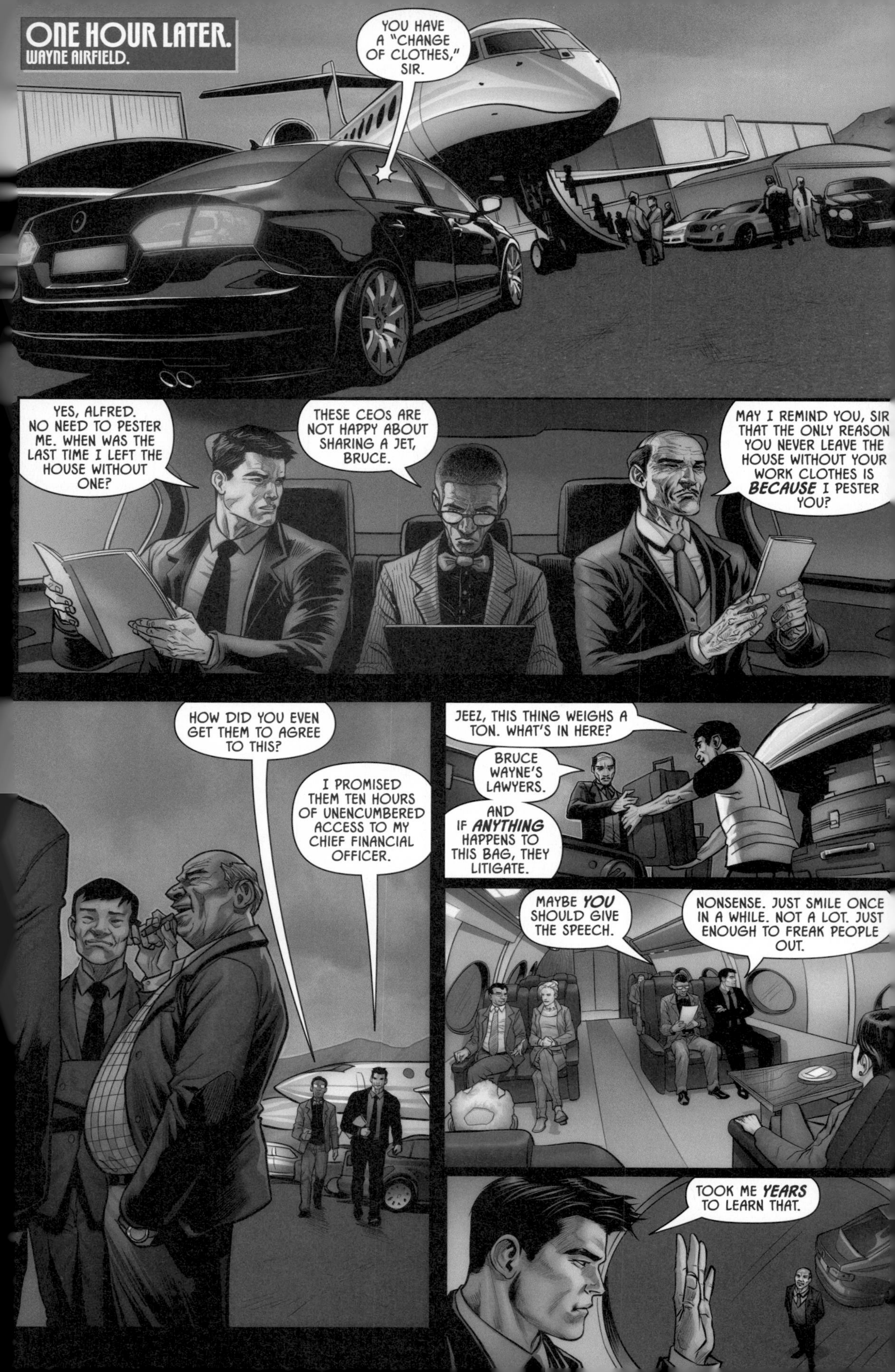
ONE HOUR LATER.
WAYNE AIRFIELD.
YOU HAVE A "CHANGE OF CLOTHES," SIR.
YES, ALFRED. NO NEED TO PESTER ME. WHEN WAS THE LAST TIME I LEFT THE HOUSE WITHOUT ONE?
THESE CEOs ARE NOT HAPPY ABOUT SHARING A JET, BRUCE.
MAY I REMIND YOU, SIR THAT THE ONLY REASON YOU NEVER LEAVE THE HOUSE WITHOUT YOUR WORK CLOTHES IS BECAUSE I PESTER YOU?
HOW DID YOU EVEN GET THEM TO AGREE TO THIS?
I PROMISED THEM TEN HOURS OF UNENCUMBERED ACCESS TO MY CHIEF FINANCIAL OFFICER.
JEEZ, THIS THING WEIGHS A TON. WHAT'S IN HERE?
BRUCE WAYNE'S LAWYERS.
AND IF ANYTHING HAPPENS TO THIS BAG, THEY LITIGATE.
MAYBE YOU SHOULD GIVE THE SPEECH.
NONSENSE. JUST SMILE ONCE IN A WHILE. NOT A LOT. JUST ENOUGH TO FREAK PEOPLE OUT.
TOOK ME YEARS TO LEARN THAT.

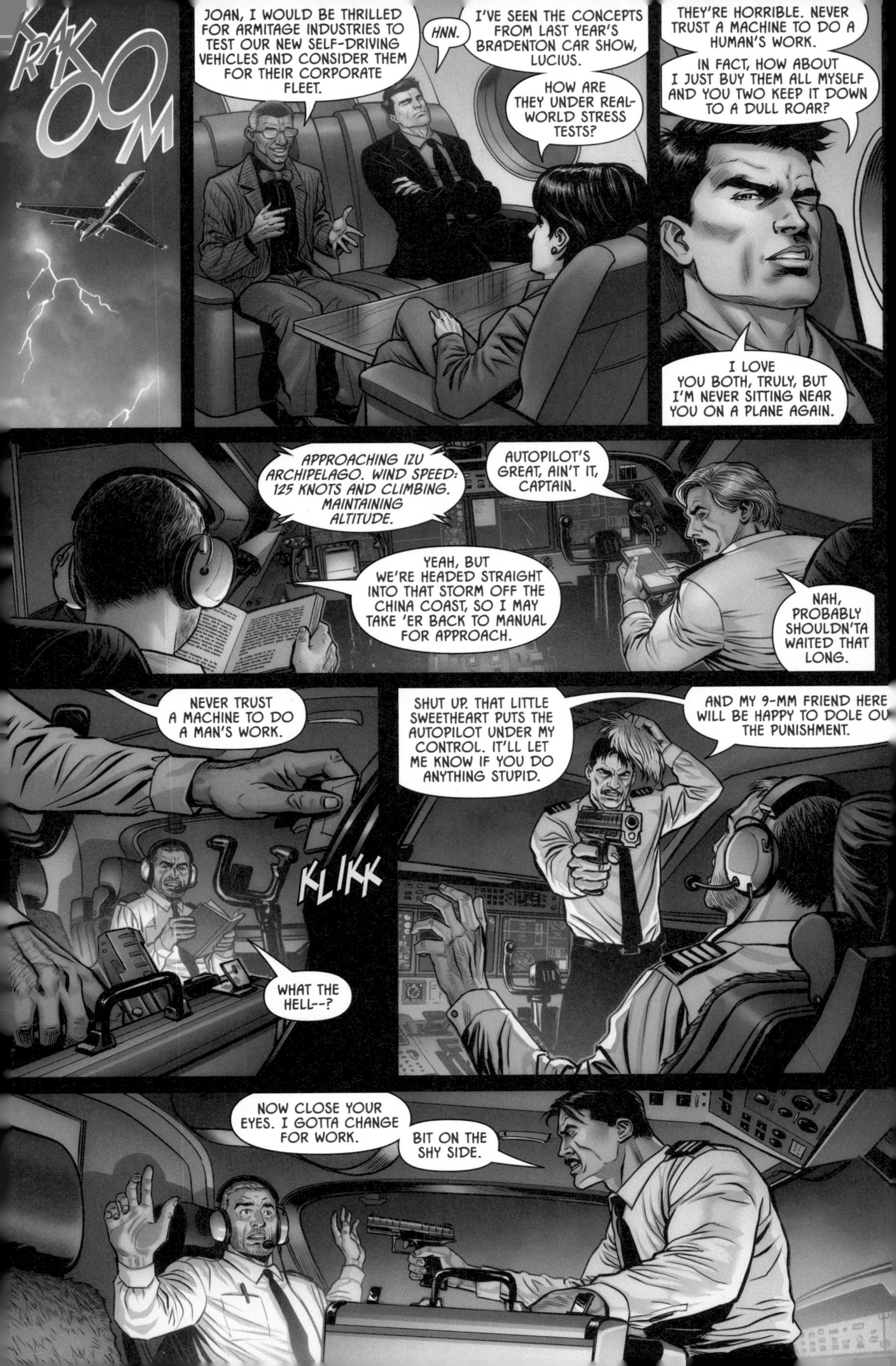
KRAKOOM
JOAN, I WOULD BE THRILLED FOR ARMITAGE INDUSTRIES TO TEST OUR NEW SELF-DRIVING VEHICLES AND CONSIDER THEM FOR THEIR CORPORATE FLEET.
HNN.
I'VE SEEN THE CONCEPTS FROM LAST YEAR'S BRADENTON CAR SHOW, LUCIUS.
HOW ARE THEY UNDER REAL-WORLD STRESS TESTS?
THEY'RE HORRIBLE. NEVER TRUST A MACHINE TO DO A HUMAN'S WORK.
IN FACT, HOW ABOUT I JUST BUY THEM ALL MYSELF AND YOU TWO KEEP IT DOWN TO A DULL ROAR?
I LOVE YOU BOTH, TRULY, BUT I'M NEVER SITTING NEAR YOU ON A PLANE AGAIN.
APPROACHING IZU ARCHIPELAGO. WIND SPEED: 125 KNOTS AND CLIMBING. MAINTAINING ALTITUDE.
AUTOPILOT'S GREAT, AIN'T IT, CAPTAIN.
YEAH, BUT WE'RE HEADED STRAIGHT INTO THAT STORM OFF THE CHINA COAST, SO I MAY TAKE 'ER BACK TO MANUAL FOR APPROACH.
NAH, PROBABLY SHOULDN'TA WAITED THAT LONG.
NEVER TRUST A MACHINE TO DO A MAN'S WORK.
KLIKK
WHAT THE HELL--?
SHUT UP. THAT LITTLE SWEETHEART PUTS THE AUTOPILOT UNDER MY CONTROL. IT'LL LET ME KNOW IF YOU DO ANYTHING STUPID.
AND MY 9-MM FRIEND HERE WILL BE HAPPY TO DOLE OU THE PUNISHMENT.
NOW CLOSE YOUR EYES. I GOTTA CHANGE FOR WORK.
BIT ON THE SHY SIDE.

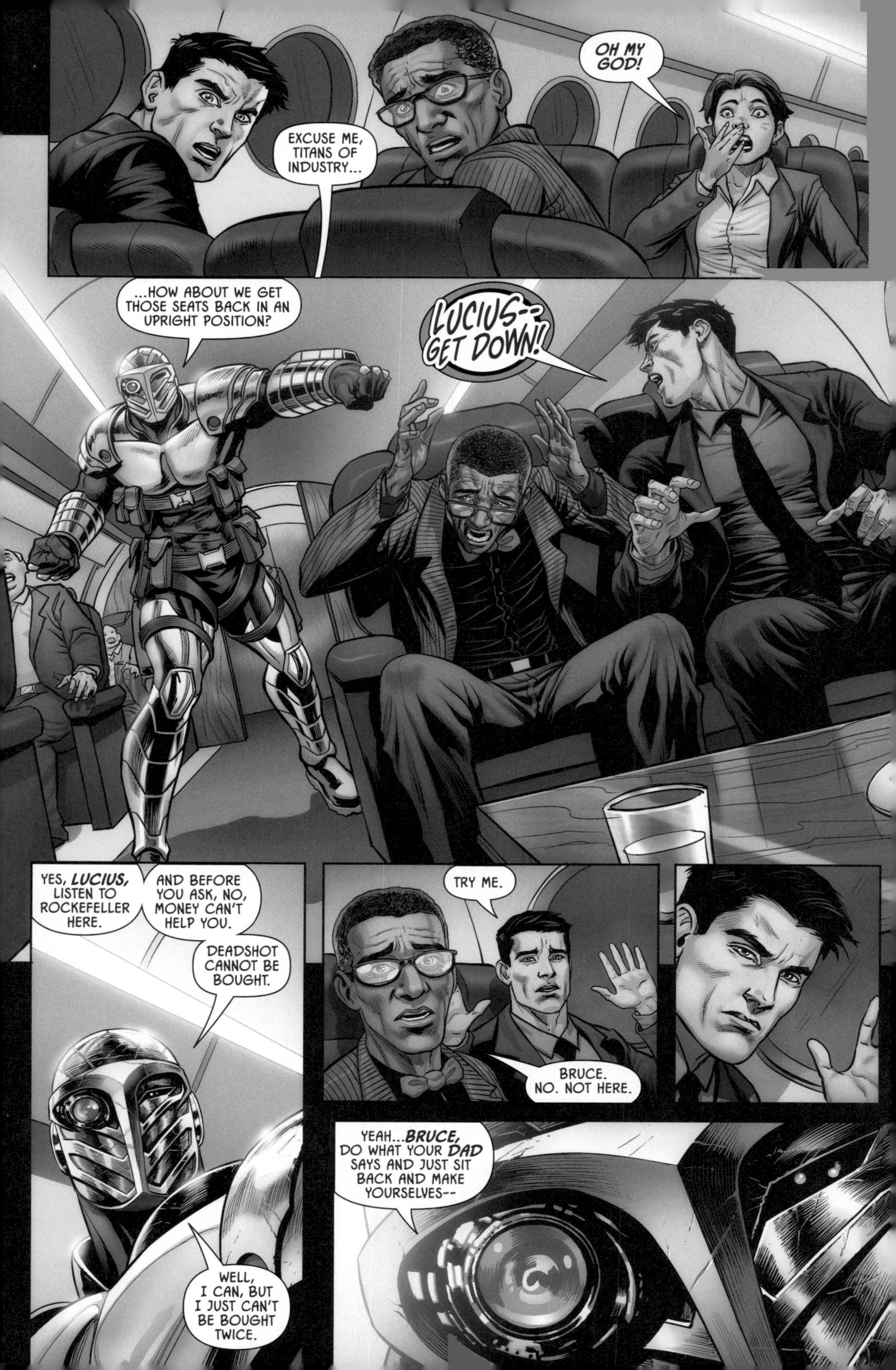
OH MY GOD!
EXCUSE ME, TITANS OF INDUSTRY...
...HOW ABOUT WE GET THOSE SEATS BACK IN AN UPRIGHT POSITION?
LUCIUS-- GET DOWN!
YES, LUCIUS, LISTEN TO ROCKEFELLER HERE.
AND BEFORE YOU ASK, NO, MONEY CAN'T HELP YOU.
DEADSHOT CANNOT BE BOUGHT.
WELL, I CAN, BUT I JUST CAN'T BE BOUGHT TWICE.
TRY ME.
BRUCE. NO. NOT HERE.
YEAH...BRUCE, DO WHAT YOUR DAD SAYS AND JUST SIT BACK AND MAKE YOURSELVES--

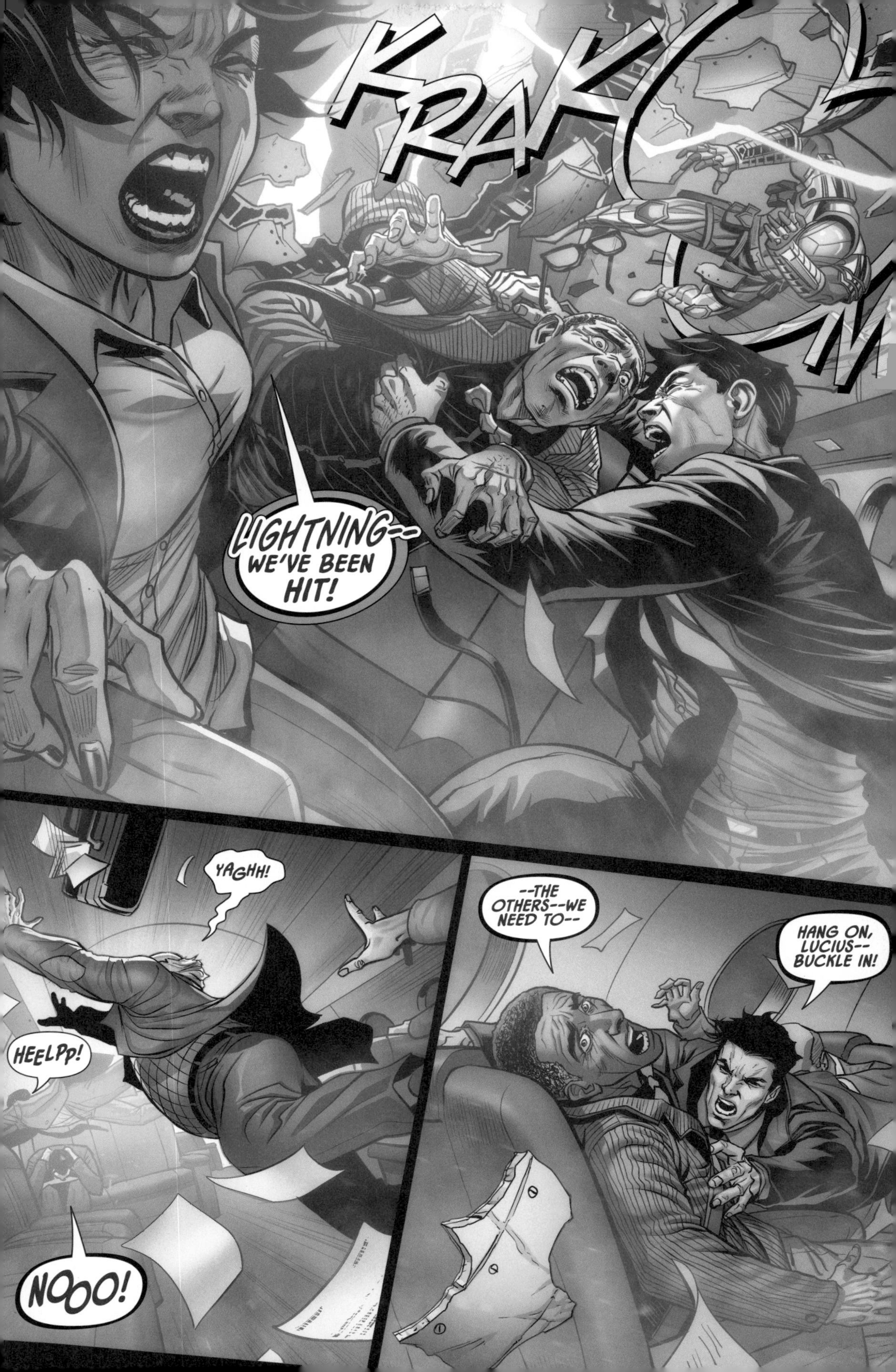
KRAKOOM
LIGHTNING-- WE'VE BEEN HIT!
YAGHH!
HEELPP!
NOOO!
--THE OTHERS--WE NEED TO--
HANG ON, LUCIUS-- BUCKLE IN!

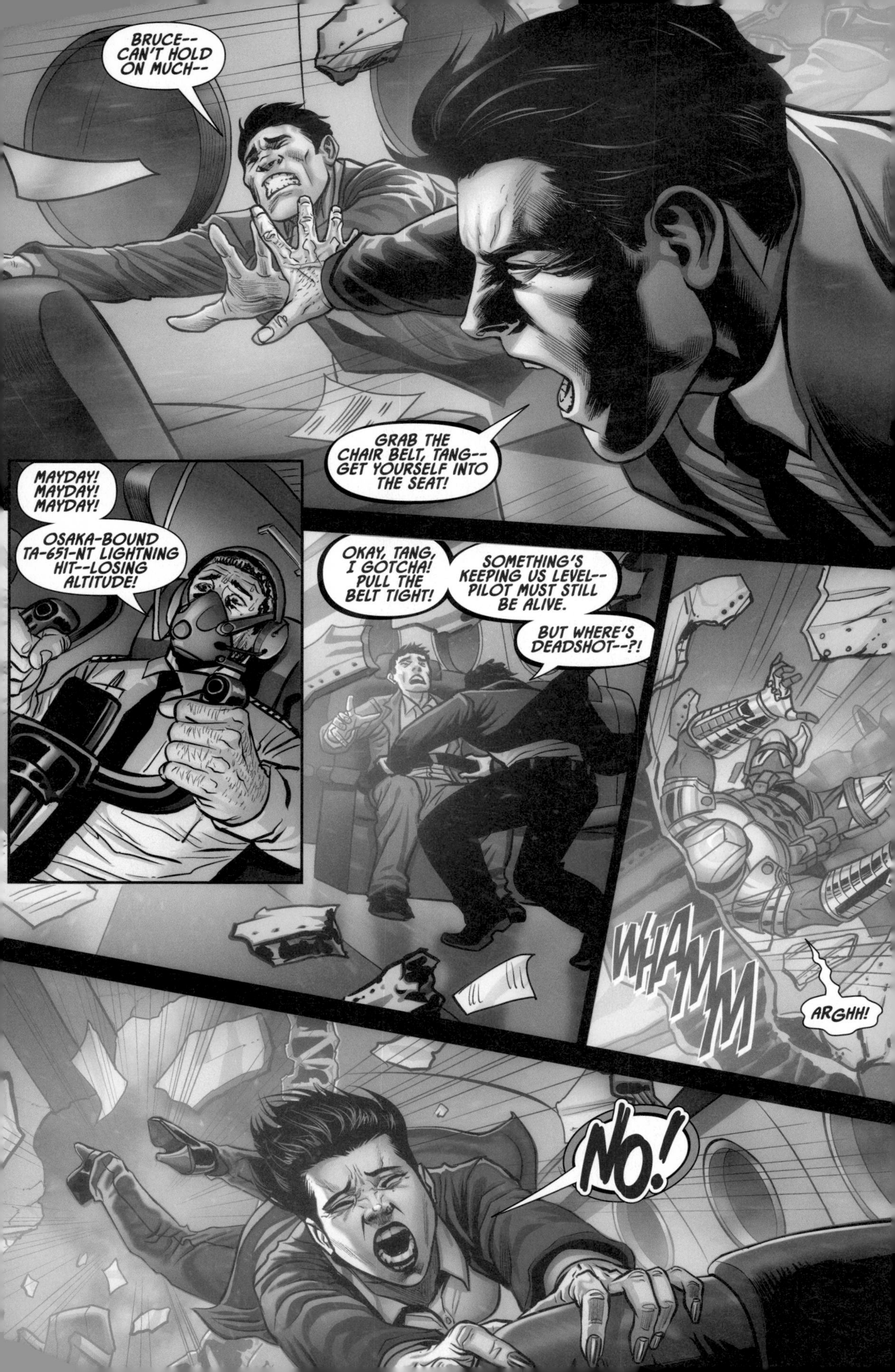
BRUCE-- CAN'T HOLD ON MUCH--
GRAB THE CHAIR BELT, TANG-- GET YOURSELF INTO THE SEAT!
MAYDAY! MAYDAY! MAYDAY!
OSAKA-BOUND TA-651-NT LIGHTNING HIT--LOSING ALTITUDE!
OKAY, TANG, I GOTCHA! PULL THE BELT TIGHT!
SOMETHING'S KEEPING US LEVEL-- PILOT MUST STILL BE ALIVE.
BUT WHERE'S DEADSHOT--?!
WHAMM
ARGHH!
NO!

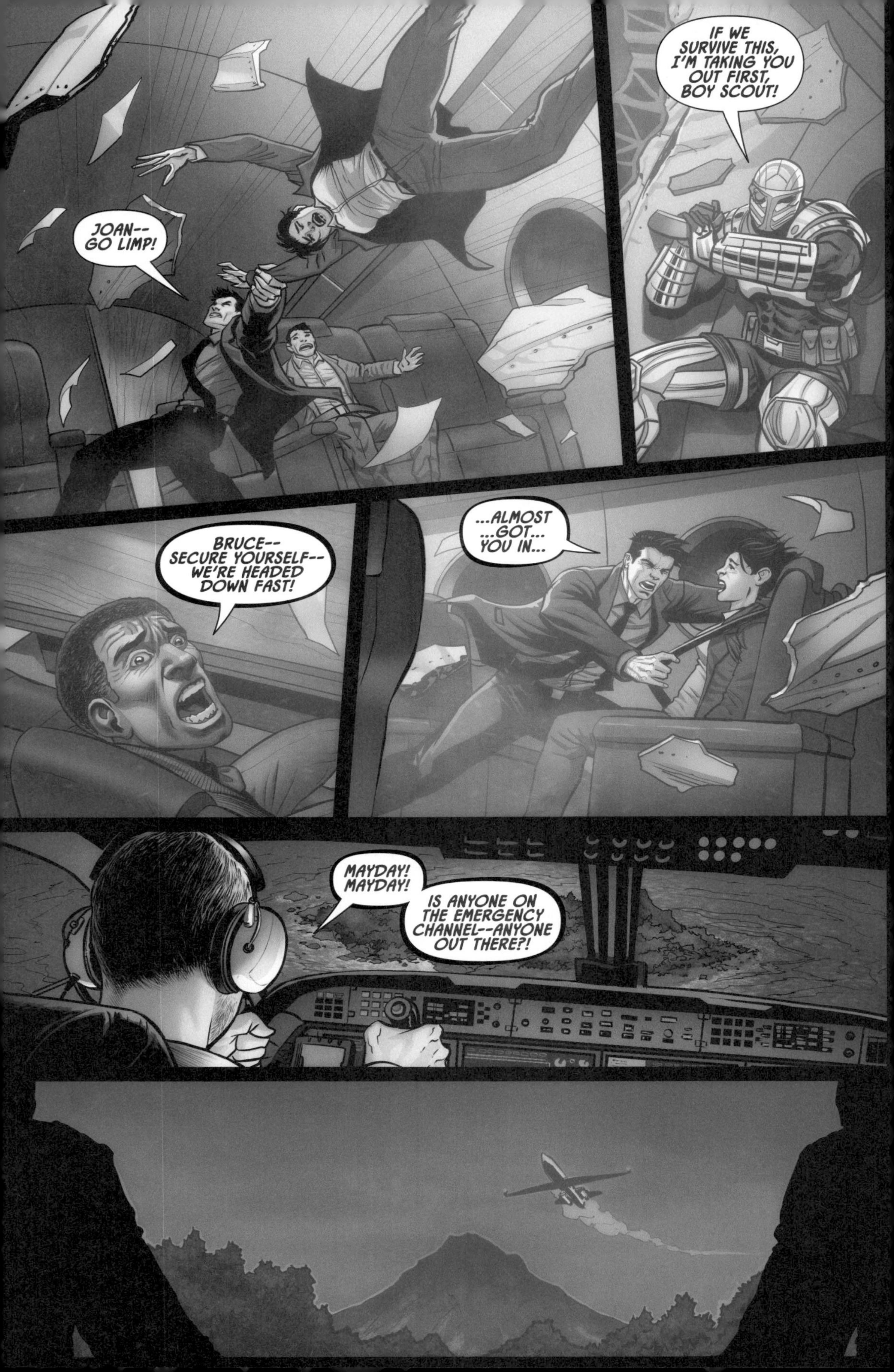
JOAN--
GO LIMP!
IF WE SURVIVE THIS, I'M TAKING YOU OUT FIRST, BOY SCOUT!
BRUCE--
SECURE YOURSELF--
WE'RE HEADED DOWN FAST!
...ALMOST ...GOT... YOU IN...
MAYDAY! MAYDAY!
IS ANYONE ON THE EMERGENCY CHANNEL--ANYONE OUT THERE?!

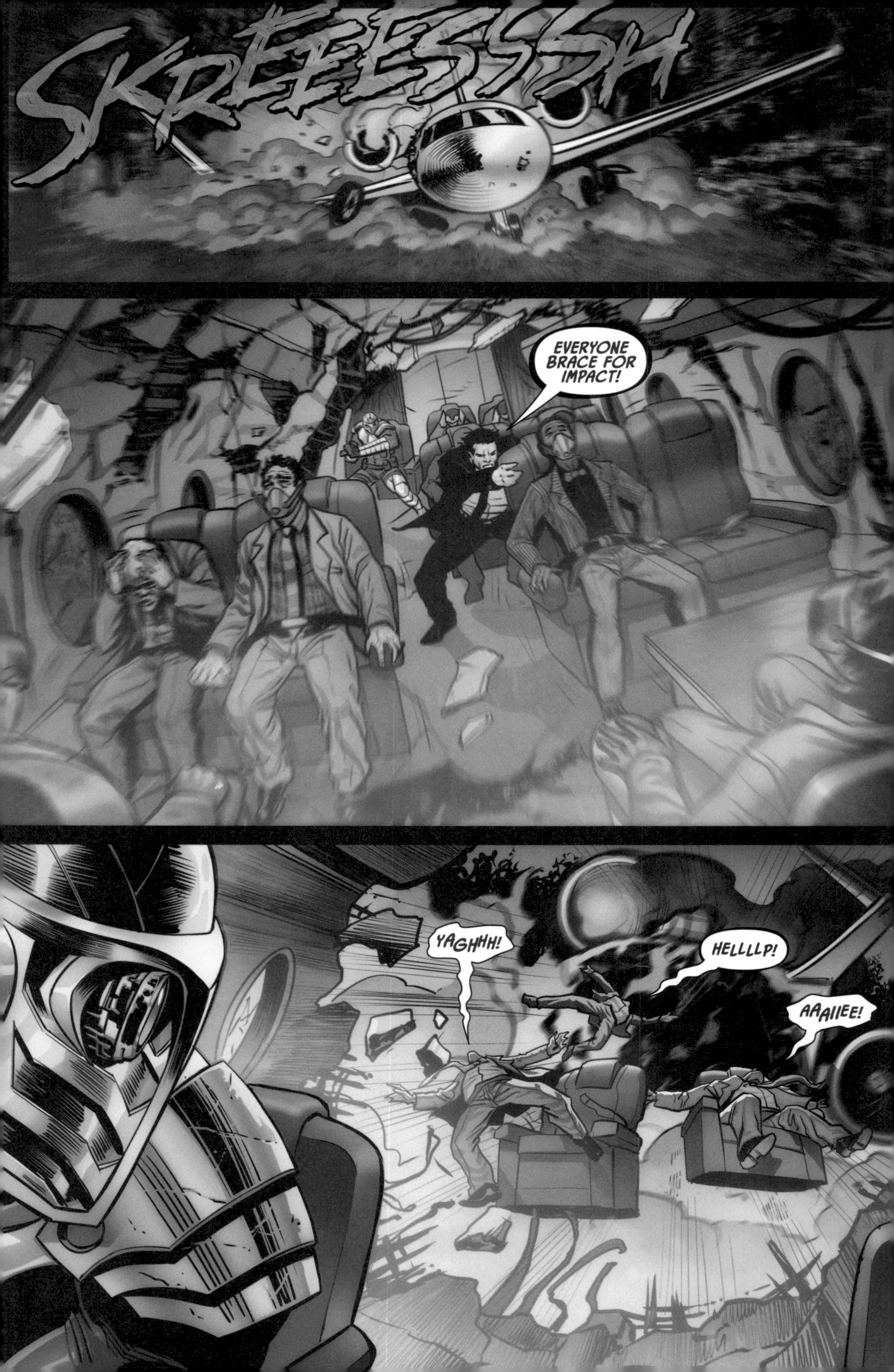
SKREEESSSH
EVERYONE BRACE FOR IMPACT!
YAGHHH!
HELLLLP!
AAAIIEE!

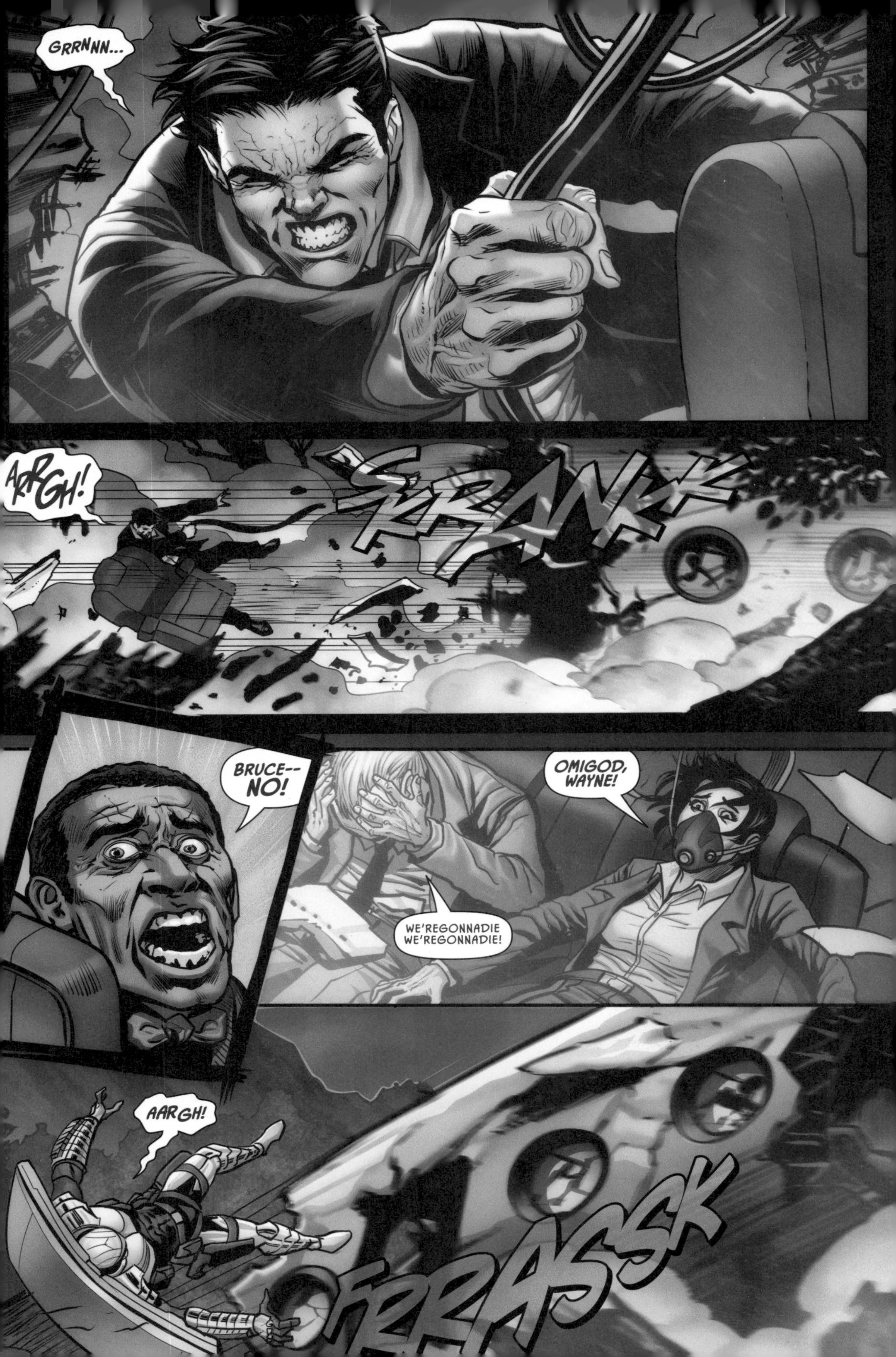
GRRNNN...
ARRGH!
SKRANK
BRUCE-- NO!
OMIGOD, WAYNE!
WE'REGONNADIE WE'REGONNADIE!
AARGH!
FRRASSK

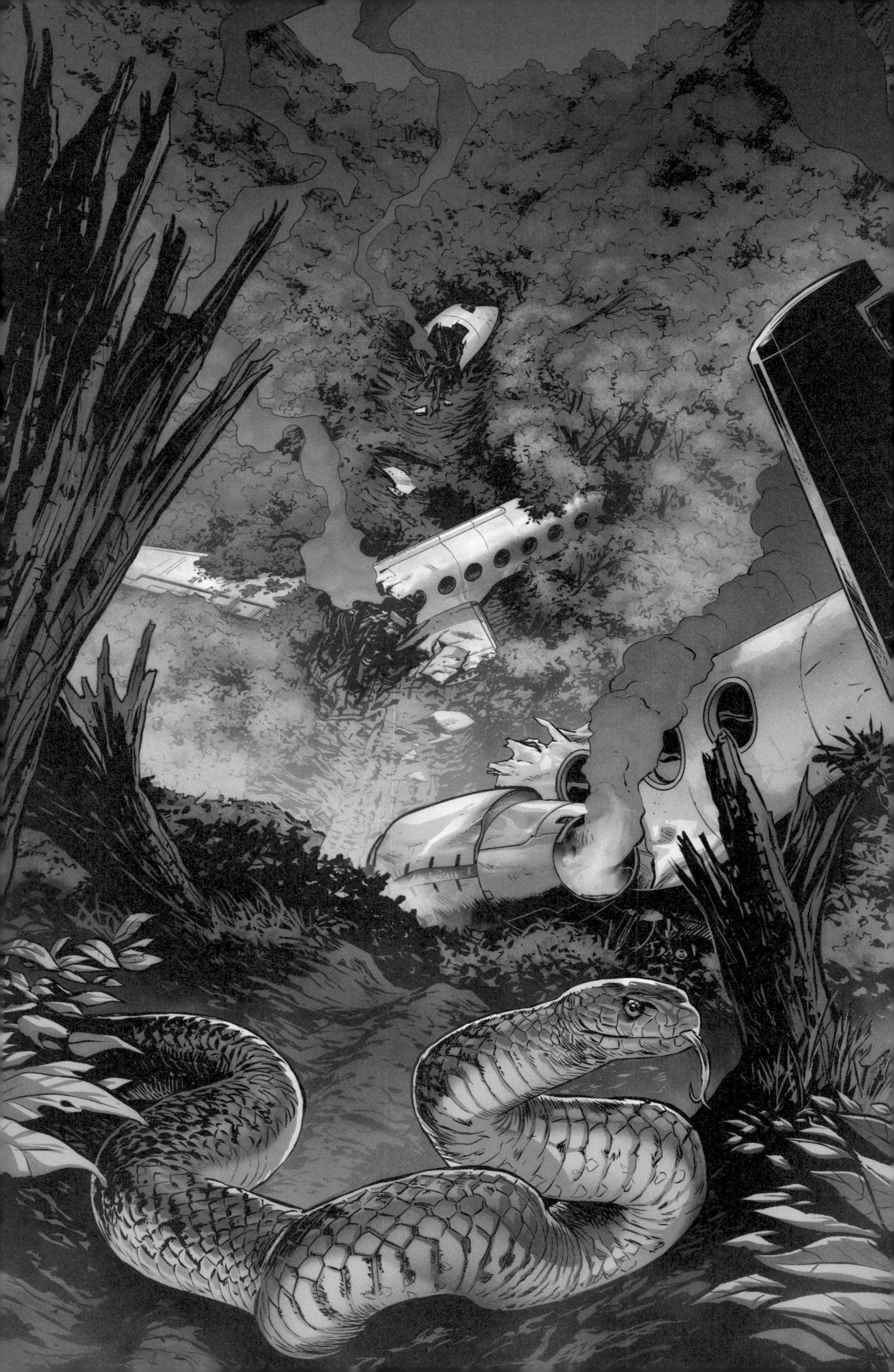

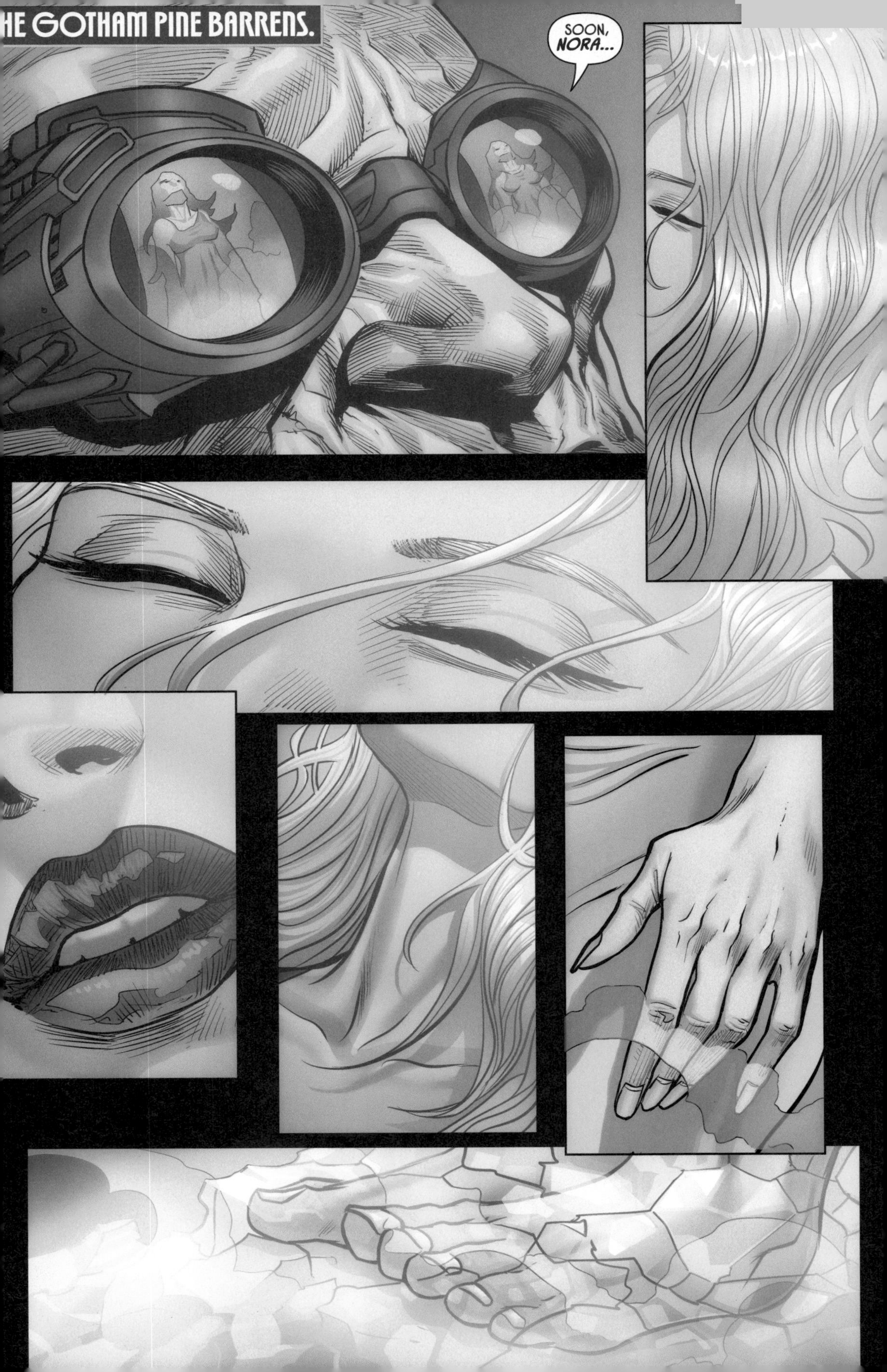
HE GOTHAM PINE BARRENS.
SOON, NORA...

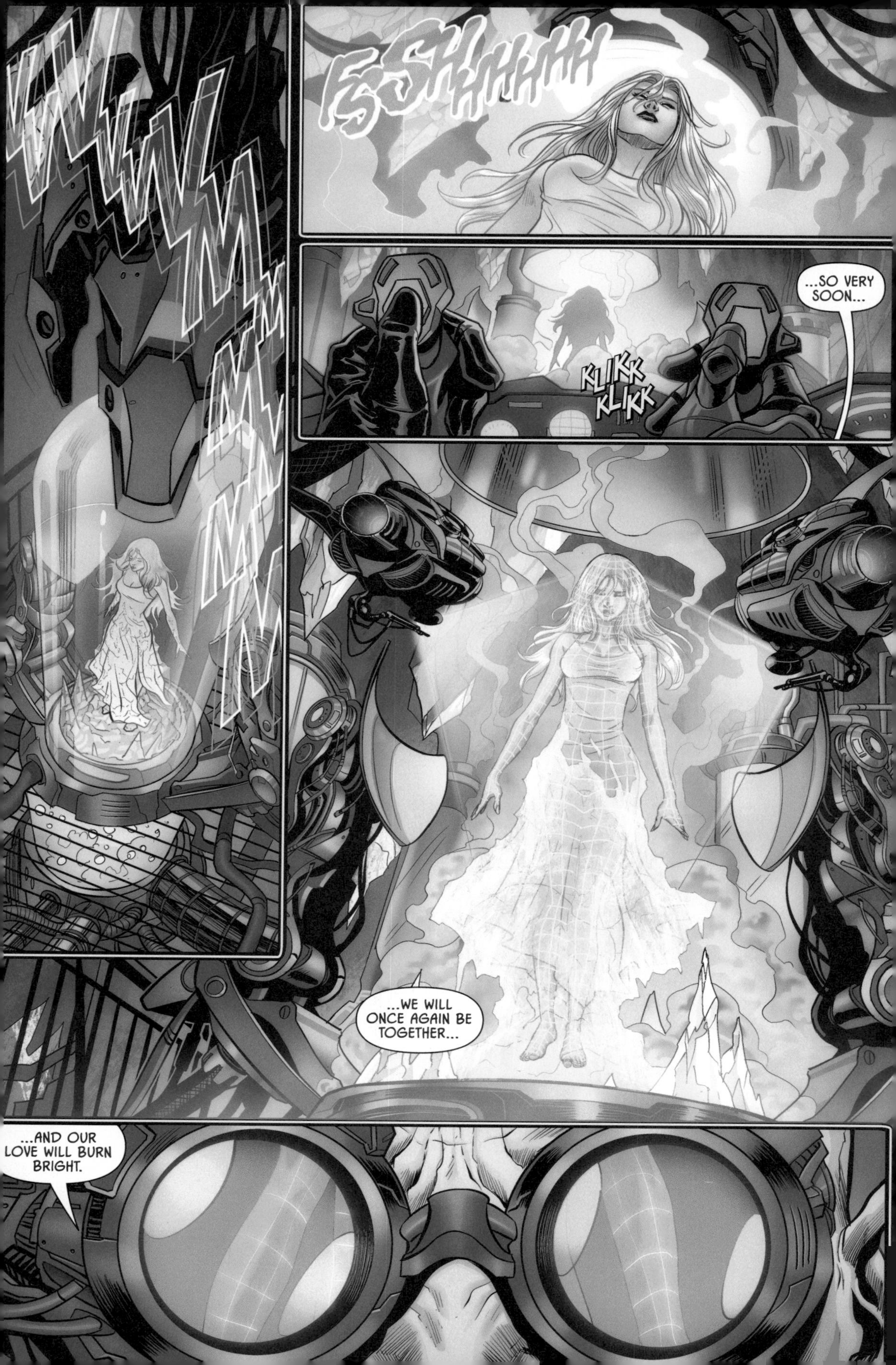

VVVVVMMMMMMM
FSSHHHHHH
...SO VERY SOON...
KLIKK KLIKK
...WE WILL ONCE AGAIN BE TOGETHER...
...AND OUR LOVE WILL BURN BRIGHT.

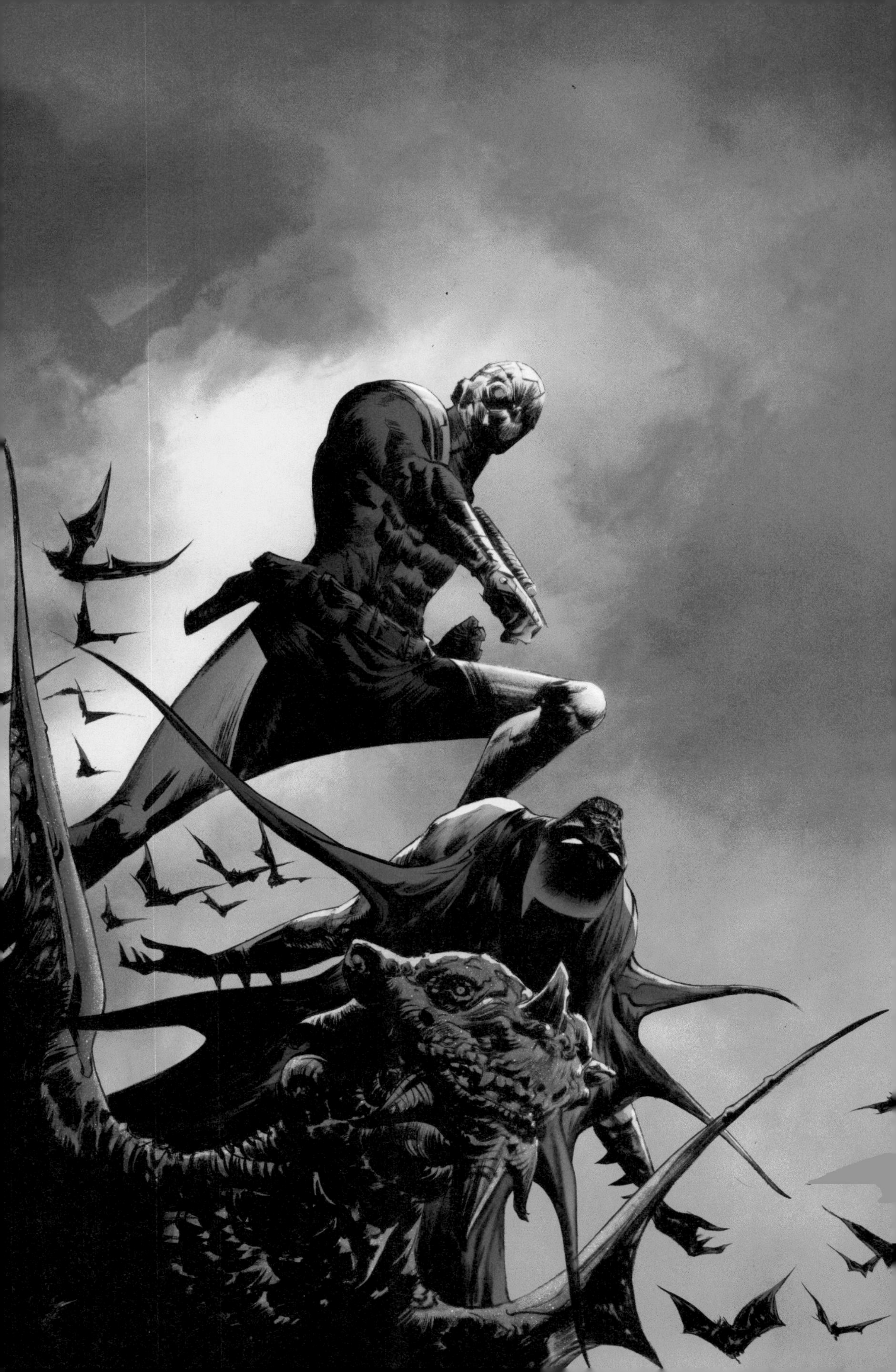

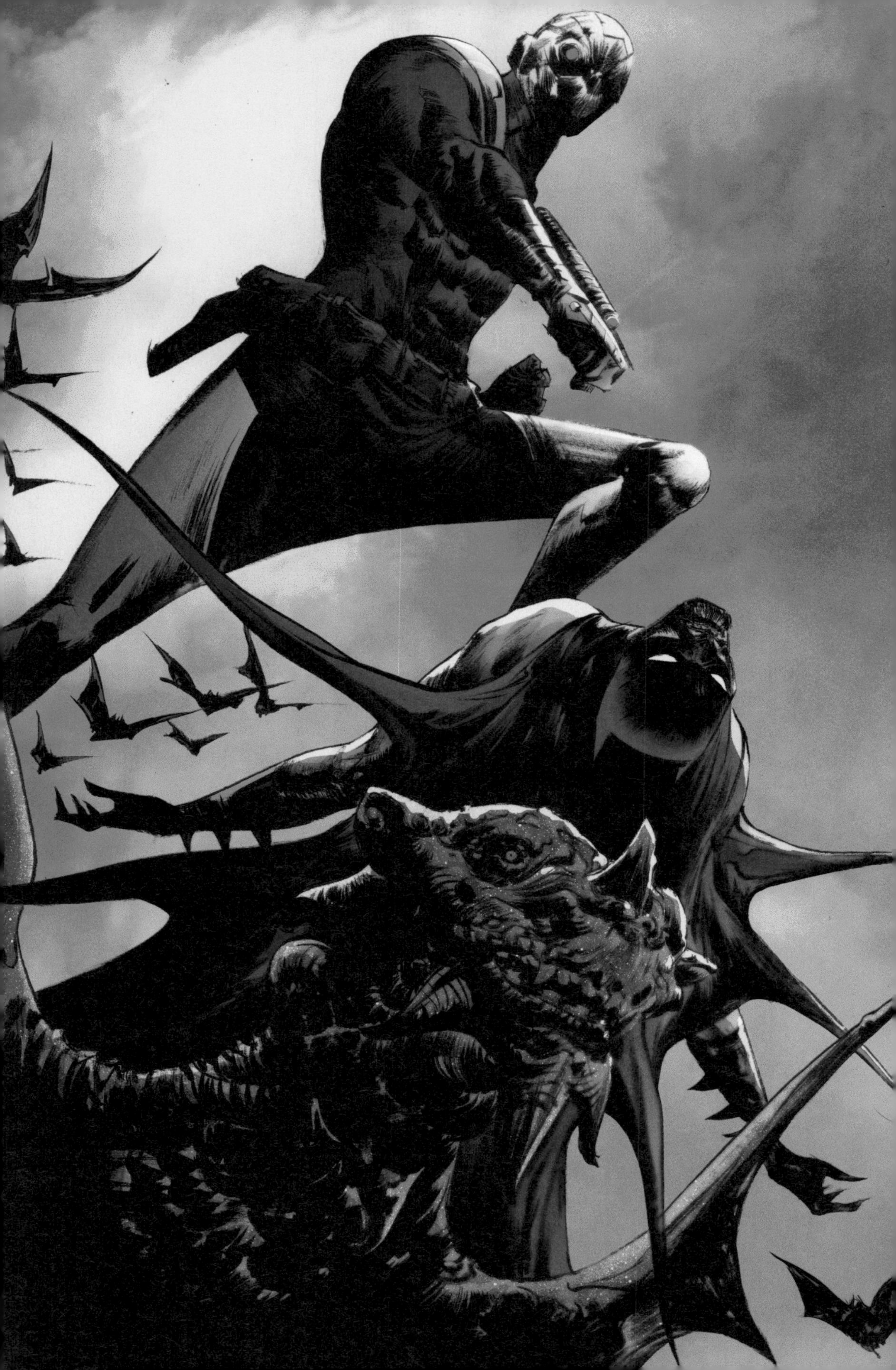

the BRAVE and the OLD

PETER J. TOMASI story & words • CHRISTIAN DUCE artist • DAVID BARON colorist • ROB LEIGH letterer
JAE LEE & JUNE CHUNG cover • DAVE WIELGOSZ assistant editor • MOLLY MAHAN editor
JAMIE S. RICH group editor

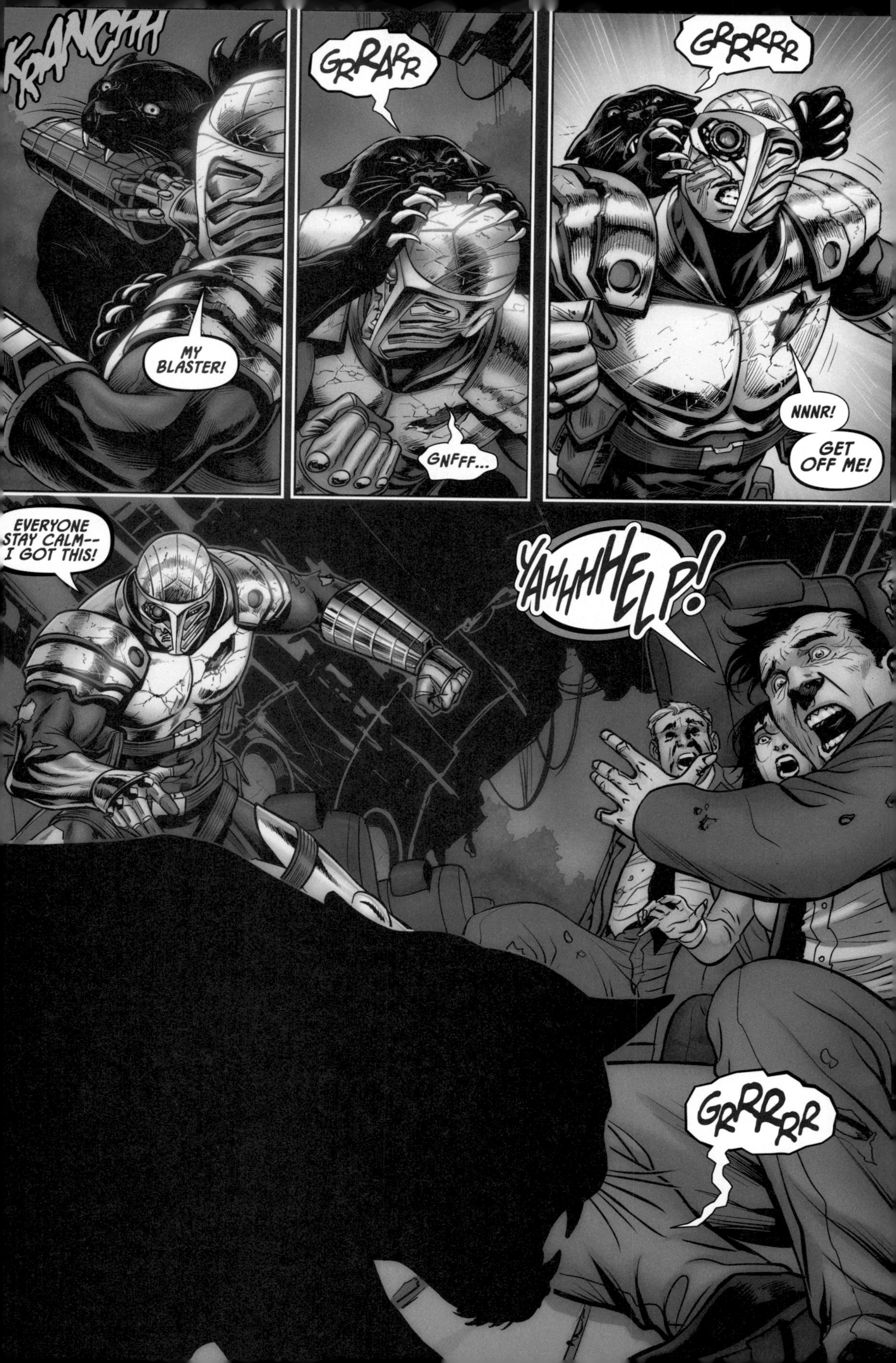
KRANCHH
MY BLASTER!
GRRARR
GNFFF...
GRRRRRR
NNNR!
GET OFF ME!
EVERYONE STAY CALM-- I GOT THIS!
YAHHHHELP!
GRRRRR

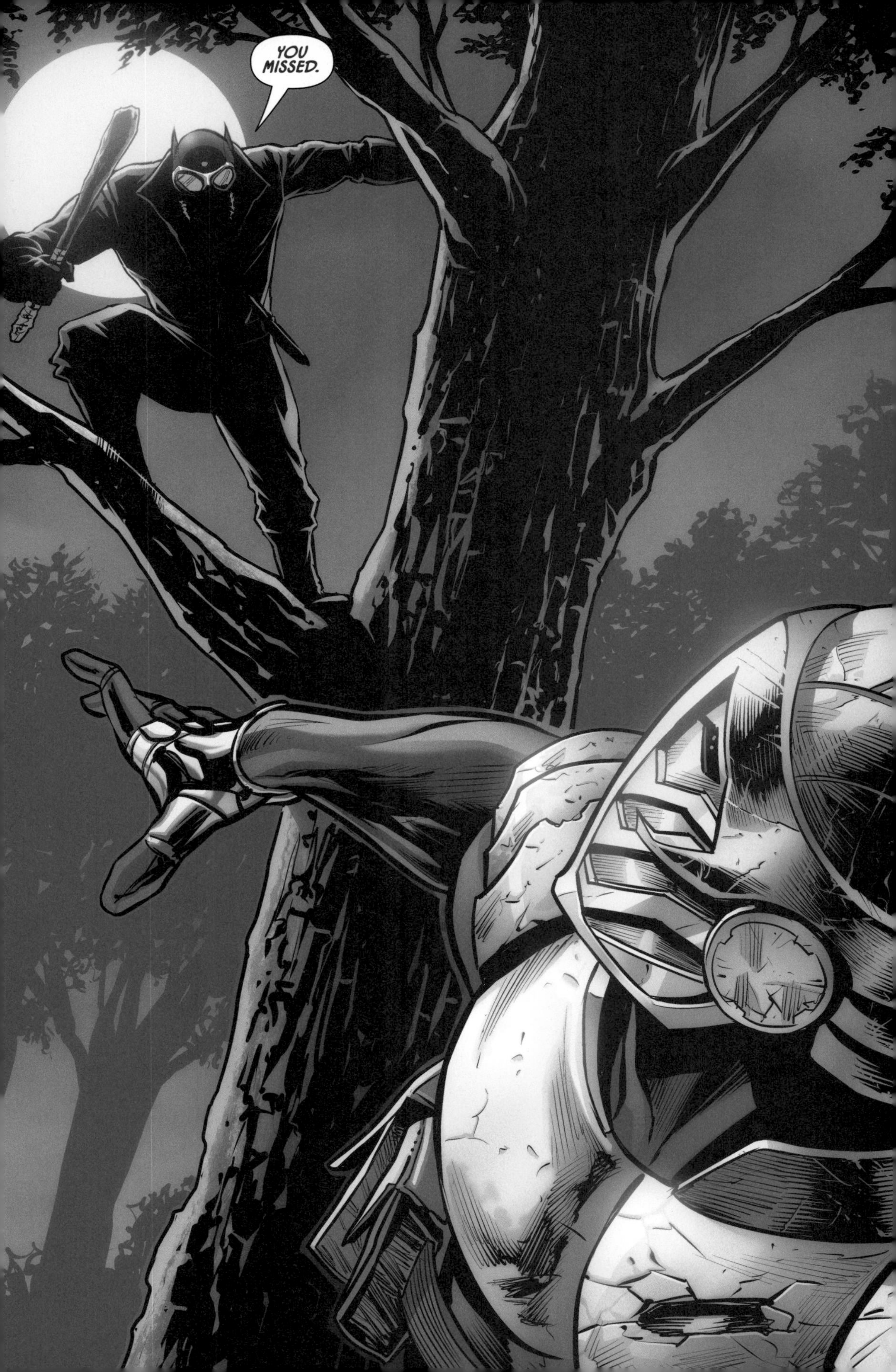
YOU MISSED.

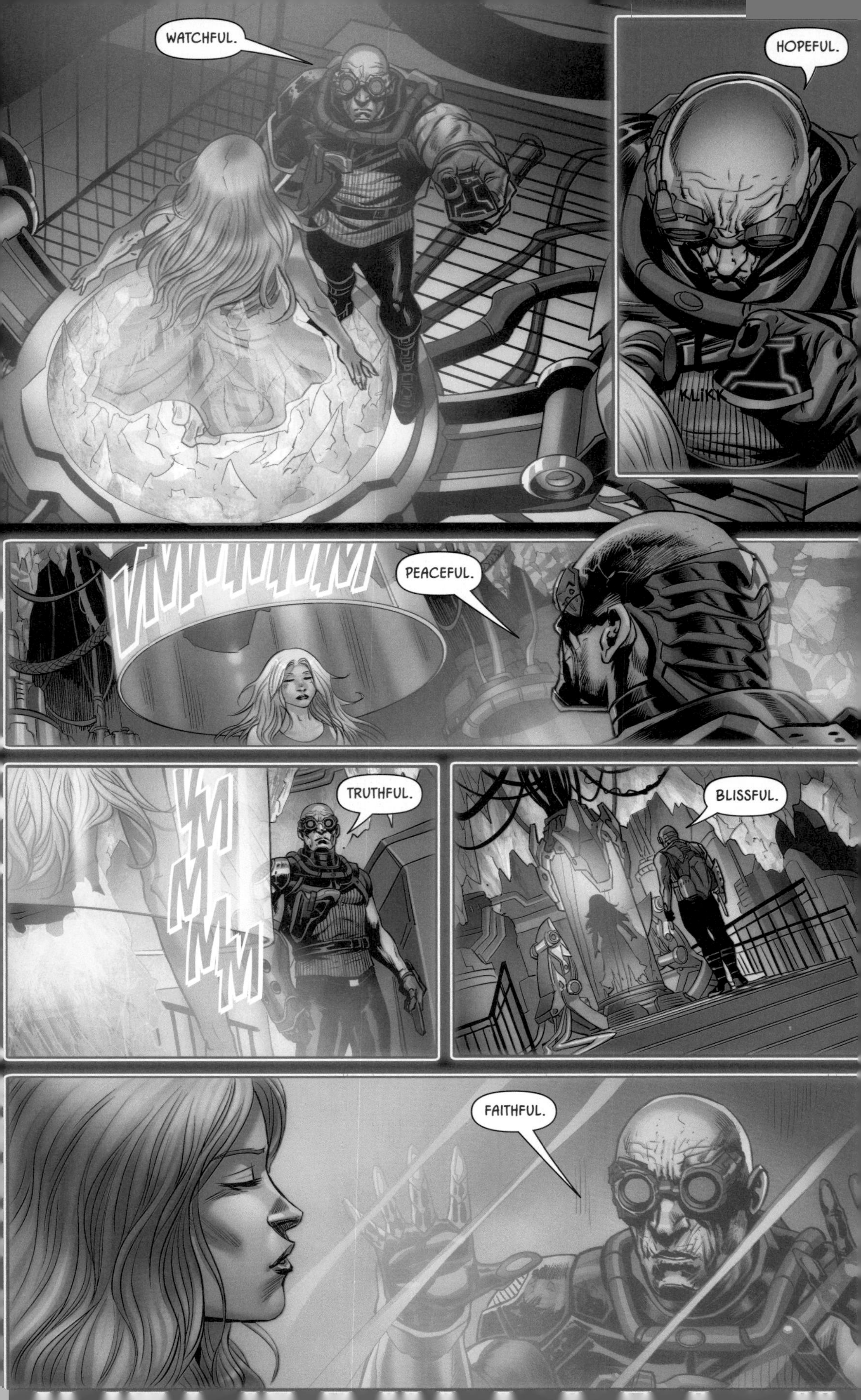
WATCHFUL.
HOPEFUL.
KLIKK
PEACEFUL.
TRUTHFUL.
BLISSFUL.
FAITHFUL.

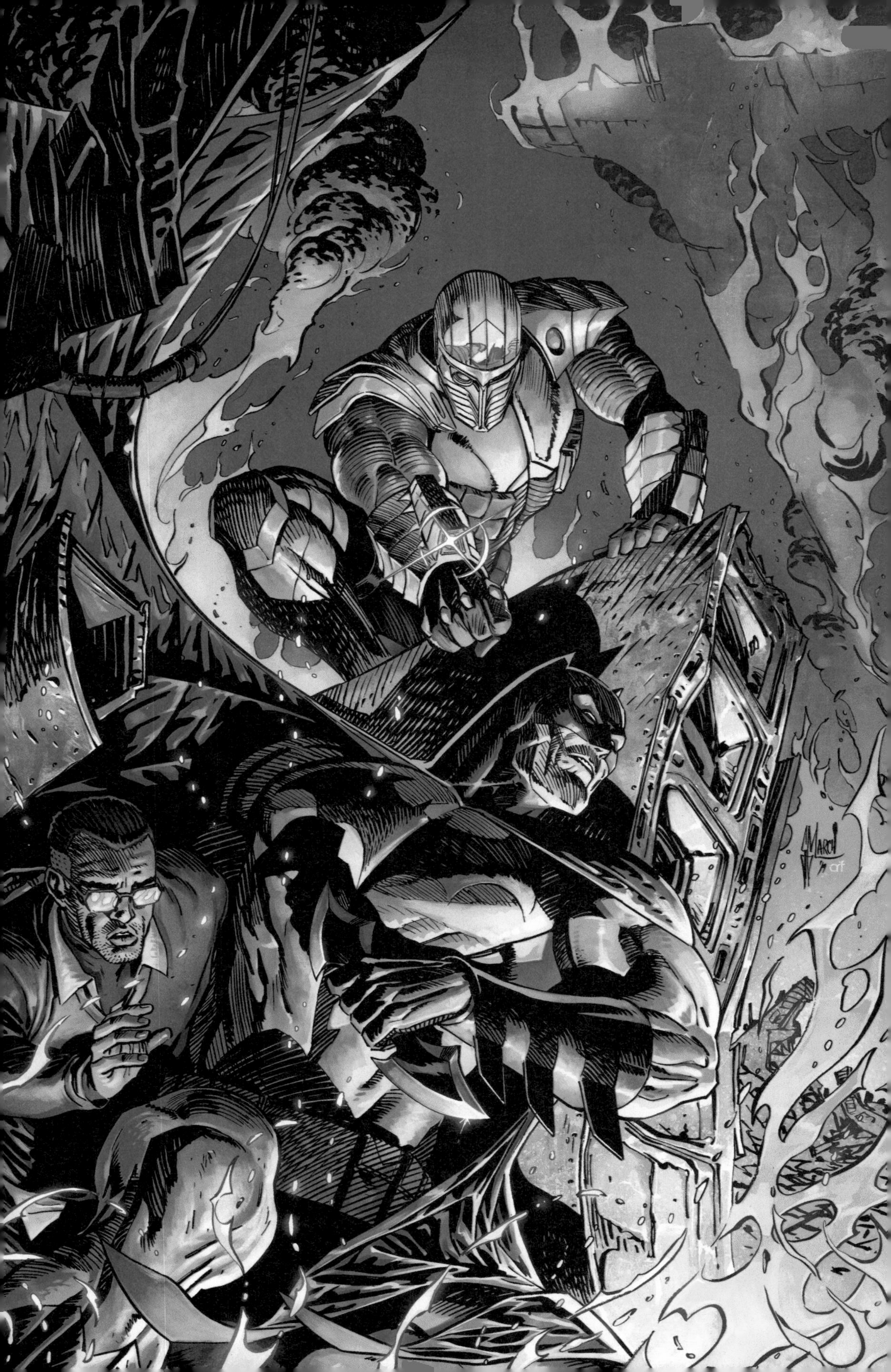

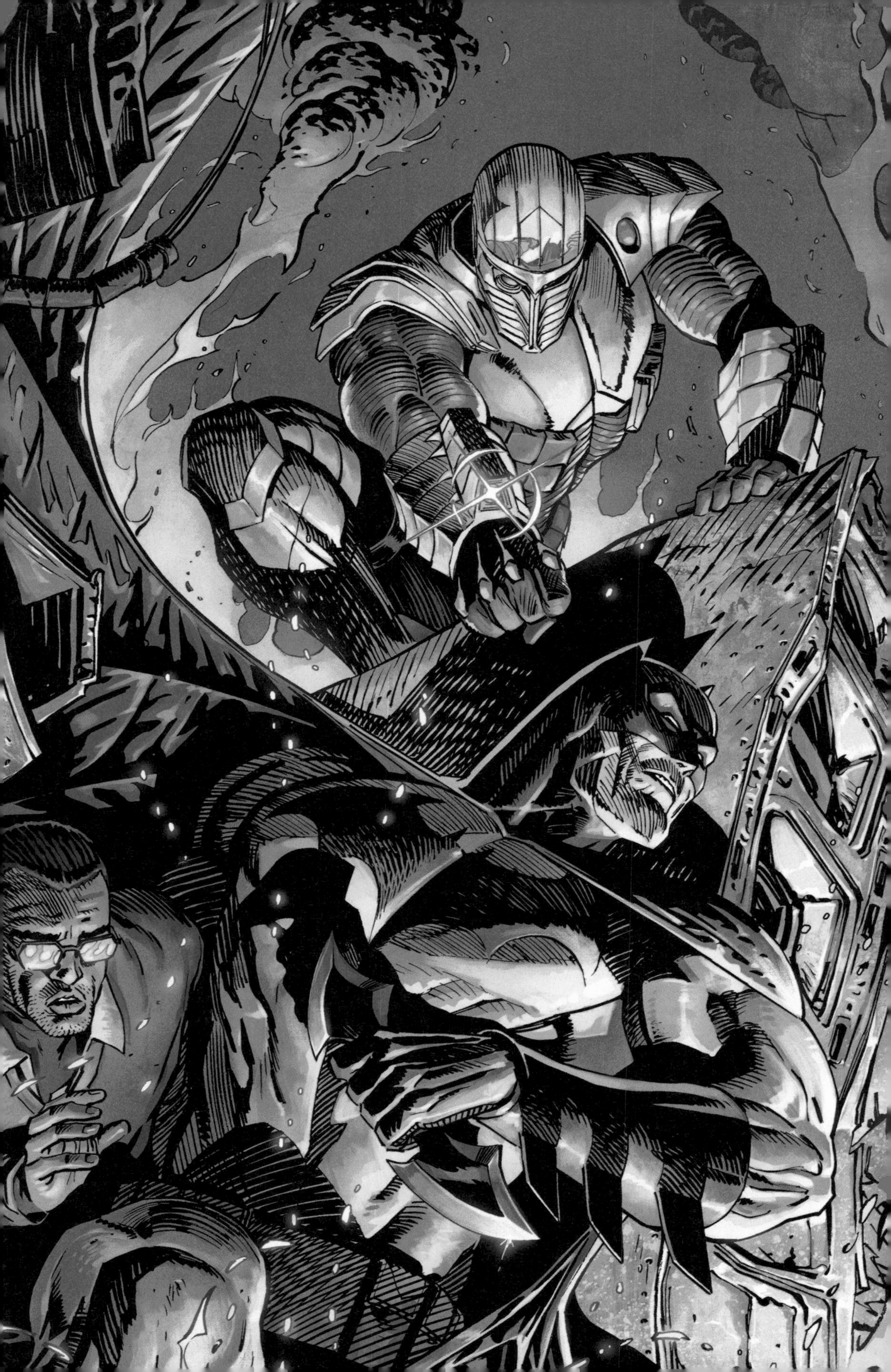

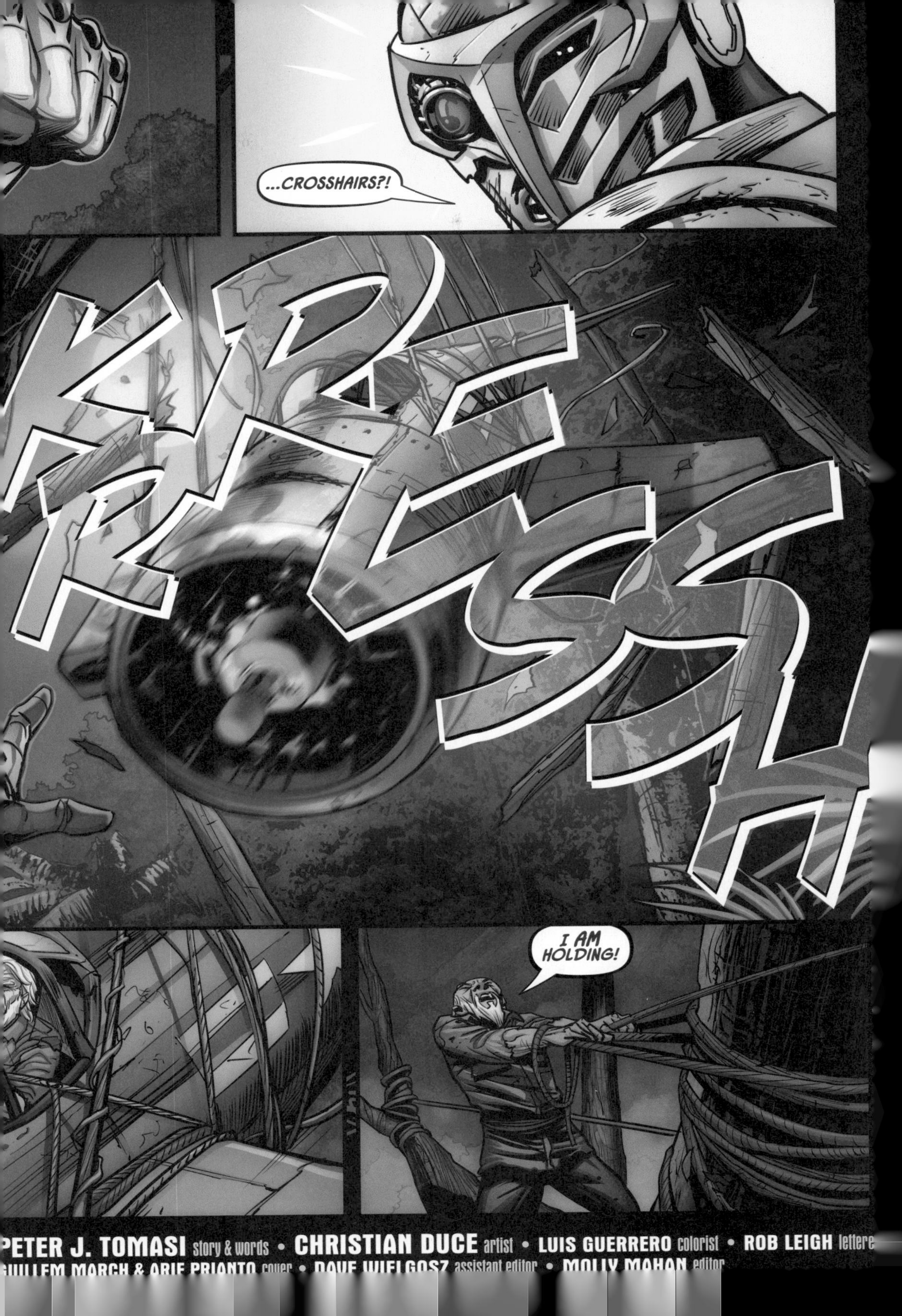
...CROSSHAIRS?!
I AM HOLDING!

PETER J. TOMASI story & words • CHRISTIAN DUCE artist • LUIS GUERRERO colorist • ROB LEIGH lettere
GUILLEM MARCH & ARIF PRIANTO cover • DAVE WIELGOSZ assistant editor • MOLLY MAHAN editor

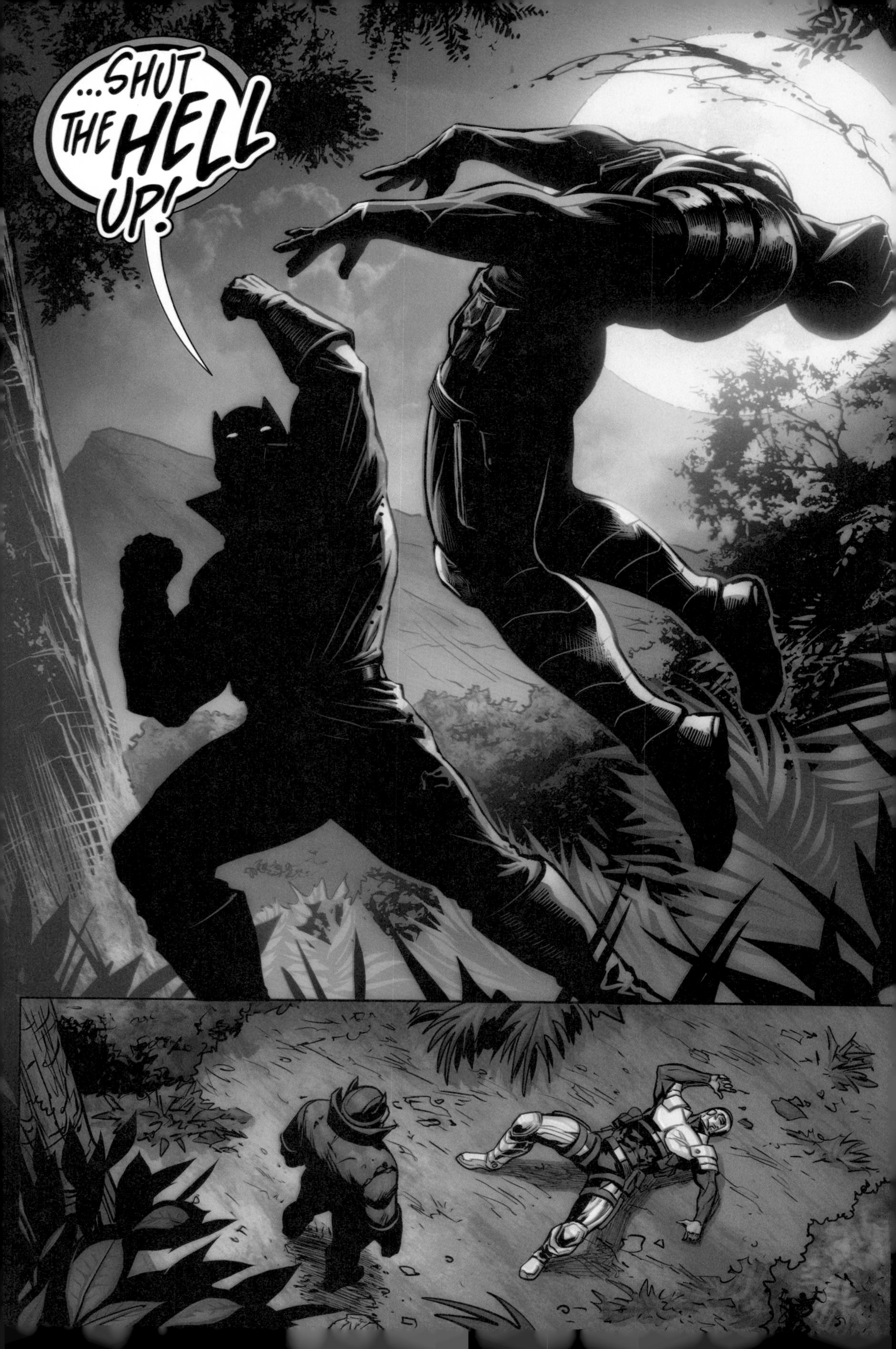
...SHUT THE HELL UP!

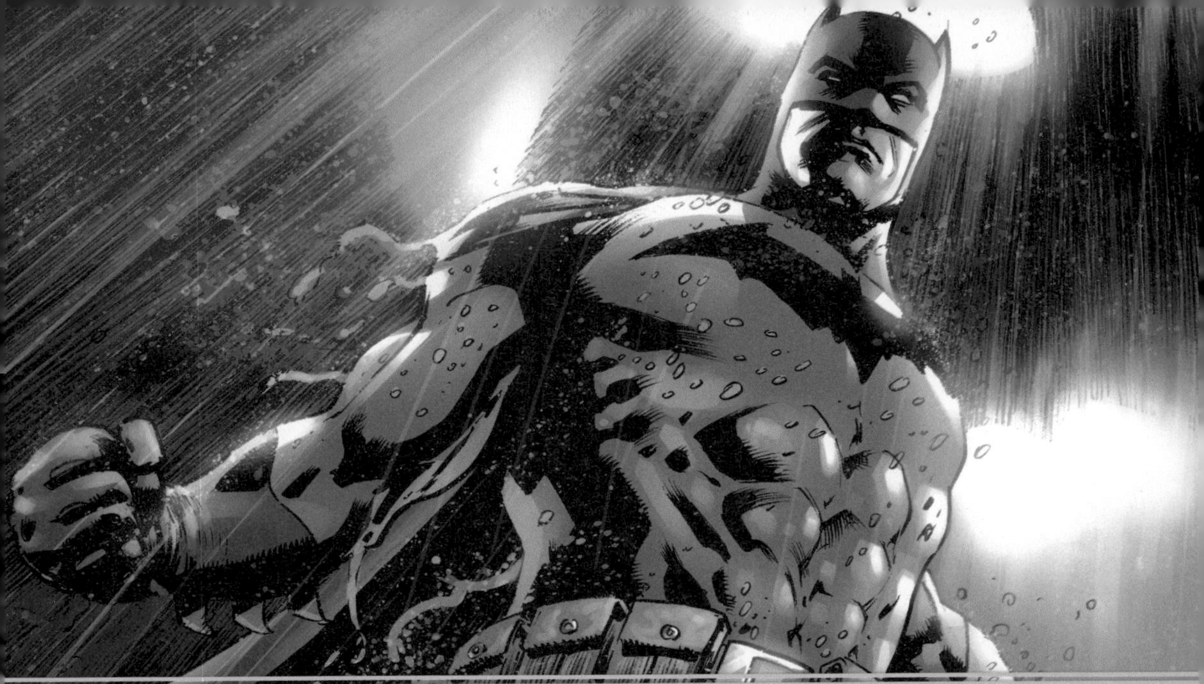

VARIANT COVER GALLERY

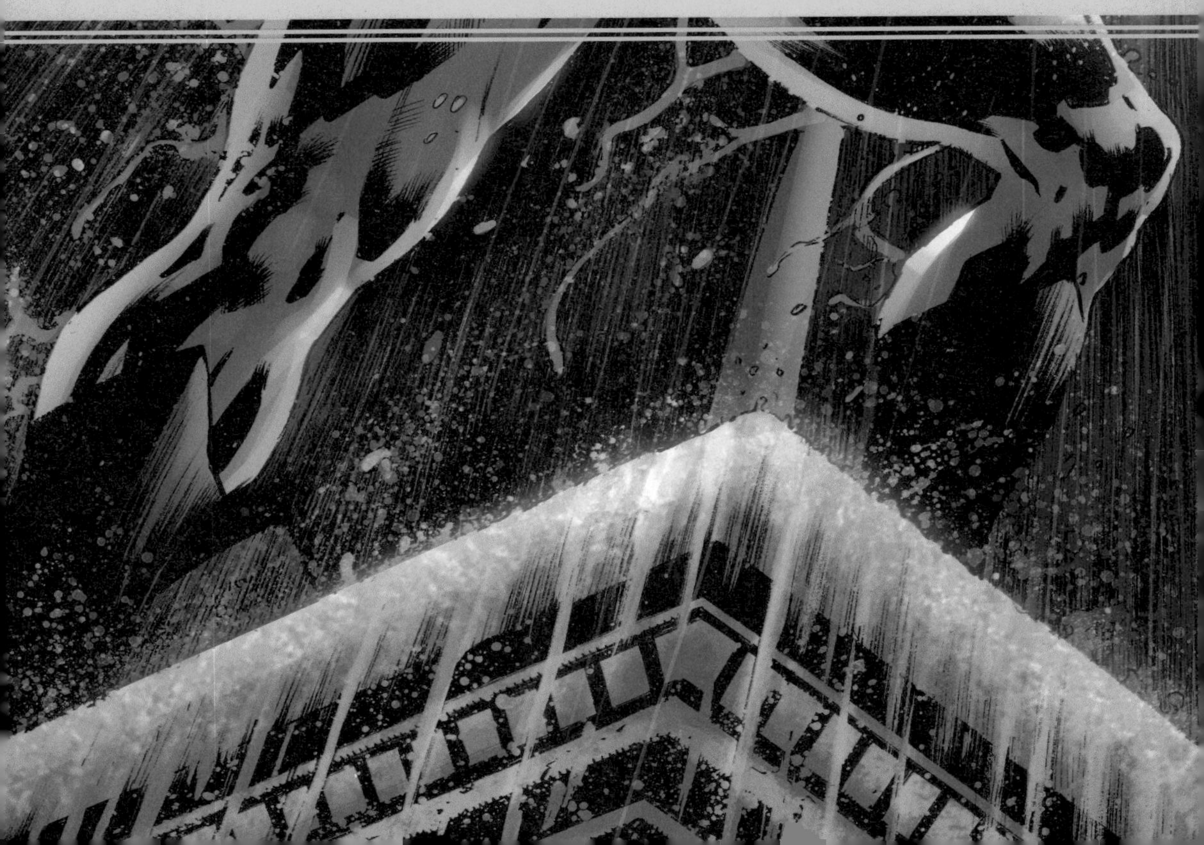

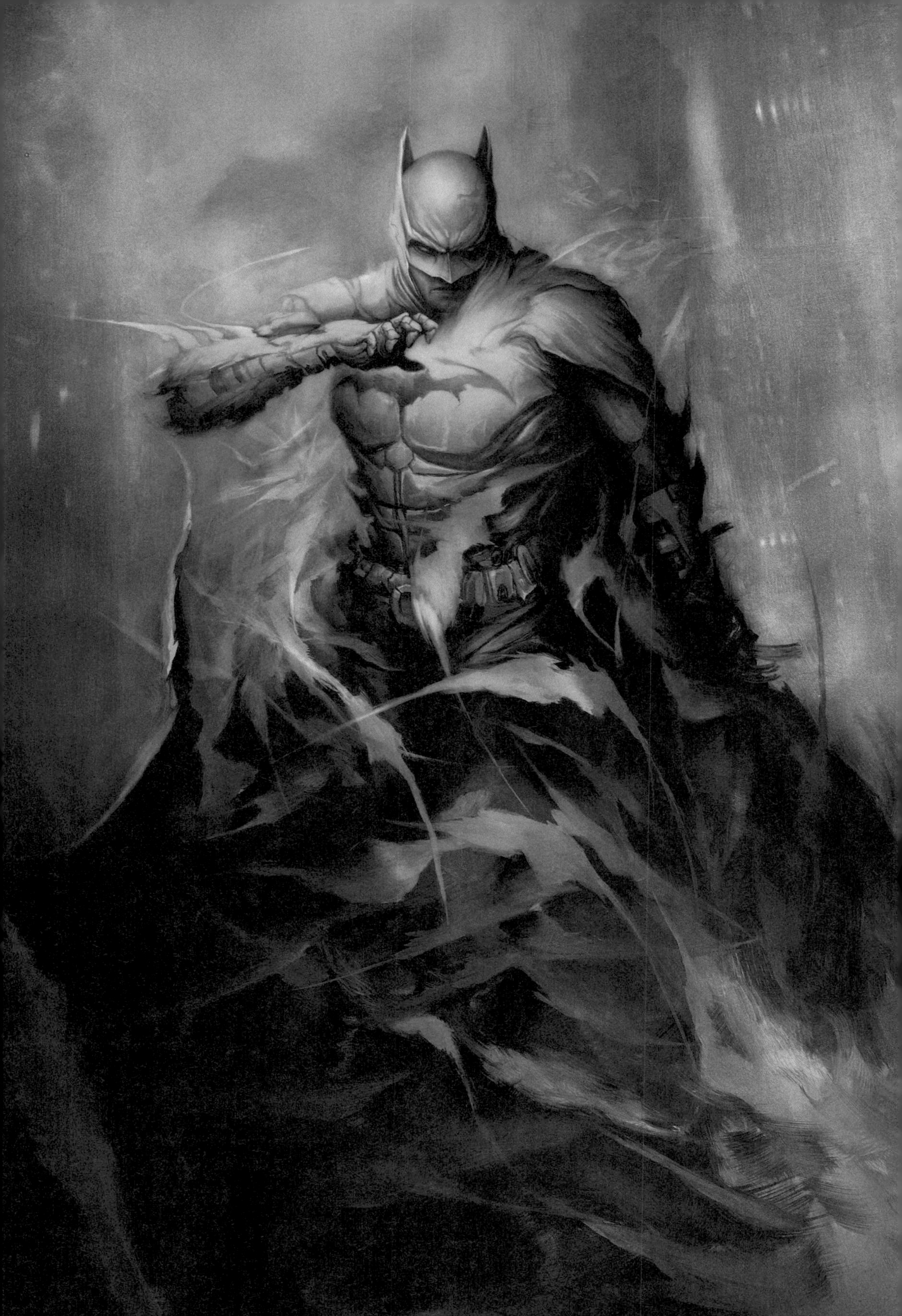

Detective Comics #1006 variant cover by DAN QUINTANA

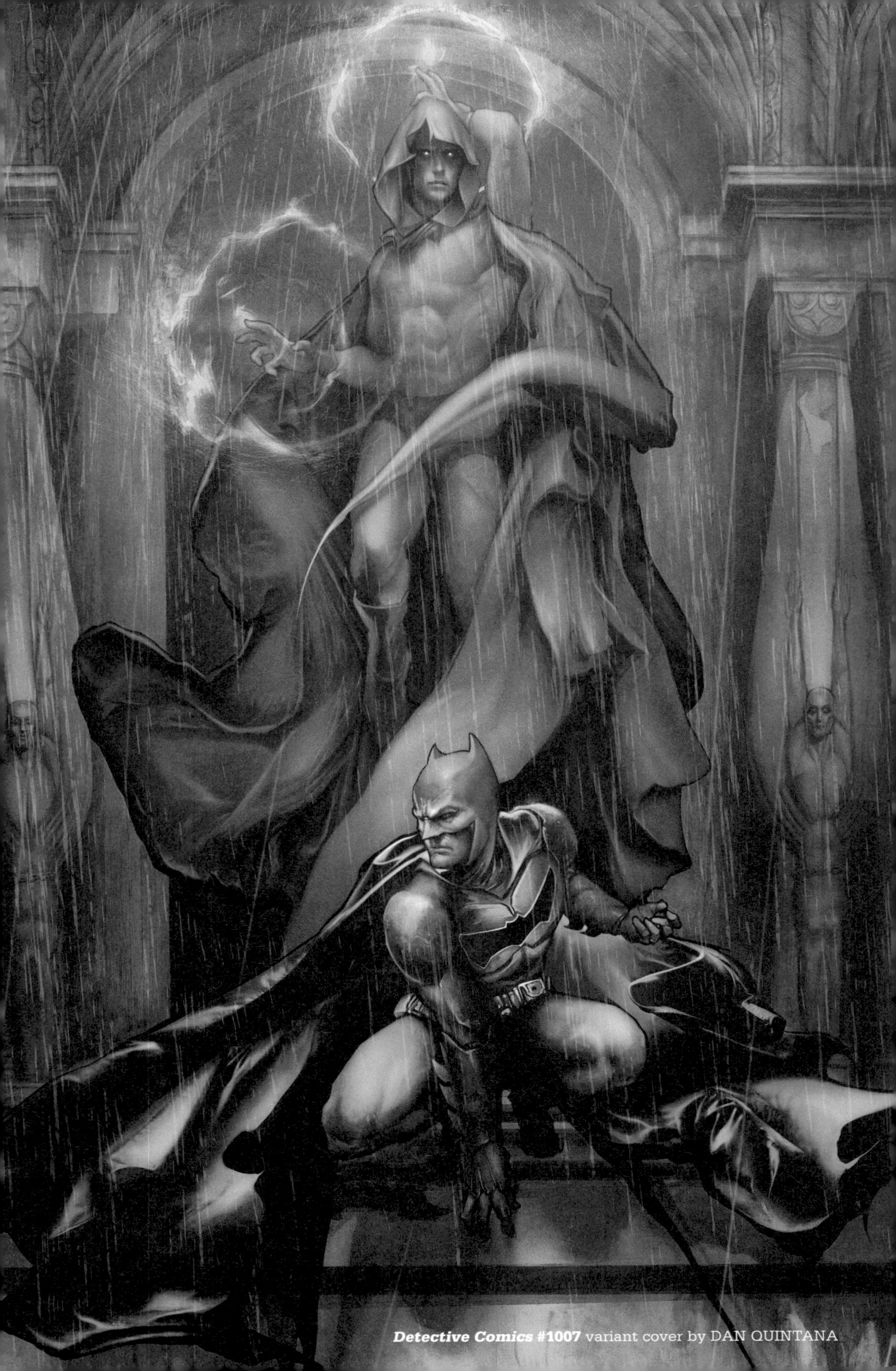
***Detective Comics* #1007** variant cover by DAN QUINTANA

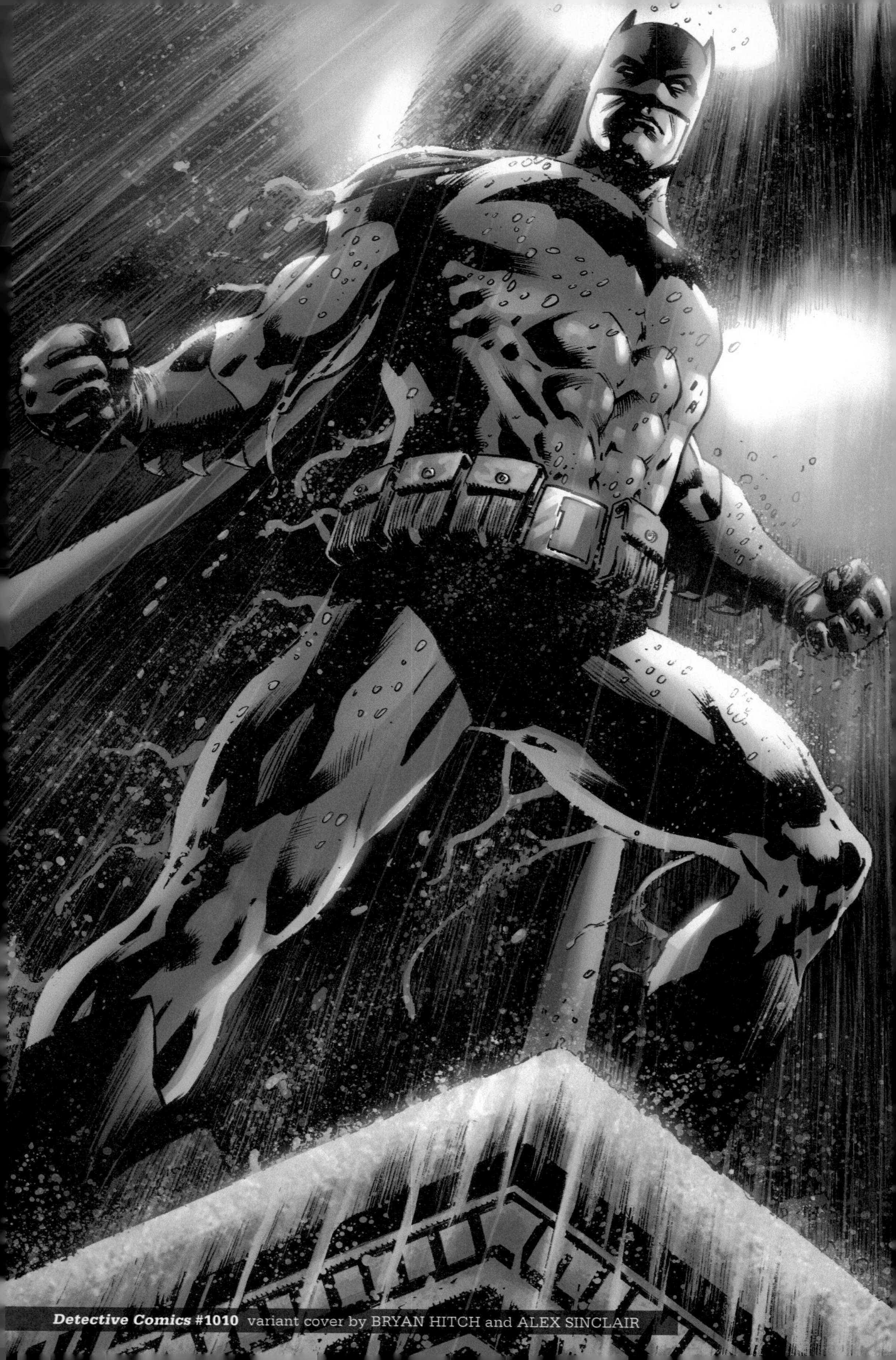

***Detective Comics* #1010** variant cover by BRYAN HITCH and ALEX SINCLAIR

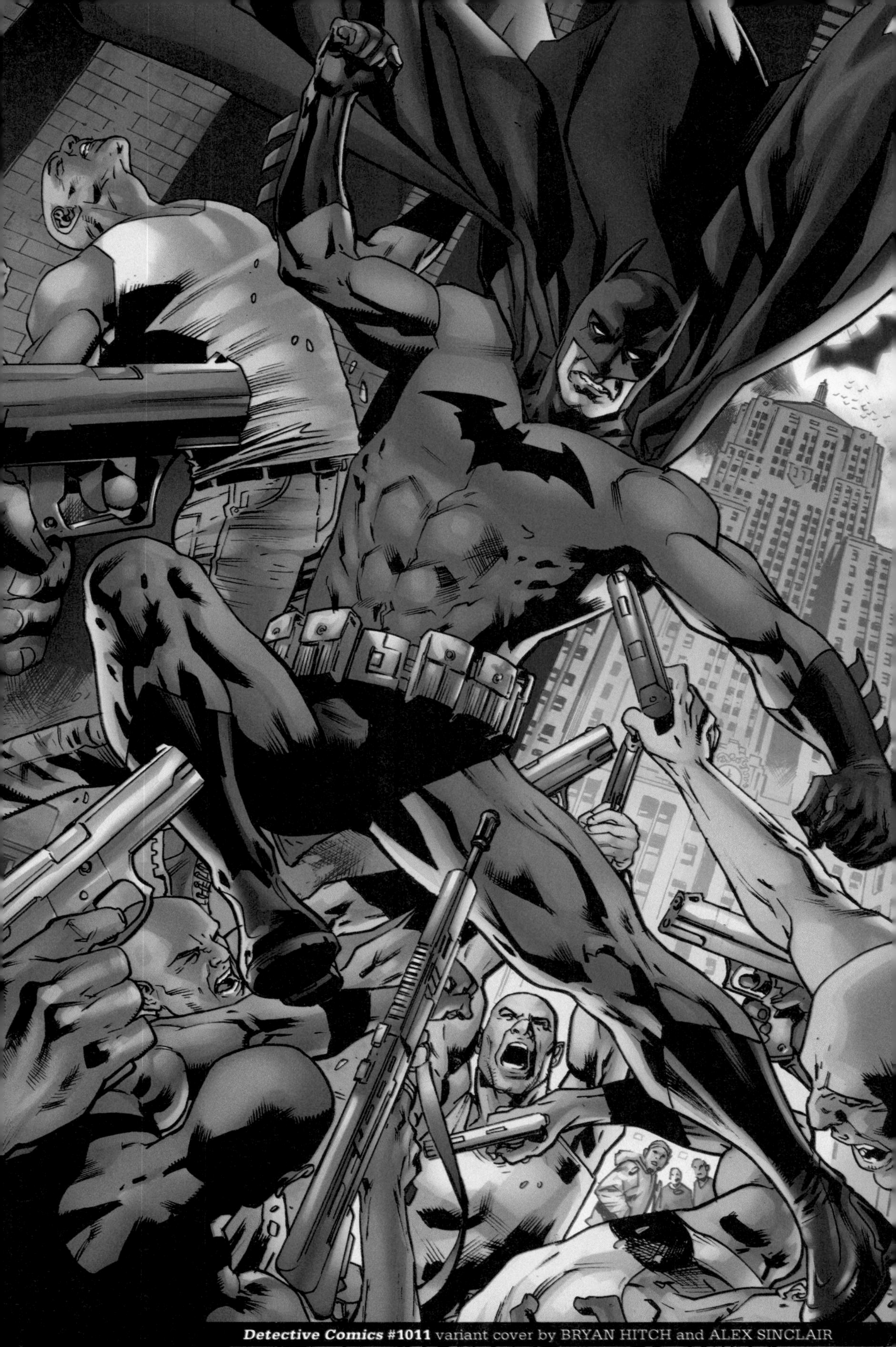

***Detective Comics* #1011** variant cover by BRYAN HITCH and ALEX SINCLAIR

"Rock solid."
– IGN

"This is the kind of Batman story I like to read: an actual mystery with an emotional hook."
– THE ONION / AV CLUB

BATMAN & ROBIN
VOL. 1: BORN TO KILL
PETER J. TOMASI
with PATRICK GLEASON

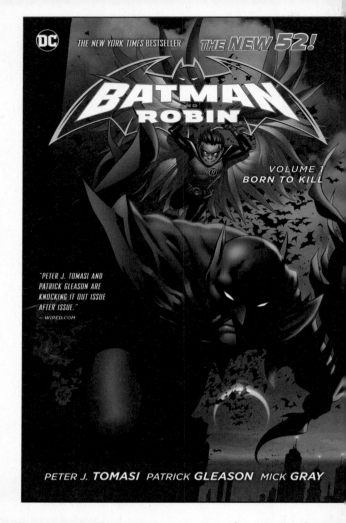

READ THE ENTIRE EPIC

**BATMAN & ROBIN VOL. 2:
PEARL**

**BATMAN & ROBIN VOL. 3:
DEATH OF THE FAMILY**